REVOLUTION
in the
PHILIPPINES

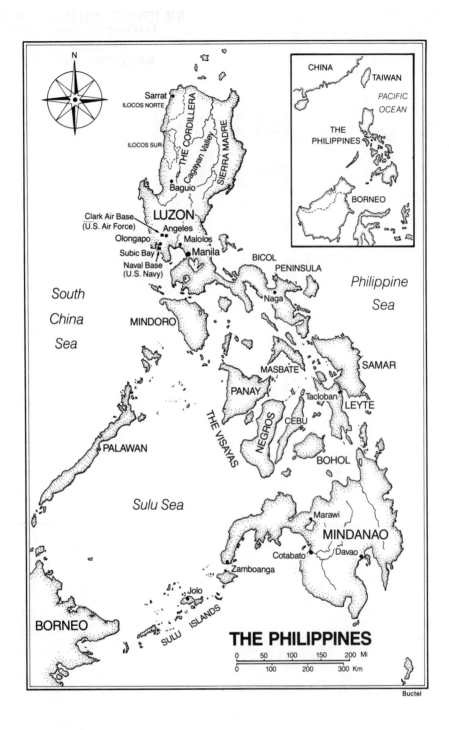

THE PHILIPPINES

Buctel

REVOLUTION
in the
PHILIPPINES

The United States in a Hall of Cracked Mirrors

FRED POOLE and MAX VANZI

McGraw-Hill Book Company

New York   St. Louis   San Francisco   Hamburg   Mexico   Toronto

1 2 3 4 5 6 7 8 9 D O C D O C 8 7 6 5 4

ISBN 0-07-050438-5

LIBRARY OF CONGRESS CATALOGING IN PUBLICATION DATA

Poole, Fred.
Revolution in the Philippines.
1. United States—Foreign relations—Philippines.
2. Philippines—Foreign relations—United States.
3. Philippines—Politics and government—1946–
4. United States—Foreign relations—1981–
I. Vanzi, Max. II. Title.
E183.8.P5P66 1984   327.730599   84–963
ISBN 0–07–050438–5

Book design by Nancy Dale Muldoon

CONTENTS

REVOLUTION
in the
PHILIPPINES

1

AN ULTIMATE ACT OF TERROR

The Death of the Dictator's Rival

ONE of us was there for the killing at Manila International Airport early on the sunny Sunday afternoon of August 21, 1983. Max Vanzi was aboard the just-landed China Airlines Flight 811 from Taipei. He was still within shouting distance of his celebrated fellow passenger, the man shot from behind while exiting and now lying in blood on the tarmac in the most shocking political killing yet in the tyranny that was the modern Philippines.

The victim, the ebullient former senator Benigno S. Aquino, Jr., a political prodigy in democratic days who was known to all Filipinos by the pet name "Ninoy," was returning to his Oriental homeland after three years and three months of exile in America. Before that he had spent seven years and seven months in solitary confinement as a political detainee in a Manila military jail. No individual act of Philippine terror could top his assassination because no Filipino still alive had had a comparable following among the 53 million people of this startlingly lush, 1200-mile-long tropical archipelago.

Vanzi had ridden with Aquino on the wide-bodied Boeing 767 because Ninoy had asked us along. Ninoy had said that the presence of foreigners at his return might give him a margin of safety—or at least assure that his story be told. Aquino had never thought it impossible that this could be the moment of his death. In the climate created by the Philippine dictatorship, his assassination, though it shook Filipinos as nothing before it ever had, was at the same time but a single thread in the carefully woven tapestry that constituted what that dictatorship proudly called the New Republic.

Back in September 1972 President Ferdinand E. Marcos had staged an internal coup d'état, proclaimed martial law, and disassembled Asia's oldest democracy. It was widely believed at the time throughout the Philippine islands that Aquino's popularity was Marcos's prime motivation: Ninoy's ultimate crime was that he had seemed a certain bet to win the scheduled 1973 presidential election.

But whatever the initial reason for martial law, the results were now plain. Among the losers were at least 100,000 Filipinos and Filipinas who had died since 1972 in guerrilla warfare against the government—many killed for tactical or political reasons, some killed at random—or just caught in cross fire. Since martial law was imposed at least 65,000 others had been sent, most solely because of their political beliefs, to special military prisons and concentration camps Marcos had set up all through the islands. Torture, rape and murder had become so prevalent in these new detention areas that the Philippines had moved toward the top of Amnesty International's list of human rights violators on the basis of cases it investigated.

Until the end of the Carter administration, America too had complained about the plight of Ferdinand Marcos's detainees. But then in 1981 Ronald Reagan came into office and embraced the dictatorship without qualification. Ever since, the conditions of political detention had been obscured. In this most American-influenced of all large countries in the world, Marcos had interpreted Washington's new position as a license to take off all restraints. What now, in 1983, caught the attention of international human rights groups was not so much the plight of the detainees as the rising number of cases of outright murder by government soldiers outside the prisons, the number of Latin American–style disappearances and village massacres unrelated to the guerrilla fighting.

We both had been closely involved with the Philippines since the 1960s, fascinated by this land on the rim of China that had once been America's only large colony—and before 1972 had been the freest and most progressive large nation of Southeast Asia. One of us had been the regionally based Southeast Asia editor of a major American news service before, during and after the 1972 coup. The other had lived for extended periods, since well before martial law, in various parts of the islands; more recently the city of Manila had become something like a second home.

Six months before the assassination we had gone back, after a two-year absence during which we had been carefully tracking the changes in the islands since Reagan became President. On that trip we had seen at first hand what the Philippines had become.

What we saw, the shambles the dictator had created of his domain, was also known to Aquino. It had strongly influenced him in his decision to return.

The nation's treasury was being drained for the personal benefit of the rulers; its people's condition was such that by most social and economic indicators they had moved from first place to last in the region; the only rising Communist rebellion in all of Asia had now spread to most Philippine provinces, and it seemed only a matter of a brief time before moderate statesmen such as Aquino would become irrelevant. Furthermore, there was growing evidence that the dictator, Marcos, was terminally ill, and he had set no orderly pattern of succession that could leave the Philippines with anything except a direct military takeover, and then civil war. Because Marcos had always spoken of his concern about his personal place in history, Aquino believed that maybe now, perhaps on his deathbed, Marcos was ready to talk of peaceful change. Maybe, despite the warnings that Marcos had issued of what might await him, it was safe, after all, to go home now.

Aquino had been in high spirits on the two-hour flight from Taipei. A youthful, even boyish, fifty-year-old, he had seemingly unlimited energy, despite recent heart trouble, and seemed always in motion. As the plane made its long descent over Luzon, he looked out and saw the electric-green rice fields, the deeper green cane fields and the blue-tinted mountains of his home island. This was the rainy season, but for the first time in days the sun was out and the view was clear. Ninoy seemed at peace. He stared through the window and smiled.

Minutes before, he had gone to the rear of the plane with Vanzi for what would be his last session with a writer. He continued to express hope. "We're racing against time, Max," he said. "We must convince the President [Marcos] to bring democracy back. I'm appealing to him to grant me an interview. He is the only man who can return the Philippines to democracy peacefully. Otherwise, we're down the road of an El Salvador."

Later he went into a lavatory to don a bulletproof vest beneath his cream-colored safari jacket. It was the same suit he had worn when he had been released from prison in 1980, under pressure from the Carter administration, to leave for emergency heart surgery in America.

Shortly before boarding Flight 811 Aquino had told a Japanese television crew, "You have to be ready with your hand camera because this action can come very fast. In a matter of three, four minutes it could be all over and I may not be able to talk to you again. So this is the big danger. Now I'm taking precautions. I have my bulletproof vest, hoping that it will be some kind of protection. But if they hit me in the head there's nothing we can do."

But he was taking these precautions, he had explained,

purely to cover all possibilities. He rated the real risk of assassination at the airport as no worse than one chance in ten.

After his last interview, with the vest in place, he took a
center-row aisle seat, 14-C, near the front of the aircraft. Vanzi
took 15-C, the seat directly behind him. Aquino's brother-
in-law, Ken Kashiwahara, an American television news correspondent traveling privately as a family member, took the
aisle seat, 14-B, across from him. Beside Ken, in 14-A, was
Kiyoshi Wakamiya, an Aquino friend traveling as the correspondent of Japan's *Shukan Sankei,* a weekly magazine published by Tokyo's large *Sankei Shimbun* group. Behind them
was Sandra Burton of *Time* magazine's Hong Kong bureau.
Roaming the plane amidst the passengers—mainly Chinese,
a few Philippine—were several Asian photographers along
with TV crews from Japan's TBS and America's ABC news
networks.

Ninoy reached into his shoulder bag, took out a small box
containing a gold Swiss wristwatch he prized. "Here," he said,
handing it to Kashiwahara, "I want you to have my watch."
Ken was puzzled, but he took it.

Just before the seat belt sign went on, the TV cameras
caught a moment of hilarity. Two pretty Filipinas on board
had recognized the famous former senator. They rushed up
to his seat. "Oh, I want to kiss you," one said, and did, on
the lips. Aquino grinned and joked, "My wife's not gonna
like this."

Then he seemed all alone for a moment. He took from
his pocket a string of rosary beads, bowed his head and prayed
in silence. As the plane was coming in on final approach he
said, "I think it's a victory if we just land."

The plane landed at 1:05 in the afternoon, and as it moved
down the taxiway Aquino noted that many other planes were
on the ground, attached to covered jetways. Half a dozen
had arrived within the past few minutes. He had scheduled
his arrival for the busiest time of day at the brand-new Manila

International Airport so that there would be plenty of people around. "The birds are all in," he said. But Vanzi noted that the tarmac was deserted of life. There was no sign of the ground crews or the ground vehicles that would normally be scurrying about.

It was not until Flight 811 turned into its assigned bay that anyone appeared. First came two ground crewmen to guide the aircraft in with hand signals. Then a blue van darted out and braked to a stop near the left side of the plane. On its side were the markings of AVSECOM, the Aviation Security Command, a special armed forces unit composed of SWAT teams to foil hijackings.

About a dozen men, wearing dark blue AVSECOM jumpsuits with visored SWAT caps and carrying M16 rifles and automatic pistols, immediately leapt out of the van. They fanned out around the nose of the plane.

Just as the passenger door at the front was opened onto the jetway, three burly men in khaki uniforms, two with AVSECOM markings and one with the insignia of the armed forces' national police arm, the Philippine Constabulary, entered the cabin. Over the plane's PA system came an appeal for all passengers to stay in their seats.

The first of the men in khaki walked right past Aquino, but the second and the third recognized him. "Where are we going?" Aquino asked, smiling and putting out his hand.

"Just down, sir," one of the soldiers said, accepting the handshake.

"Okay," said Aquino.

Kashiwahara said, "Ninoy, can I come with you?"

"Yeah, come on."

Kashiwahara turned to the nearest soldier and introduced himself. "I'm his brother-in-law. I want to go with him."

"You just take seat," the soldier ordered.

While they were talking, Vanzi saw the largest of the guards slip a huge hand, with fingers like sausages, down Aquino's back and help him up from his seat. With one of the men on each side of him and one behind, they rushed him to the door.

At the point where the accordion jetway tube met the entrance to the fuselage, a service door on the jetway was now open, with steps leading down to the tarmac. The soldiers hustled Ninoy to the steps. Instantly five big men—dressed identically in dark trousers and loose, short-sleeved, embroidered white shirts—threw up their brawny arms, blocking the view to the outside. They were roughly shoving back the reporters, photographers and TV cameramen, knocking some down. Wakamiya was on the floor, poking his head between their legs.

But the cameras kept rolling. The first gunshot, as timed later on videotape, came only forty-nine seconds after Ninoy had left his seat, only nine seconds after he had disappeared through the service exit.

Four seconds after the first shot, the one believed to have killed Ninoy, there were three more shots, apparently meant for his supposed assailant. Then after twenty seconds there was a flurry of six shots, and then another rapid burst of many shots together. Wakamiya was still poking his head through the white-shirted guards' legs. One of these guards had been standing all along at the top of the stairway at the service exit. His head was turned and he was watching what the reporters, held back by the other guards, could not see down on the tarmac. When the firing was over, the guard calmly turned back to face the cabin, expressionless.

Passengers were diving for cover. Burton was screaming. Kashiwahara was shouting, "Goddamnit, goddamnit." One woman wailed, "He's dead, he's dead!" Another was shouting, "Watch out for the children."

And now Vanzi and the other reporters got to the service door. Aquino was lying face down on the tarmac, a fountain of blood gushing up from a wound behind the left ear that looked at first as if it had nearly severed his head. Inches away from his head was another body, face up, riddled with bullets, dressed in the light blue shirt and dark trousers of an airport mechanic. There was no sign at all of the three guards in khaki who had gone off with Ninoy.

But the men in blue AVSECOM uniforms down on the tarmac showed no sign of panic. They were as collected as the white-shirted man who had watched the killing from the top of the steps. They were all in fixed positions with their guns drawn, as if securing an area after a military operation had been carried out precisely as planned. Two, crouched in the two-handed shooter's stance, had their .45s pointed directly at Vanzi. He saw two more heft Ninoy's body like an animal carcass into the van. The van sped away. Seemingly out of nowhere yet another white-shirted man appeared on the killing ground, reached down, picked up a handgun lying near where Ninoy's body had been, and slowly walked away.

Wakamiya, speaking moments later to Vanzi in the jetway, said that after Ninoy was shot the man in the mechanic's uniform was hurled from near the van, and shot seconds later.

In the ten days that followed, Ninoy's body was taken to his Manila home for viewing, then to a nearby church, then to another church seventy-seven miles north in his home province of Tarlac, and back to Manila for the funeral and burial. In these ten days the country came to a standstill. The largest crowds in anyone's memory, at one point several million, turned out for the various processions with the casket. Some thought the moment of the revolution had arrived, though for now there was more mourning than rioting.

Meanwhile at the presidential mansion—the old Spanish colonial Malacañang Palace, set in formal gardens along Manila's Pasig River—what was visible to the public distinctly lacked any air of mourning. For many days there had been no sign of Marcos, who had announced he was going into seclusion for three weeks to "write two books" on the history of the Filipino people. It was widely assumed that he was out of view because he was dying. Marcos suffered, it was widely believed, from systemic lupus erythematosus, a debilitating disease which can go into remission for long periods but, because it prevents antibodies from working, always results in death, usually from kidney or lung failure. It had been reasonably established that for years he had been on dialysis and now it was rumored that, though medically dangerous, a kidney transplant would be attempted.

And when he appeared on government television the second night after the killing, Marcos indeed looked close to death. His enunciation remained clear and methodical, but his voice was weak. His bearing, once ramrod military straight, was that of a shrunken old man. His face, recently taut and handsome with high cheekbones and piercing eyes, was puffy, with the look of a death mask, and his eyes were dull—though one palace official told a reporter, "If you think he looks bad now, you should have seen him three days ago."

But Marcos, known throughout his career as a humorless man who rarely made small talk and hardly ever joked, was in a jesting mood. He was surrounded by his entire cabinet, his wealthiest business cronies, tame journalists and the top generals of his armed forces. He made light of rumors. He said, without being asked, that his most powerful cabinet member, his flamboyant wife, Imelda, who headed something called the Ministry of Human Settlements, had not been involved in the killing. He ridiculed the idea. Pointedly, as if in warning, the government camera then panned to the only other person in the country whose power equaled Imelda's, Marcos's former driver and bodyguard, once the suspected head of a paramilitary unit of convicts and now Chief of Staff of the bloated Armed Forces of the Philippines, Marcos's relative, Gen. Fabian C. Ver. From Ver had come the last and most specific in a series of warnings to Aquino that "unknown" killers might be lying in wait for him should he attempt to come home now.

The screen image of Ver seemed a silent threat. Then

all cameras again fixed on Marcos, who sat on a raised golden chair, in effect a throne, as he made light of the absurd notion that the President of the Philippines would kill Benigno Aquino. His cabinet members, generals, and journalists from the controlled press all laughed. They nodded sagely as he went on to say that what had happened was very likely "a Communist rub-out job."

Two nights later, with the nation in mourning, Marcos went on television again, this time specifically to squelch rumors about his health. In a gesture reminiscent of Lyndon Johnson, the fastidious dictator stepped out of character and raised his shirt to show unbroken skin on the side of his belly at the place, he said, where there would be marks if a kidney machine had been attached—though actually that place would be lower than the area he exposed, and dialysis does not always leave such marks. Showing his skin was another occasion for general glee and laughter from the aides, cronies and soldiers who again surrounded him.

Filipinos watching the state-controlled broadcasts did not laugh. Marcos had reigned since before half his people were tiny children or had even been born. There was a mystique that he had supernatural powers, plus a general belief now that America would step in if he needed saving. Ninoy Aquino may have been the most popular man in the country, but Ferdinand Marcos, despite his physical deterioration, was at this point still the most feared.

No Filipino believed that anyone outside the government could or would have masterminded the killing of Aquino. Some did not accept every detail of the version of the Japanese correspondent who said he'd seen the supposed killer thrown from the direction of the van and killed after Aquino was shot by a soldier. But the only place in Manila where anyone not employed as a government propagandist was heard to accept Marcos's version of the assassination was at the American embassy.

2

MANILA BEFORE THE MURDER

Images in the Hall of Mirrors

THE chain of islands between the South China Sea and the Pacific, some so large they feel like a mainland, that make up the Republic of the Philippines had always presented puzzles. The archipelago, with its thick jungles, high mountains, sweeping plains and even urban sprawl, had always been intensely disorienting to outsiders. Its mix of cultures—Malay overlaid with Spanish, overlaid with Chinese, overlaid with American—its clash of customs, its startling combinations of hype and tradition, high life and low life, earnest striving and wild abandon, had always given visitors the feeling of being in a fun house hall of mirrors.

But the disorientation felt in the Philippines of the past was as nothing compared to what it had become when we went back six months before Aquino's killing. To enter the particular part of the hall of mirrors that is the huge capital, Manila, was by February and March 1983, at the start of the Philippines' hot, dry summer season, a matter of suspending disbelief while stepping through the looking glass into a time warp.

There had been elements of this disorientation for us during the preceding two years while, in our absence from the islands, we had been drawing ever closer to the exile opposition in America. At first, between 1981 and our return in the 1983 summer season, we had been bemused to find ourselves dealing with revolutionaries who wore pearls and diamonds. Then, after making our way through a morass of hazy, amateurish far-left splinter groups, we had been surprised to find ourselves dealing with intense, brilliant, and highly sophisticated and organized Filipino Marxists who believed with apparent solid foundation that they would one day be governing their country.

But still bigger surprises came as the Reagan era dragged on. Soon we were attending meetings, in places ranging from church conference rooms to run-down old union halls, at which everyone was coming together. The glittering silk-stocking revolutionaries, who represented democratic leaders from before Marcos's 1972 coup, were now sitting side by side in meetings, and marching side by side in protest demonstrations, with jeans-clad Marxist intellectuals who saw the Philippines as a future workers' paradise. And meeting and marching with them were Filipino priests and Filipina nuns.

When we did go back in 1983—one working the government side and one the underground—we knew enough about the direction the Marcos government had taken since Reagan so that we were not caught off guard when threatening phone calls began. And we were not surprised when certain Philippine government functionaries we knew in Manila took one of us aside and showed how we had been tracked in San Francisco and New York, just like the opposition figures, by Philippine secret agents whose main mission it was to harass the exiles. Indeed, we had already been felt out by a man close to Marcos (whose identity we must protect), to see if we could be paid to drop our book project.

After two years of Reagan and two years with the opposition, we knew enough so that all this was expected. And after nearly two decades of familiarity with the Philippines we had thought it unlikely that when we went back there would be anything more that could startle us. But our sense of reality was strained past reasonable limits by what we actually did see, six months before the Aquino assassination, upon our first return in 1983.

It is difficult for anyone without an Oriental sensibility to take in the scope of the flashy surface manifestations of the costly excesses that had been carried out in the Philippine capital. The physical signs of the excesses by now way overshadowed anything done by an Eva Peron in Latin America or even a Shah and Shahbanu in Iran. By 1983 this Third World city of 8 million people, recently at the top of the heap in Southeast Asia, was going through such economic hardship that international relief groups were comparing it not to the cities and nations of its region but to Bangladesh. And yet parts of Manila had suddenly, almost overnight, become a crazed modern Oriental version of something that Louis XIV, as played by one of the Marx Brothers, might have created.

What was particularly disorienting was that so much of the new rich side of Manila was either a blatant flaunting of the rulers' new wealth or had no direction. There were, for example, shiny new skyscrapers housing new government or semi-government banks and agencies designed to skim personal profits for the rulers from all economic activity in the archipelago. There were also equally grand skyscrapers housing new government agencies that had the announced plans of carrying out programs for the poor. These programs ranged from providing land to Filipinos who were landless—the vast majority—to housing for those who were homeless or lived in makeshift urban or rural hovels—the vast majority—to food for all who suffered from caloric and protein malnutrition—the vast majority. But all such programs had been discarded almost as soon as they had been thought up and publicized.

The new skyscrapers for abandoned programs were the

least of it, but they provided a starting point. On a typical day in a typical such skyscraper—this one built to house a new bureaucracy whose stated purpose was to make every Filipino a prosperous entrepreneur—one of us got off the elevator at the wrong floor. He found himself not in offices where antipoverty plans were being laid but rather in an erotically dark, government-financed discotheque, complete with strobe lights and girls in scanty dress. Behind the girls, whose makeup looked caked in the daylight from the hallway, there was a sign indicating which credit cards this particular government agency accepted.

Discotheques like this one existed all over the city in other government buildings, we would find. There was even one in the President's mansion, Malacañang Palace. But this was only a tiny part of the construction programs that dramatized the widening gap between rich and poor. More illustrative were the sleek hospital buildings dotted around Manila that constituted the most recent gifts from the very rich rulers to their very rich cronies. These mammoth, always well guarded, specialized hospitals—the Children's Hospital, the Heart Center, the Lung Center—had luxury suites, the newest miracle medical equipment, and high-paid staffs that would be the envy of hospitals anywhere. There was nothing remotely like them elsewhere in Asia, not even in Japan. But they were pay-as-you-go health facilities, more costly to patients than any others in Asia.

As we moved about the city we next came upon the luxurious campus, its architecture combining old Spanish and late American shopping mall, of a brand-new educational institution. It was called the University of Life. Not long ago the Philippines had clearly been the leader in higher learning for all of Southeast Asia. It still had a half-million college and university students. But the University of Life was not for ordinary students; it was for those who, like its founders, the rulers, had decided it was time to reject all traditional learning.

Like some California cult, it had replaced professors with something it called "facilitators" and had come up with such notions as putting sports on a par with housing and drinkable water as one of the newly identified "Eleven Basic Needs of Man."

By rejecting the old, the facilitators explained, a course of development could be directed from Manila that would revolutionize the entire Third World; but when one of us spent days at the University of Life listening to the conflicting new philosophies that were supposedly guiding the rulers, he was unable to get anyone there to point to a single development program with any record of accomplishment. What blueprints there were for economic uplift were ludicrous. Most representative, perhaps, was the strange earthworm program. Facilitators had gotten their hands on foreign scientific papers saying worms were full of protein. They had decided that a great new domestic and export market was beckoning. Immediately new buildings appeared throughout the country, set on fenced-in, sweeping lawns with signs announcing "Earthworm Station." No foreign markets had been found for the worms, however, and at the University of Life it was admitted that no one there, or even passing through from the provinces, had yet seen a Filipino eat one. Outside the University, the plan came up in conversation only in rumors that the local McDonald's franchises were sneaking them into their hamburgers.

But the University of Life with its silly schemes was only a small part of the new Manila we found in 1983. Its campus, the new skyscrapers and the new luxury hospitals, although highly visible parts of the changing face of the city, were not nearly so visible as the physical plants aimed at promoting not health and uplift but the fun of tourism. In various parts of the city there were large new deluxe hotels, built all at once at a cost higher than some Third World countries' annual budgets—including a dozen with 500 rooms or more in the international five-star class. They were beginning to dominate the skyline.

Yet Manila and the Philippine islands were hardly a place great numbers of foreign travelers were choosing for conventional vacation play in 1983. Even in its tourism, the place had become a battleground between the people and the armed forces of their rulers. Slum dwellers had been sent away by soldiers so their shacks could be torn down to make room for inner-city golf courses. In the provinces, land had similarly been confiscated in order to set up Caribbean-style beach resort complexes for use by the dictator's business associates.

With tourism a part of the oppression, the tourism sector had suffered from the violence that was breaking out in response to government terror. For several years urban arson and bombings, aimed at scaring foreigners away, had been commonplace. In 1980 a young employee of the Marcoses' new Ministry of Tourism, Doris Baffrey, had set off a bomb in the midst of an international travel agents' convention which Marcos himself was attending. Although no one died, the convention was immediately disbanded, and ever since nearly all the more respectable international travel agents had been warning their clients away. And yet the new Manila hotels flourished in a way. One of them had become a well-guarded gambling casino, made legal by the rulers and owned by the cronies. It had replaced one recently burnt down by urban guerrillas. Most of the hotels were used, in effect, as high-toned state brothels for the new monied local elite, and also to accommodate regularly scheduled foreign sex tours, such as an Australian tour called "The Randy Rams."

But even the odd new resort facilities, along with the skyscrapers with discos, the luxury hospitals and the University of Life, all paled as symbols of the beserk new Manila before what had been erected along Manila Bay. For a mile out into the bay from Roxas Boulevard, the great palm-lined esplanade that used to follow the water, land had been filled in to accommodate a series of new edifices that, more than any other new buildings we saw, boggled the mind. Tyrants in other Third World countries had squandered state funds to erect cultural centers as monuments to themselves, a matter of life imitating the art of Evelyn Waugh. But this sort of thing, like the creation of instant philosophies, was associated with various largely illiterate states in Africa, never before with a large and predominantly literate Asian nation. And never in modern times had it taken place on such a scale.

The first of the landfill area projects was a great, stark, stone and glass complex, simply called the Philippine Cultural Center. It was used regularly to present such non-Filipino state guests as Van Cliburn and Margot Fonteyn, and it surpassed in grandeur New York's Lincoln Center and Los Angeles's Chandler Pavilion. But one cultural center had not been enough.

There was the adjoining, equally lavish Philippine Folk Arts Center, the expense of which, the rulers said, had been justified for it had added to the glory of what they variously called the New Society and the New Republic by bringing to Manila such non–folk arts events as the second Muhammad Ali–Joe Frazier fight and the 1974 Miss Universe Pageant. It had been built in a hurry, specifically to interest the American Miss Universe promoters. There was also, built later while we had been away in the early 1980s, thrown up so fast for an international film festival that workers had died in construction accidents, the Philippine Film Center. It was made of marble and modeled precisely on the lines of the Parthenon, to be used in annual ceremonies honoring such state friends as George Hamilton, who had conceived the festival, and other stars out of a "Where-Are-They-Now?" column, such as Leif Erickson and Virginia Mayo.

There was, in addition, the Philippine International Convention Center, the biggest conference center complex in

Asia. It lacked conventions for the same reasons—torture, terror, bombings, insurrection, a new military run wild—that the hotels lacked mainstream foreign tourists. This was where Doris Baffrey set off her bomb. Most foreigners did not dare use the Philippines any more for big international gatherings. But the Convention Center did not stand vacant: it was used most often for parties, such as wedding receptions and fashion shows, and kept so cool that here in the tropics the women of the Philippines' new elite, arriving in stretch limousines with their bodyguards, could show off their minks and sables while strolling through its marble halls along miles of parquet floors.

Slightly to the north of the Convention Center was the curious multimillion-dollar Coconut House, a lavish mansion with inlaid murals and great chandeliers, built entirely of coconut products. It had actually been hailed as the symbolic fulfillment of a government plan (already dropped) to show that the people's inadequate housing could be remedied with clever new uses of the Philippines' largest export crop. It too had been thrown up fast while we were away: it had been built to provide Pope John Paul II with a worthy dwelling on his early 1981 swing through the Far East. When the Pope refused to set foot in it, the Philippines' miffed rulers had arranged to have it inaugurated by Brooke Shields instead.

And among much else between the Film Center and the plush marble and hardwood Philippine Plaza Hotel, which was used for state guests who did not rate the Coconut House, there was something called the Tourist Pavilion, just opened when we got to Manila in 1983. This massive, meticulously tended series of gardens was used solely for state evening entertaining. On flowered acreage running to the new shoreline were gazebos, fountains, bars, food tents, stages, rare plants, little hills and valleys, and a large artificial lake with full-size, brightly painted decorative boats—a theatrically lighted, seemingly unending ersatz landscape, both grandiose and precious, that was something out of the reveries of the region's long-dead ancient empires.

But these and other extravagant projects were not the only part of the new Manila that so staggered our imagination in 1983. Just as life at the top was hard for the non-Oriental mind to take in, so was life at the rapidly expanding bottom. At first after the 1972 coup the slide had been gradual; but in the two years preceding 1983 Manila had, despite its new imperial edifices, gone from a somewhat seedy but still vital tropical metropolis to something like what today is known only in travelers' tales of the nineteenth century. It had suddenly, for the first time, become the old stereotyped Oriental city where the powerful live by trafficking in human flesh, a place where, as the nineteenth-century travel writers loved to say, life is cheap.

The crowding was like Calcutta. Everywhere, on all streets and sidewalks, on every corner and down every alley, were masses of people, many of them able-bodied, simply hanging around at any time of day or night for lack of anything else to do.

And much of Manila looked as though there had been some great upheaval that entailed saturation bombing. Part of it had to do with the homes that were being bulldozed in the name of those development schemes that were later abandoned. Some of it was the result of public services breaking down. Also, miles of streets had been torn up and great pipes set beside the trenches in a plan to bring clean water to the people. The streets remained torn up. The people had barred workers sent to put the pipes in place, for it had turned out that the pipes, sold by members of the ruling elite to themselves through private companies they controlled, were made of asbestos—asbestos for drinking water.

Certain main thoroughfares were still kept clean for appearance' sake. They were swept constantly by people who constituted another symbol of the new order, men and women in bright red bandanas and bright orange and red T-shirt and pants uniforms, the T-shirts labeled "Metro-Manila Aide." But in most of the city the aides, a part of now-neglected beautification plans, were in similar but by now old, faded, torn and patched uniforms; they swept dust and debris back and forth, back and forth, not bothering to bring carts or bags to take the litter away.

Aside from the physical shape the city was in, and aside from the cultural centers and other arrogant structures that rose above the shambles, the most striking change in downtown Manila had to do with something else that was out of a past forgotten elsewhere in Asia. It entailed such depravity as to churn the stomachs of the most pleasure-bent of old Asia hands.

Back in the 1960s one of us, who used to roam all parts of Manila as a bachelor, had had some success with a paperback book for an American publisher that took a lighthearted look at the city's all-pervasive, and then almost always lighthearted, nightlife. But the amusements of the past had little to do with what now, in 1983, had become Manila's most noticeable downtown nightlife scene.

This new scene was set outdoors, in streets and alleys and in a small park in the area called Ermita, which when we were last in town had still been the most gracious of the old Spanish-flavored residential districts. Ermita runs south from the great old park called the Luneta, where the government buildings of democratic days, examples of American Greek-revival courthouse architecture, languish. It borders Manila Bay at the point where, across Roxas Boulevard along the water, the American embassy stands, one of the largest embassy establishments America runs anywhere in the world. Before the landfill projects farther south, the embassy had been the bay's dominant structure, and in the 1980s it was still an imposing beacon of American influence.

But a stone's throw from the protected corridors of the

U.S. chancellery building there was now something that did not exist in the open this way anywhere else in twentieth-century Asia, not even in Bangkok, not even in Calcutta. The new downtown open-air scene was centered around masses of prepubescent girls and boys, many ten years of age or younger. Nightly these children paraded before, and were fondled by, men of particular tastes who were now flocking to Manila from all over the world. And in parked cars and along walls on the side streets the child prostitutes were performing sex acts upon their patrons, often in view of strolling visitors from the nearby luxury hotels.

All through Ermita the once-immaculate streets were now filled with garbage left for weeks in the tropical sun, giving the whole district what the nineteenth-century travel writers used to describe as the old Orient's horrid stench of festering excrement and flesh. Small children and old women poked through the garbage for their daily food. And surrounding the child prostitute parade area that gave Ermita its new focus, the new grand hotels coexisted with the dingiest of massage parlors, brothels, sex-show arenas, and homosexual dives and girlie bars where the price of oral sex was the same as the price of a drink.

And so there was nothing lighthearted about most of the new Ermita entertainment establishments. It was not so much that they offered sex as the kind of sex they offered. There had always been erotic undercurrents in Manila, as in all other big Southeast Asian cities. As a group, Filipinas are widely considered among the world's best-looking women. It has to do with the racial combinations: The dark-skinned people of Malay culture who had come from China in prehistory and moved into the Philippines by way of what is now Indonesia had taken on many other non-Malay strains. The islands had been visited by Arabs and Indians. Chinese tradesmen here, as in the rest of the region, had long ago settled in the towns and cities. There had been the Spaniards, especially the friars, who commonly had Filipina mistresses and Filipino children. Later there had been voyaging Japanese who settled to farm and intermarried, and then the Americans, who had spread out everywhere.

It was a land where the culture demanded that every man of any importance have a mistress whether he wanted one or not. You saw them all about, even in government offices where the official with whom you were talking might be having a neck massage or a manicure during your interview. The pretty girls were also in the big nightclubs where the old politicians used to do most of their business, and they were in bars in every part of the city.

Since anyone could remember, Manila had had such bars, catering more to Filipinos than to foreigners. These were places where a man could stop by for a San Miguel beer and a chat with the bar girls, or just possibly wind up taking one of the girls home. But this was only after it had been established, usually after several visits and always after many hours, in a face-saving way for all concerned, that what was going on was not a mere financial transaction.

Such relative innocence was something out of the past now. What two years before had been a half-dozen Ermita bars aimed at tourists had become two solid miles of bars in 1983. A few remained entertaining, but most were grim. Most had been turned into out-and-out, and highly specialized, whorehouses: they now had back rooms, or just curtained-off areas, where the house specialties were carried out by teenage prostitutes, male and female. These specialties took in the entire range of sexual preferences known to man. There was no longer any pretense that what was going on was light-hearted and casual: the customer was hustled from the moment he approached the door with highly specific promises of what awaited him. It was an indoor scene as hard-core in its way as the child prostitution scene outside.

Everything got back now to the desperate need for money.

Beggars, often carrying maimed children, had suddenly turned up in every part of town. Like so much else in the Manila of 1983, this was something that used to be associated with the subcontinent, and with bygone centuries, not with the verdant lands of present-day Southeast Asia. For the first time, entire families were seen sleeping in the streets.

The Philippines in the Marcos era had become, despite its overlay of modernity, one of the most destitute large nations of Asia. Before Marcos, Filipinos had been as well fed as the people in any neighboring tropical countries. Now, according the Asian Development Bank, their average caloric intake was lower than that of the Indonesians, the Indians, the Bangladeshis, or any other people in Asia. The government itself admitted that 30 percent of preschool children were malnourished; international agencies generally put the figure at over 70 percent. The Food and Research Institute of the Philippines said 40 percent of all deaths in all age groups in the islands were related to this malnutrition.

According to the World Bank, real wages in the Philippines had dropped by over 25 percent between 1972 and 1979; with a faltering economy and further inflation, which at one point had gone over 40 percent, wages were still falling. Rice production had increased as the population rose, but at the same time the Philippines had become an importer of wheat, and most rice farmers were impoverished. U.S. AID officials said that despite some overall increases in food productivity, most poor families had been getting poorer and hungrier. By the government's own figures, some 70 percent of the people had by now slipped beneath the poverty line—which as defined by the government was considerably lower than the line set by the UN Food and Agriculture Organization— and in 1984 that percentage would rise.

At the time martial law was declared, plantation farming and foreign ownership of plantations was encouraged, and plantation workers, who came to comprise 50 percent of landless workers, were removed from the protection of minimum wage laws. Much-vaunted land reform decrees issued by Marcos had proved worthless pieces of paper since farmers supposedly given land had had to pay for it in installments and some 80 percent were in default. And in any case, big landlords who did not have another income and all landlords in the armed forces had been exempted from land reform. U.S. AID considered Marcos's land reform so ineffective that it had refused to participate in it in any way.

As for city workers, the early martial law decrees had removed legal protections against the exploitation of women workers and had repealed child labor laws. The workday had been made longer with no increase in pay, and then wages in general had been cut. For many, there was no longer overtime, since by presidential decree Sundays and holidays were now normal workdays.

The previously sometimes favorable balance of payments had been turned into a $2 billion annual deficit by 1982. The foreign debt, $600 million when Marcos was legally elected in 1965 and $2.2 billion when he declared martial law in 1972, rose to over $25 billion in 1984, much of it in short-term loans—the kind of debt more common to Latin America than Asia. The payment of interest had long since passed what the World Bank and the International Monetary Fund considered the danger point. And the country's annual growth rate average of 6.5 percent during most of the first decade of martial law was now by far the lowest in Southeast Asia, having slipped beneath 2 percent for 1982 and 1983, projected as negative growth for 1984 and 1985.

The government claimed a fairly high employment rate by counting anyone who worked at anything for even a few hours a week. But drastic underemployment, so drastic as to have the effect of unemployment, was at 40 percent at the end of 1979, the last year for which figures had been assembled, and it was still rising, according to the World Bank.

A business-supported research group in Manila, the Center

for Research and Communications, reported that whereas in the year before martial law 10 percent of the country's families received 30 percent of the nation's income, that figure ten years later had gone up to 45 percent of the income. And the bottom 70 percent, whose share was 48 percent before martial law, had seen that share drop to 31 percent. Even the government in its own reports predicted that in the 1980s the lot of the impoverished would get worse.

It was this overall economic situation that had led Ninoy Aquino into a certain optimism concerning his personal situation: he had said he thought Marcos might be willing to talk of change if only so that a transfer or sharing of power would permit historians to spread around the blame for the country's having fallen apart.

But despite what had happened to the Philippines economically since the start of the dictatorship in 1972, it was still possible in 1983 for a visitor in Manila to miss it. At the recently completed Manila International Airport, an official with an ID badge would steer you to an illegal taxi charging an illegally high rate. Then you could drive to Roxas Boulevard and on to certain hotels or the Convention Center and see nothing but clean, wide avenues, tidy houses, spectacular high-rises, neat parks. You might notice, too, that you were passing a great many gaily painted or whitewashed concrete walls and wooden fences.

Behind these walls and fences were old and new squatters' shanties where people, often crippled from disease and brain-damaged from malnutrition, were packed tight in tiny rooms with neither ventilation nor sanitation, much less such amenities as electricity and running water. The rooms into which they were crammed commonly had makeshift ceilings so low that an adult could not stand upright. Many a child who wound up in the center of town parading his or her body for sale considered that this was a step up in the world—as a number told us when we talked with them.

Of course we had seen other cities in other parts of the

world that had horrible slums. And in a few cases, such as Beirut, we had seen slums that had been fenced off from view. But the additional cosmetic touches that had appeared in Manila by 1983 were a further challenge to the visitor's imagination.

For example, if you dared wander through the rugged slum area called Tondo, north of the Luneta and the Pasig River, you would turn a corner and all at once find yourself in what appeared to be an unusually rarefied world. Here suddenly was a romantic park square with neatly trimmed lawn and hedges and lovingly cared-for flowering trees and plants. And surrounding the park, here in the unlikely setting of Tondo, was what appeared to be a complete, and also highly romantic, little Mediterranean town, made up of lovely pastel-colored townhouses with red tile roofs and flower-filled ironwork balconies. Such townhouses also lined many of Tondo's main streets. But then if you would go a step farther you would see that in truth there were often no buildings at all. The townhouses were merely the facades of townhouses, like those on the streets of old Hollywood studio lots.

And surrounding the fake town, backed up right to the rear of the facades, were the shanty people, who were officially considered nonpeople by the government. The government had long since announced that these slums, no matter that your eyes told you otherwise, had been eradicated. Although the World Bank said that a third of all Manilans were slum dwellers, by government logic these people did not exist.

And the odd mixure of the real and the perceived got crazier than that. If you ducked down into one of the shanties you would discover, as we did over and over, that the people had not, after all, been totally put out of mind by their masters. In many huts at least one wall now contained—at the strong suggestion of officials who had recently come visiting—a large four-color poster or calendar. This poster or calendar was the only thing the typical Manilan had ever received from his current government. It depicted a scene from the previous autumn: four people standing together, dressed in tuxedos and ballgowns, with great grins on their faces. The four people were Ronald and Nancy Reagan, and the Philippine dictator and his powerful First Lady, Ferdinand and Imelda Marcos.

3

AN EMOTIONAL RELATIONSHIP
The Americanized Islanders

DENIZENS of some of the world's worst slums encouraged to hang color pictures of a dazzling social scene involving the American President on the packing-case walls of their shanties? It was enough to make a sane person, fearful of losing sanity in the hall of mirrors, give up and retreat to the impeccably appointed new international airport that Imelda Marcos personally had built. And yet if you knew the Philippines, if you returned as we did in 1983, then took another look from outside and returned again, formal Reagan-Marcos pictures in the slums began to make a certain twisted sense.

Manila may be 10,000 miles from Washington, yet there is no country in the world quite so close to America as the Philippines. But although American economic and military aid was actually increased between the start of martial law in 1972 and the coming of Reagan in 1981, America had drawn certain lines between itself and the Philippine dictatorship. During Henry Kissinger's time as secretary of state, both presidents Nixon and Ford did go so far as to make brief stopovers in martial-law Manila; but they instructed their ambassadors to keep their distance in public from Marcos and Imelda. And although Carter kept the aid money flowing, he also began pressuring Marcos to do something about his appalling human rights record. Imelda, on her regular private trips to America, was practically pounding at the doors of the White House, but neither Nixon, Ford nor Carter would issue the Philippine dictator and his wife the official invitation to Washington they sought.

By the time of our first 1983 trip back to the islands, two years after Reagan's election, the policy of quietly keeping the Marcoses at arm's length had been ripped apart and abandoned. Since his election, Reagan and his administration had moved official Washington as close to official Manila as the two capitals had been at any time since the Philippines was an American colony. Now in 1983, as we saw the deadly contrasts between that part of Manila built for the rulers and that part left to the slum dwellers, we also found that Filipinos had gotten the point of what Reagan had done. American and Philippine official policies were now so inextricably linked in the Filipino consciousness that in the view from the islands they were indistinguishable.

It was not, however, that the relationship had had its start with Reagan. The American interests in the islands, real and perceived, were long standing. But what Reagan had done by his third year in office was to create a climate in which Filipinos had something even bigger than the hated dictatorship to bring them together in often violent opposition. Reagan had managed to convince large parts of Philippine society that America was not so much behind the Philippines in general as it was behind the leaders who had killed democracy and were operating a gulag, ruling by terror.

In 1983 we would see among the opposition in the Philippines precisely what we had seen in New York and San Francisco among the exile opposition. We would see all parts of the society, from far left to old right, from students to clergy, intellectuals to aristocrats, slum and rural organizers to scions of Manila's old families and the landed gentry, all coming together. And we would see signs that what brought them together was something bigger than the Marcos family.

Before 1981 the most common graffiti line in towns throughout the archipelago had been "DOWN WITH THE MARCOSES!" By 1983 what we would most often see scrawled on walls was "DOWN WITH THE U.S.–MARCOS DICTATORSHIP!"

The linking of America with the homegrown tyranny in the islands had been so thorough that we would become convinced that, American newspaper headlines of the time to the contrary, another Vietnam in some small country in Central America or the Middle East was not the greatest threat facing Americans. What America had to fear most right now, it seemed to us, was another Vietnam in a large country right out here near Vietnam itself.

The Philippine military, which Marcos had doubled and redoubled in size after establishing martial law, had from its very start been an American creation. America had always provided its weapons and much of its training and planning. American forces, some permanently on the scene at the giant U.S. bases in the islands, had regularly participated with Filipinos in war games and other joint maneuvers.

But Reagan by now was trying to double the military aid to the Philippines, and everyone knew how that aid was used. What fighting the Armed Forces of the Philippines did was 100 percent against Filipinos and it would stay that way since America still, by treaty, maintained responsibility for the islands' defense. And the Philippines had no external enemies.

American private businesses had long been the principal foreign investors in the islands, although until 1972 they had been held in check by nationalistic Philippine presidents and members of the Philippine Congress. Since the enactment of martial law, however, virtually all restraints on foreign investment and ownership, as well as all restraints against taking profits out of the country, had been lifted. Cheap strike-free labor, usually not covered by minimum wage laws, had been guaranteed to foreigners, primarily Americans and Japanese, who moved in to operate factories, mines and plantations in the new climate of the martial law Philippines.

Thus American and Japanese private interests, operating through Marcos cronies, had won effective control over large parts of the economy. Direct Japanese investment, forbidden by law until Marcos abolished the Philippine Congress, had suddenly, in 1972, been made legal by presidential decree. Japan, which with America had already become one of the Philippines' two largest trading partners, now had major interests, from copper mining to plantation farming, throughout the islands. America too had increased its share. Another martial law presidential decree had set aside court decisions that would have brought to an end the special postcolonial privileges American businessmen enjoyed. America's approximately $3 billion in direct investment had now become an incalculable figure because since 1972 the Americans, like the Japanese, had also been investing with local capital.

After 1972 Marcos had set up free trade industrial zones, where no effective law could touch the foreigners, for assembling and then exporting manufactured goods made from duty-free imported parts. With the new postcoup emphasis on foreign factories, plantation agriculture and foreign exploitation of timber and minerals, Marcos had brought the Philippines all the way back to a colonial economy. In the words of a prominent American academic specialist in Philippine studies, Prof. Robert B. Stauffer of the University of Hawaii, Marcos had accomplished the "refeudalization" of his domain. Together, America and Japan had brought about, with the help of Marcos, what Japan alone had failed to pull off in the Philippines in World War II when it tried to bring the islands into a Greater East Asia Co-prosperity Sphere.

But it was not so much American investment that had

kept Washington in the picture after the imposition of martial law. Private investment constituted only a small and relatively insignificant part of the American stake in the islands, and American corporations had similar interests in other politically harsh and volatile parts of the world. But in no comparable dictatorship, and in no land so unstable that a widespread guerrilla rebellion was in progress, did America have such a serious military commitment.

In 1984, Subic Naval Base, along with its Cubi Point Naval Air Station, which supported and was the forward base for the Seventh Fleet, was America's largest naval base in the Far East. Clark Air Base, home of the Thirteenth Air Force, was likewise the largest American air base in Asia. Both had been the key logistical support centers for the wars in Korea and Indochina. Together they were a key link in America's worldwide network of strategic installations, responsible for covering an area that took in the Pacific and extended all the way to the Indian Ocean and the Middle East. The Philippines was also an American military communications hub for all of Asia, covering everything from satellite and conventional intelligence gathering to the deployment of nuclear submarines and the guidance of long-range missiles situated throughout the Eastern portion of the world.

Some 80,000 Americans were still in the islands. At any one time some 15,000 of them were uniformed servicemen and another 25,000 the dependents of servicemen, an interesting prospect to anyone considering taking hostages.

And the visible signs of the American connection went way beyond the presence of American installations, American factories, and American businessmen, airmen and sailors. Long before the close ties between the new Reagan administration and the Marcos dictatorship began, the Filipinos looked upon themselves as participants in the American way of life. They had always considered the Americans their benefactors, as the people who had helped them into the modern world, given them the basis of an educational system unrivaled in the Third World and, not least, taught them the workings of democracy.

The U.S. connection began in 1898 as a sideshow to the Spanish-American War when Commodore, soon to be Admiral, George Dewey sank Spain's ragtag Far Eastern fleet, without the loss of an American life, in a single busy day in Manila Bay. But the sideshow became the main event when it turned out that the Filipinos, who had been fighting with great success against troops sent from Spain to hold a colony it had possessed for 350 years, wanted full independence, not a new colonial master. It took three and a half years of fierce counterinsurgency warfare all through the archipelago, often guns against bolo knives, to suppress the guerrillas of the Philippines independence movement, and the bloody mopping-up operations continued until 1913.

In 1898—in fact in 1984, too—many Americans were hazy about just what the Philippines was. Perhaps it was a kind of sardine, a nineteenth-century newspaper commentator had joked. The commander of the American forces during a key phase of the Philippine-American war, Gen. Arthur MacArthur, father of Douglas MacArthur, told of how when he first steamed out to Manila in 1898, "There was little or no literature aboard from which instructive information could be obtained. One writer to whom we had access advised all travelers to carry coffins, as few returned alive from Manila. Another and more optimistic writer cited an Eastern epigram to the effect that for romance and adventure the entire Eastern world relied upon Manila. These two facts constituted about all we could learn by investigation.

"As a general proposition, when the command entered Manila Bay everybody was in a totally ignorant but especially sensitive and receptive state of mind. It was apparent, however, that we had entered a new world of various and great resources, teeming with a dense population that was in a paroxysmal state of excitement."

MacArthur was to discover for himself how that population,

when finally provoked beyond its customary patience, could unite even though its territory was so vast. He and his men knew they would be fighting in parts of the north, on the 42,000-square-mile island of Luzon, which was also the most populous island and contained the seat of government, Manila. They had thought that what they considered to be tribal rivalries would keep the rest of the country out of war. But they soon found themselves also fighting in the central Philippines, in the heavily populated group of islands called the Visayas—including Leyte, Samar, Panay, Negros and Cebu—which seemed on the surface a storybook version of a tropical paradise. They also found themselves at war in the southern Philippines, on the 38,000-square-mile, frontierlike Mindanao, and on the smaller islands running farther south from it.

The Philippines starts with the small Batanes Islands in the far north, which are in sight of what was called Formosa, later Taiwan. Running south for the 1200 miles of the nation's length, the chain, about 700 miles wide, ends, after Luzon, the Visayas and Mindanao, with the Sulu islands, which are within sight of Borneo. The logistics of subduing such an entity were naturally nothing at all like subduing a Cuba or a Puerto Rico. To go into the Philippines, it turned out, constituted a major war of conquest.

That faraway war, entered almost by chance, also turned out to be the harshest foreign war yet at that point in America's history. Atrocities committed by both sides were a harbinger of Vietnam. And yet vicious though the fighting became, the Americans wound up being remembered by Filipinos less as enemy invaders than as partners in putting together the first democratic nation in the Orient.

Before the war was over, responsibility for the Philippines had been transferred from the American military to American civilians. Even as the war was in progress, boatloads of American schoolteachers were arriving, and soon the American soldiers turned their attention from killing to building roads and schools, digging wells and distributing food. In 1907, with mopping-up operations still in progress, the first nationwide legislative elections were held. In addition, Filipinos were also placed in most top administrative and judicial positions.

As of 1935 the Philippines, now a U.S. Commonwealth, had its own elected President as well as its Congress, its own constitution and an all-Filipino Supreme Court. In all matters except foreign affairs, it was essentially self-governing, with American-style democratic elections, Bill of Rights protections and a clear separation between the executive, legislative and judicial branches. Throughout World War II the Filipinos, unlike any of the other mainstream Southeast Asian peoples, fought fiercely against the Japanese. The year after the war ended, keeping strictly to a schedule set up in 1935, the Philippines became the first colony anywhere in the postwar world to receive full independence.

The Americanization did not vanish with independence. It remained the dominant foreign overlay in a nation that still retained elements from ancient days of other Oriental cultures. It was more immediately apparent even than the Spanish overlay, although the people mostly had Spanish names and were 85 percent Roman Catholic, constituting the largest Catholic country in Asia. But the American influence, after half a century of colonial rule, was what was most striking. Among much else, the Republic of the Philippines had become an English-speaking country, the largest in Asia after India and the fourth largest in the world.

The other Malay countries, Indonesia and Malaysia, after their independence each created a new national language, a simplified form of the many Malay languages, for use as a lingua franca. The Philippines, however, gave official status only to Tagalog, the Malay language spoken around Manila, even though Filipinos too spoke many distinct Malay languages and dialects. The reason was that the Philippines did not need a new lingua franca: it already had one. For decades now, English had been the medium of instruction in the schools, the first language of government and major commerce, and also the official language of the courts and the military.

But language was only one of many outward signs of what bound the Philippines to America. The bond was deeply emotional as well. For American right-wingers the Philippines, much like the Panama Canal, remained a symbol of American might, a reminder of an age when America had been able to flex its muscles, a piece of living imperial history. To other Americans it was the one place in the Third World where American ideals had taken hold, not just the free enterprise system but also concepts of democracy and freedom. And to Filipinos—even those on the left who decried American colonialism and "neocolonialism"—America and all things American continued to have a special place in their lives.

When we returned to Manila in 1983, the contrast between the royal life and the life of squalor that Marcos had created simultaneously had been intensely disorienting. But even before Marcos and martial law in the Philippines there were factors, because of the American veneer, that made Americans constantly seek reassurance that what their senses told them was true. Much of Philippine life then, as now, seemed to Americans a peculiarly distorted reenactment of life at home.

Back in democratic days when there was a Philippine Congress, there was also a House Un-Filipino Activities Committee. The Philippines did not recognize the Soviet Union, much less China, until the 1970s. At Christmastime, "I Saw Mommy Kissing Santa Claus" had the status almost of a carol. Mother's Day and Valentine's Day were near-sacred national holidays. Prudish Protestant homilies, such as "The Family That Prays Together Stays Together," glaringly inapplicable to such a hedonistic and Latinized macho Oriental society, were tacked up in schoolrooms and appeared on billboards erected by the Rotary clubs that flourished in all towns of any size. The products used by those who could afford manufactured goods were usually American brand-name products, often made locally under license.

The men, women and children of the Philippines brushed their teeth with Dr. West toothbrushes and Colgate toothpaste, shampooed with Prell and deodorized themselves with Mum and Arid. Hamburgers and hot dogs were served along with the Indian-influenced native food of the region and Spanish and Chinese dishes. Despite the tropical fruit growing all around them, Filipinos offered canned Del Monte fruit cocktail to their most honored guests. Baseball and then basketball took over from cockfighting and jai alai as the best-attended spectator sports.

The lively newspapers of the pre-1972 era of freedom gave heavy play to the World Series. They were also quick to follow American papers in referring to Presidents' wives with the capitalized honorific "First Lady." When boys shouted "Hey, Joe!" at you on the street, there were overtones of wartime camaraderie passed down through the generations, rarely insult. The fast-moving traffic of the towns and cities was dominated by another reminder of war days, the open mini-buses called Jeepneys, which had first been made from surplus U.S. Army Jeeps; now the bodies were made locally, covered with chrome, decorative figures and tassels, and painted in brilliant tones, though the old frontal shape of the Jeep was maintained.

Darting daringly through traffic that might include animals as well as little Datsun taxis and Cadillac limousines, the Jeepneys, blaring music from their stereo speakers, were part of the color of the islands, and even considered uniquely Filipino. It may have seemed a hall of mirrors, but before martial law it was, at the very least, a place where people commonly smiled with pleasure, not with the Oriental smile of nervousness that came back later. The Philippines was a place where residents and visitors alike nearly always seemed to be relishing life.

There was music everywhere—on vehicles, in offices and workshops, in the parks and streets, coming from farmers' fields and everyone's homes. It was not the singsong music of the Orient but rather a precise replica of the best of American popular music, whether jazz, soul, acid rock or the big band sound. Filipinos had long been noted throughout the region as entertainers. All through non-Communist Asia it was a matter of prestige to have a Filipino band playing in a nightclub or hotel lounge, and as often as not the American-seeming sounds these groups produced had been composed by Filipinos.

Any fad or phenomenon that caught on in America was likely to catch on in the Philippines. In 1983, for example, everyone, whether they had the money or not, was talking about the pleasures of home videotaping. Advertising and public relations had long been professions much more respected in the Philippines than in the America that had invented them. In 1983 we saw giant U.S.-style billboards sticking up from behind the walls that concealed a particularly squalid slum adjoining the road between the Malate and Makati sections of Manila. The billboards carried such messages as that "SWISS QUALITY KNORR SEASONING" is a taste enhancer that "PERKS UP FOOD," and that "YOU'LL LOVE THE FAMED WHITE SANDS OF MATABUNGKAY," an elite beach resort.

But the unintentionally ironic and piquant touches of America that were, and remained, a part of everyday life in the Philippines amounted to much more than comedy. They were outward expressions of the deep inner ties felt by Filipinos with America. And Americans, even in the dark later years of the Marcos dictatorship, even as political opposition to them grew, remained personally popular in the islands. That popularity could be attested to by any American who had recently been on the receiving end of the hospitality for which the Filipinos were always noted and of which they were justly proud.

The popularity lingered because, for all the mirror-image distortions, the Philippine-American connection had to do with more than trivial manifestations of the American way of life. Much of what was best about America was also best about the Philippines.

Not everything was perfect after independence, but the Filipinos had taken to the business of self-government with a spirit that was still remembered nostalgically in the 1980s, even by Marxists who opposed liberal democracy as much as they opposed the dictatorship. Whatever the complaints about the society, the people had known they could kick the rascals out. Presidents were commonly voted out after a single term in office. Members of the House and Senate too, and also provincial governors, mayors and other local officials, knew they would be one-termers if their performance did not match their promises. Institutions that had grown up during the American era, including government pension plans and a social security system, were honored. The judiciary, by and large, was respected; and the Supreme Court was considered absolutely incorruptible.

Political campaigns were always exciting, much like those in America before the days of television. They featured such hoopla as combination mass rallies and picnics and torchlight parades. The press was by far the freest in Asia and never hesitated to criticize, even blast and insult, the highest officials.

There were inequities between rich and poor, though not so vast as they would become after the dictatorship. As in the rest of Southeast Asia, there was corruption on all levels of government, but never like that brought in with the dictatorship when corruption became nationalized, in effect, with all illicit as well as licit economic activities in the country controlled from the presidential mansion, Malacañang Palace. Interest groups prevented Congress from passing implementing legislation to carry out plans to redistribute the land. But at least land reform was gaining a certain momentum—in glaring contrast to the situation under the dictatorship in which Marcos, after beginning land redistribution schemes, dropped them and was consciously steering agricultural development into a colonial export plantation pattern.

Before 1972, in almost every sphere the Philippines was leading the large new nations of its region. Not only were its universities the leaders of Southeast Asia, its population was nearly 90 percent literate, a figure that approached 100 percent in the larger towns and cities. It had far more doctors per capita than any other nation in the region, and the same was true of all the professions.

In addition to being the region's educational center, Manila was in many ways the financial center too. Long before the berserk building programs of the dictator and his wife, Manila already had the most impressive array of new skyscrapers of any city of the region, including those in the Makati section on Ayala Boulevard, widely known as the "Wall Street of Asia."

Certain Filipino figures had already achieved international renown. There was Carlos P. Romulo, the author and statesman who had served as a nonvoting member of the U.S. Congress in the 1930s, later was on MacArthur's staff, and was serving as president of the United Nations General Assembly at the time of the Korean War. There was Ramón Magsaysay, a former bus mechanic, who as secretary of defense in the early 1950s put down a Communist challenge through reform combined with force of arms, and went on to the presidency.

And there were others, better known inside the Philippines than outside, who had taken up the challenges presented by the modern world. One was Aquino himself, who had served with Magsaysay and knew that democracy in the Philippines could be saved only by much greater reform than had been accomplished so far. There was the Jesuit-trained academic and one-time foreign secretary and senator Raul Manglapus, who set up a new reform political party, the Christian Social Democrats, that had been winning the allegiance of more and more students and young professional people just before martial law. Earlier there had been the nationalist senator Claro M. Recto, who had convinced much of the country that if it was to realize its potential it had to shake off its image of being a military appendage of the United States.

In the years just before martial law the voices calling for reform and for development along lines that put Filipino interests over those of America were becoming louder and were being heard. The workers in the cities, the nation's subsistence farmers, the laborers on the plantations, were all organizing. They were founding cooperatives, federations and unions. When challenged by the wealthy, court decisions were going in their favor. In mid-1971 a Constitutional Convention was convened at which the delegates were articulating their desire for a policy of internal development and more equitable distribution of the nation's income, and also a foreign policy that reflected nationalistic feelings. Meanwhile the church, which in the past had been considered a voice of conservatism, was increasingly becoming a voice for reform. The old-fashioned, business-as-usual politics of the by then lame duck Marcos and the group around him seemed headed for extinction.

Later an American Franciscan missionary asked, "Could this have been the reason why martial law was declared: because democracy was just beginning to work [and] the grievances of the masses were finally being organized, getting aired, bringing pressure to bear on the political institutions?"

Most Filipinos saw martial law in more personal terms. They believed that it resulted from nothing more than intense, driving personal ambition at work—the ambition of Marcos, his wife, Imelda, and those who depended upon them for their share of the nation's wealth and their positions of power.

During democratic years there had been a certain amount of ballot-box stuffing; there had been cases of voters being paid, even cases in the provinces of voter intimidation, before Marcos came along. The big political families maintained troops of bodyguards so large they sometimes amounted almost to private armies. But it was nothing like one man having a full national army at his personal disposal, as was the case after martial law. And anyway voters had redress through the workings of the widely respected nonpartisan Commission on Elections that had been given solid enforcement powers, including powers over the police and the military, at the time of independence.

Incidents of tampering with elections notwithstanding, Filipino politicians had for the most part played by the rules since Commonwealth days. Then, in November 1965, a new sort of man was elected President.

4

UNDOING AMERICA'S WORK

A New Breed in the Palace

FERDINAND E. MARCOS was a former congressman and senator who had first come to public attention in the 1930s, while still in his teens, when he handled his own defense to beat the rap for the murder of a successful political rival of his father. Having seen life from both sides of jail bars when very young, he approached politics, and eventually the presidency, in both old and new ways.

On the one hand Marcos was a typical old-line politician, a one-sided man of steel nerves who lived and breathed politics, always concerned with voter opinion and legal niceties. On the other hand, as it turned out, he was a man willing to overturn all laws, a man with ambitions of becoming the first Filipino caudillo.

According to the picture he drew of himself, he was in many ways a creature of America. Periodically throughout his career he claimed that he deserved respect, and in the long run obedience, because he was virtually America's representative in the region—what Lyndon Johnson, at the time Marcos agreed to send a battalion to Vietnam, called "my strong right arm in Asia."

He developed the habit of labeling every political foe a

Communist, as if the use of this scare-word would please the Americans, upon whom he depended to arm his military and save his country from bankruptcy. When he imposed martial law in 1972 Marcos said he needed the extra powers to go after the Communists, but first he went after the liberals and moderates instead. Toward the end, the word "Communist" had almost no meaning at Malacañang Palace. By now Marcos had called such people as bishops of the church, distinguished old senators and congressmen, planters in the provinces and industrialists in the cities, either Communists or Communist tools.

He said what he was doing to his country was for the sake of American prestige in the region. Yet America's one apparently solid historical achievement in Asia, the creation of a functioning democracy in a large nation, was the very target of his campaign, begun with the 1972 coup, to rip apart all of the Philippines' national institutions that America had helped build.

Ferdinand Marcos was a peculiarly secretive man who came from the narrow strip of inhospitable farmland that lies between the mountain chain called the Cordillera and the South China Sea in northwestern Luzon. It is an area called the Ilocos provinces. The people of these harsh provinces, the Ilocanos, are related to warriors of Sumatra, from which they originally emigrated. Finding themselves on bad land in the Philippines, from the start they lived by their wits, trusting only each other, trying to best peoples from more bountiful provinces. They became the most tight-lipped and clannish of all Filipinos, and among the most enterprising.

Because their lands could not support them, they moved out into other provinces, though they kept ties to home and stayed apart from other ethnic groups. In Manila the Ilocanos were sometimes looked down upon by high society as a race of chauffeurs and maids. But they entered the military in large numbers, since it meant a chance to escape poverty and perhaps get a free education. Whenever and wherever possible they aimed at bettering themselves by education and getting on the government payroll. Many went further as distinguished academics and professionals.

Ninoy Aquino, a man of Luzon's fertile central plains who admired spontaneity and had the common touch Marcos lacked, used to speak with us at length about what motivated the dictator. In his exile Aquino was a visiting scholar, first at Harvard and then at MIT; in addition to his city home he kept a lake house, with no phones, in an old mill town west of Boston, where one of us used to spend days and nights talking with him. Aquino was obsessed with Marcos—just as, palace visitors told us in Manila, Marcos was obsessed with Ninoy. Although Aquino was fifteen years Marcos's junior, they had in common the promise when very young of one day becoming President of the Republic. But while Marcos was the son of a failed politician, Ninoy had illustrious forebears. He was the son of a renowned senator and the grandson of a hero of the Philippine-American war. Like Marcos, he had become a national celebrity while still a teenager.

Aquino was the Philippines' leading foreign correspondent at seventeen, covering the American war in Korea and the French one in Indochina. He then became the youngest city editor of a major newspaper in Manila and, simultaneously, the story editor of the Philippines' largest movie company. Next he was elected mayor of his hometown, Concepcion, at twenty-three the youngest mayor in the country. As a personal emissary of President Magsaysay in the early 1950s he had accepted the surrender of the main leaders of the Huk rebellion, which was centered in his home province of Tarlac but directed at Manila; for this he received the Philippine equivalent of the U.S. Congressional Medal of Honor.

Aquino was still in his twenties when he became governor of Tarlac and under thirty-five when, in 1967, he was elected by the nation at large to the Senate, where he quickly established himself as the leading critic of the then only two-year-old Marcos administration. There were love-hate aspects to the Marcos-Aquino relationship; ever since they had come to each other's attention in the early 1950s as likely future presidents, they had been on a collision course.

Ninoy liked to tell of how "Marcos had the advantage of the clannishness of the Ilocanos and the spread of the Ilocanos all over the machinery of government. Marcos was a very distinguished young man. Even as a young man when he topped the Bar [the nationwide annual bar exam for new law graduates], there was no doubt in the minds of people that Marcos would one day be President. As a young Congressman he was already selected by his peers to be a leader. . . .

"He was known to be very loyal to his friends. . . . But in spite of that, he was a very private man. He never really confided. He played his cards very close to his chest. He was a womanizer, but he never displayed it; he was very discreet. I remember we were both delegates to [an international conference for men of public affairs in] Geneva; he was screwing around, but he kept it to himself. He would listen, but he'd never give his part of the story. I found that queer. I never liked him at that point. I never trusted that bastard. He would listen but never give anything. Somehow, when you made a deal with Marcos he gave you the impression he had something up his sleeve. He was two or three steps ahead of you. . . .

"He would never, never move until he was very, very sure. So long as he could use you, goddamn it, he would use you. He'd embrace you like a cobra. He was a sneaky bastard. He was not an open man, but he was cunning. He was brilliant and he knew how to use power. He knew timing and he built on that myth."

The myth was that he was always a step ahead of his rivals and always knew at any given moment what they, and also the people he governed, were doing. But between his first election to the presidency in 1965 and his coup that changed the system in 1972, Marcos's political life had begun to go sour.

It was not that he had failed in a material sense. Already, before martial law, he had made more money out of the presidency than had any of his predecessors. It had begun when he was in Congress. He had, as we traced it with one of his closest pre–martial law officials, established a racketeer's stranglehold on the Ilocos provinces; he had made fortunes through kickbacks from the Virginia tobacco business that started there, and further fortunes from selling citizenship papers to Chinese merchants; he had also worked foreign exchange scams for his political contributors. Large-scale graft became part of the Marcos way. But money was not enough.

Unlike his wife, he wanted money only for the power it gave him and the power it denied those he took it from, not for the pleasures it could buy. He was a man who lived only for politics and had no pleasures, except golf while conducting business and a bit of secret womanizing, outside the political power game. But he was limited by the constitution to two terms as President.

"Now don't forget," Ninoy said, "Marcos became President when he was only forty-eight. Assuming he would serve two terms, he would be only fifty-six and what does a guy of fifty-six do at the peak of his health?"

Aquino had concluded back in 1966 that even then Marcos had decided that "he was going to be the first president for life." He was from the very start secretly scheming to overthrow the system, in part by placing Ilocanos in key posts, Aquino said. And this was why when Aquino entered the Senate in 1968 he used his maiden speech "to tell the Filipino people to beware of this President because this guy is making a state where we will end up in a huge concentration camp."

Soon after Aquino's warning, Marcos suffered a major embarrassment when he was caught—and exposed personally by Aquino—setting up a small secret commando army to snatch territory in Borneo from Malaysia. He had been exposed as having had the commandos killed to cover up what he had done. Stories began to circulate about murders he had ordered elsewhere, especially in the Ilocos provinces, to silence opponents. Then shortly before the 1971 Senate elections, three explosions went off in rapid succession during a rally for the opposition Liberal Party candidates at a Manila church square called Plaza Miranda.

A score of people lost their lives in Plaza Miranda and some eight dozen, including the candidates themselves, were wounded. A reform-minded senator from Marcos's own Nationalist Party, José W. Diokno, produced evidence, never refuted in any court, showing that the explosions came from grenades that could only have been obtained by government law enforcement officials. Diokno, who was to be one of the first men jailed under martial law, resigned from the Nationalist Party in disgust. Marcos blamed the bombing on Communists, but produced no suspects.

Two years earlier Marcos had spent so much in state funds for his own reelection that he had had to devalue the currency right afterward. By 1971 even the unlimited money at his command was not enough, and his party lost seven of the eight Senate seats that were contested.

Then came massive student demonstrations that would continue to plague Marcos until he staged his coup and put a halt to free assembly. Day after day the students marched. Their slogans could be heard in Malacañang, as could the sounds of police firing into the crowds and the screams of young men and women being beaten with truncheons. Yet the students were back in the streets each day, and Manilans had the feeling that Marcos had lost control of his capital. But they wrote it off, since he was a lame duck and would soon be replaced.

He was quarreling with other power brokers and many

were deserting him, considering him impotent now as a force in national life. His Vice President, Fernando Lopez, no longer bothered to come to work.

Personal humiliation mounted. With freedom of speech still virtually total, a tape recording surfaced. It carried what was said to be the voice of Marcos singing love songs in his native Ilocano tongue, sounding like a love-struck W. C. Fields, while he was in a bed with a blonde Hollywood starlet, one Dovie Beams. Later at a news conference, Miss Beams herself told of the affair with Marcos. Copies of her under-the-mattress tape made the rounds; it was even broadcast by the campus radio station at the University of the Philippines.

Marcos was being laughed off as his legal term ended. Despite reform-minded opponents, a Gallup poll showed that increasing numbers of Filipinos were coming to the belief that conventional politics had been so debauched that it was time for the people to petition America for state-hood.

But up and down the country Aquino was on the stump. He was exposing not just Marcos but also Imelda, who had begun the first of her bizarre building projects. It seemed clear that there was no one around who could stop Aquino from winning the 1973 presidential election.

In 1983, one of Marcos's best-known and longest-standing supporters, newspaper columnist and Malacañang habitué Teodore Valencia, told us it was Marcos's very failings as a legal President that had led to martial law. Using the peculiar twisted reasoning that had become so common in Malacañang, Valencia said that if Marcos had followed the constitution and stepped down after the end of his second legal term, he would have been remembered "as a do-nothing president—and no one wants that!"

The pettiness of the rulers and the justifications they gave for what they did were as bizarre as the physical signs of their excesses and failings in 1983. Just before we got to Manila,

Marcos had had a large group of authors, journalists and middle-of-the-road and conservative politicians arrested and
thrown into jail. They had been picked up on Presidential
Commitment Orders, meaning they were personal prisoners
of Marcos. Their crime was that they had ties to a publication
that had questioned Marcos's World War II record.

Although Marcos had been a decorated wartime guerrilla
fighter, he had also, as Aquino and others put the story together, spent a good part of the war under the protection
of collaborators with the Japanese. He claimed to have won
a great many medals from both America and the Philippines,
but it had long since been proved beyond a doubt that many
of the medals were for feats of valor that had never taken
place, many of these claimed feats in actions that had gone
unrecorded in any dispatches. In the New Republic, however,
to question even the most egregious lies of the rulers was to
be guilty of "subversion," which was the charge under which
these men were being held. And now it came to light that
in a series of presidential decrees issued two years previously
but held secret until 1983, the very act of criticizing the government in general, or the President specifically, had been
made punishable by death.

By now, in 1983, Marcos hardly ever left the palace for
any reason. His people seldom saw him except on television.
He stayed in Malacañang brooding, palace visitors said, concerned about his personal place in history. More than anything
else he talked about the medals that historians said he did
not deserve. Much of his time was now spent supervising large
batteries of researchers and writers who were churning out
locally printed books under the Marcos name. No one, not
even in the Ministry of Information, also known as the Office
of Media Affairs, which was his publisher, could give an accurate count of how many volumes had come out. They covered
everything from the saga of the Filipino people since prehis-
toric times to the philosophies expounded at the University

of Life, from organizational charts of the New Republic bureaucracy to the Marcos war exploits and the historic significance not just of his own presidency but also of the presidency of Ronald Reagan.

When he attended to business in 1983, it was literally business, ordering that government funds be used to bail out companies whose titular owners were always relatives and friends. But even this, according to those who saw him most frequently, was secondary to his attempt literally to rewrite the history of the Philippine archipelago with himself and his wife as the central figures.

Yet he was apparently still plotting, as Aquino must have known at the moment of his death. With the help of his relatives, such as General Ver, the military chief of staff, he was ordering arrests here, loosening up there, ordering killings one day, the release of prisoners the next, constantly tinkering with the strange new state he had created.

Right after he had declared martial law in September 1972, Marcos had begun to build up two institutions to replace all the others he was tearing down. One was the military machine, now at his sole disposal, which had no function other than internal security. He raised its manpower from 60,000 to 300,000. Ilocanos were given the most key commands. And now officers swore loyalty not to any nation or republic but personally to the President himself.

What slack was left by the military was taken up by the second institution: a personal conglomerate, controlled directly or through front men by the President and the First Lady. Filipinos called it "the Octopus." Unlike other strongmen who began by attacking corruption, Marcos let it be known right at the start that corruption was fine with him so long as it remained under his personal control. Through the Octopus he and Imelda made themselves the wealthiest couple in the Far East by skimming from virtually all activities, whether inside or outside the law, that involved money in the Philippines—including the production and sale of sugar, coconuts, and other commodities, the issuance of letters of credit for foreign transactions, gambling, and tourism involving prostitution.

Because simple greed and power for its own sake, not fascist ideology, appeared to be the main motives, many foreigners tended at first to miss how thoroughly he was running his country by terror. Indeed, we had been visiting the Philippines periodically after 1972 and it was not until 1983 that we found people there commonly comparing what was happening to an El Salvador.

In the early years of martial law there was the widespread use—for the first time in the Philippines since the Japanese occupation—of political detention, torture and murder. There were military checkpoints at major intersections. There was an overseas travel ban for Filipinos and a national nightly curfew for everyone. But there were no tanks in the streets, nothing yet that was anything like the all-pervading terror so common in Central America.

And yet gradually the Philippines was becoming the equivalent of El Salvador, and on a grander scale. As the Communist guerrillas, the New People's Army, established fronts on all the major islands, the new military responded with increased torture and killing.

At the time Reagan came into office, Marcos had already become remote from his people, staying behind the walls of Malacañang Palace, already brooding on history as he directed that the military step up the terror. Increasingly the only people he dealt with besides his ghostwriters and business cronies were his Ilocano generals, whom he could trust because of blood ties, and his tall, fair, parvenu First Lady, Imelda, who right from the beginning of martial law had been entrusted with important state duties.

Imelda had started out by assuming the role of her husband's principal emissary to foreign countries. After three years—three years with no Congress to block presidential appointments—he began to give her official titles and specific grand-scale domestic duties and power. In 1975 he named her to a new post he created as "Governor of Metro-Manila," handing her life-and-death power over the 8 million people in the nation's urban core.

A CIA report prepared at the time for the eyes of President Ford and a select group of high officials spoke of the appointment as "further evidence of her growing strength as a political figure in her own right." The report went on to describe how "increased centralization of power since martial law was declared three years ago has given Mrs. Marcos a chance to form her own political coterie and to expand her personal influence into many new areas of government policy. She clearly hopes to exploit her enhanced power to build a political base that would enable her to take over in the event of her husband's abrupt departure from the scene."

"Mrs. Marcos is ambitious and ruthless," the report said. It called her the "presidential understudy" and stated that her "desire to become governor [of Manila] evidently stemmed from her belief that she needed to demonstrate her administrative talents. Her husband acceded to the idea. . . . Many Filipinos believe that Marcos has left a political will naming his wife his successor."

The report said that because Imelda was born "a poor cousin of landed aristocracy, she has a thirst for wealth, power and public acclaim, and her boundless ego makes her easy prey for flatterers. Although she has little formal education, she is cunning."

But the CIA analysis pointed out that "Manila's middle and lower classes . . . have never liked the Marcos clan," and doubted that Mrs. Marcos would accomplish much of anything for the benefit of Manilans since "she has a short attention span." It continued: "After only a week on the job, she left town for a visit to the U.S., explaining that her new domestic job could not be permitted to interfere with her foreign policy interests. Part of Mrs. Marcos's problem in being taken seriously as a successor to her husband is her freewheeling lifestyle featuring world junkets and jet set friends."

The CIA report had put it mildly. In February and March 1983, while one of us was exploring the slums of Manila and the Communist strongholds in the provinces, the other was attending state functions in the capital, sometimes at the new Tourist Pavilion in the royal complex on Manila Bay. Late at night at the Tourist Pavilion, with honored guests from home and abroad in their jewels and formal attire, disembodied voices would fill the air long before her arrival: "The First Lady has left the Palace. . . . The First Lady is on her way. . . . The First Lady has reached the Convention Center." An orchestra playing popular tunes would increase its volume and tempo. Then there would be a pause, all lights would dim, and spotlights would go on, directed to a far corner of the gardens.

She would appear as if from some fairyland, wearing a brightly colored gown with butterfly wings, a star's made-up face beneath a huge tiara, sweeping into the pavilion as everyone stood. At fifty-three she retained the bearing she had exhibited as a successful young beauty pageant contestant. Behind her came hundreds of people—government ministers, lackeys and lovely girls—who would fan out to drape garlands around the necks of the more noted guests. Instantly, camera crews would appear all over the gardens.

A Philippine cabinet minister would take the microphone and give a long rhapsodic speech of praise: "I just cannot believe what this great woman has accomplished in so short a time. I look around me here at what used to be water and I see the works she has performed. . . ."

Imelda would speak too. Then she would sing. Then she would coax a minister from Indonesia or Thailand to the bandstand to join her in a duet. Her performance could last minutes, or it could last hours.

Then suddenly she would depart, loud music rising in tempo as again everyone stood to pay homage. Once she was gone you felt as if you were awakening: had this apparition been an actual person or was it a sequence from a dream?

But this woman was not just a dream. She was the driving force behind the construction projects that had so changed the face of Manila, although much of the time she continued to flit about outside the country. While abroad, as at home, she was spending part of her time on political missions but most of it in the pursuit of pleasure. For these trips she routinely used two airplanes, DC-10s or Boeing 747s from the Philippine Air Lines' fleet, to transport her vast retinue of security forces, international hangers-on, and homegrown sycophants. If her husband was presenting his version of the New Republic through ghostwriters and vanity publishing, she had entrusted hers to the world's gossip columnists.

Her retinue, which could take in almost anyone who might interest paparazzi, usually included Henry Ford's ex-wife Cristina, who by the 1980s had a house of her own on the grounds of the Marcoses' Malacañang Palace, where she was usually seen with, among other gifts from Imelda, young macho Philippine movie stars. The size of the retinue had expanded as Imelda's powers increased. By now, in addition to her other duties, she was Minister of Human Settlements, a vaguely defined new cabinet position that virtually gave her control over nearly anything she wanted to control, not just in Manila but all through the land.

In the retinue there were royal pretenders of Europe, such as Count Mario D'Urso and Princess Maria Gabriella of Savoy, as well as whatever Hollywood has-beens she had recently decided to take up. They were always accompanied by scores of protectors from the Presidential Security Command of the Army, the elite military unit that supplied troops to guard the palace, and also NISA, the National Intelligence and Security Authority, the all-powerful secret police system her husband had created as his equivalent of Iran's old SAVAK. Also included were the newly rich wives of her and her husband's martial law business cronies, who served as ladies-in-waiting, with special blue dresses to so designate them. And the "Blue Ladies" were always joined by scores of lovely young Filipinas chosen purely for decorative purposes.

These women and girls, Philippine businessmen, European aristocrats and American beautiful people acted, quite literally, as a chorus, often speaking praise in unison in the sort of language servants use in the Philippines: "Oh yes, Mum, you're right." The chorus came in as she expounded on how the bulk of Filipinos, whom she called "my little people," loved her for her excesses because, as she frequently repeated, "they want to see a star." She would say of her little people, "If they had money they'd only spend it on drugs and alcohol. What a bore."

While abroad with her entourage, it was routine for Imelda to have an entire department store closed to the public, or opened after hours, so that she could spend hundreds of thousands of dollars in a single outlandish, purely personal shopping spree. And all over the world she was constantly picking up real estate, some of it expensive downtown commercial property but much of it townhouses and country manors to house her new possessions.

Just as it was difficult for someone without a nineteenth-century Oriental mind to take in the grandeur of the new Manila built by and for the rulers, and also to take in the scope of the country's human suffering, so was it difficult to believe what you were seeing when you saw Imelda in action.

But as it turned out, Imelda, who had played such a central part in destroying the American-style democracy in the islands, was not too much for the imagination of Ronald Reagan.

5

WASHINGTON RAISES THE STAKES

The Embrace by Reagan

THE FIRST CLEAR and specific signal that radical change in the American-Philippine relationship was ahead actually came in December 1980 during the interregnum between Reagan's election and his inauguration. Imelda Marcos, in the course of one of those two-jet trips she turned into royal processions, was in New York, staying at the Waldorf Towers. Ronald Reagan, along with George Bush, was at the Waldorf Towers too, conducting the business of the transition. He knew Imelda from the past. Back when he was governor of California he had been to Manila on a junket for the opening of the first of her cultural centers. Now he agreed to meet with her again.

Aside from parties and shopping, Imelda had come to America this time with politics on her mind. In addition to looking for a chance to see Reagan, she was hoping to negotiate with prominent non-Communist exile opposition leaders. She wanted to tell them that Reagan's election meant the game was up, since henceforth there would be a man in the White House who would collude with Marcos to bring about their downfall. Although these exile figures were all under death sentence or charged with capital crimes in the Philippines, she was offering them safe conduct home if they would recant and swear fealty to her husband.

After her meeting with Reagan Imelda saw, among others, the former senator Ninoy Aquino, who had gone into exile that year after his long solitary confinement; he flew in from Boston to find out what the lady at the Waldorf was thinking. Then a few days later, a tall, bearded Greek-born American citizen named Steve Psinakis, a longtime pre–martial law resident of Manila, flew to New York from San Francisco for an appointment with Imelda. Psinakis was the exile activist most consistently attacked and threatened by the agents, inside and outside the Philippines, of the Marcoses. His wife, Presy, was the daughter of a formerly wealthy entrepreneur whose holdings Marcos had seized through extortion, the sister of a former Manila newspaper publisher whom Marcos had held hostage to get at the family's wealth, and the niece of the Vice President who had quit before martial law was established. Steve and Presy had been the most vociferous of the activists from abroad working for the overthrow of the dictator. Steve was said to have his own agents in the islands acting to destabilize the regime, and two years earlier he had been the mastermind of an intercontinental Hollywood-style escape caper in which his brother-in-law had been sprung from one of Marcos's most secure military jails.

As soon as Aquino finished his session with Imelda he got on the phone to Psinakis, who had still not made up his mind whether or not to see her. Summing up the meeting in his typical rapid-fire fashion, Ninoy said, as Steve recorded it:

Number one: It was a good friendly meeting. Number two: She did almost all the talking for more than four hours. . . . Number three: She tried to appear confident and impress me with her contact with Reagan. I understand Reagan and Bush were also staying at the Waldorf and she met with them. She told me they spent more time with her than with [West German Chancellor] Helmut Schmidt. Number four: You won't believe this but she gave a dinner for Nixon in her suite last Sunday and she videotaped the whole affair. She showed me the program. Nixon couldn't praise her enough. He referred to Imelda as "the Angel from Asia" who came to him when he was down and out. . . . Number five: She told me that you and I have sent assassination teams to Manila to knock off some of her people. . . . Number six: She sounded confident that the Reagan administration will go after us here, especially you. . . . That's it in a nutshell.

Psinakis, our first prime contact when we first began tracking the changes in the Philippines, had feared the election of Ronald Reagan. Marcos had been blaming Psinakis, along with Ninoy and other exile figures such as the former senator and foreign secretary Raul Manglapus, for the urban arson and bombings that had been carried out in the past year to destabilize his regime. Recently a Philippine-American businessman, Victor Burns Lovely, Jr., had blown himself up in his hotel room in Manila, losing an eye, a hand and most of his hearing. He had been interrogated mercilessly in a hospital, then presented live on Manila television giving a transparently rehearsed confession saying he was an agent of Psinakis and Aquino, and that Psinakis had personally given him the bomb.

Later Psinakis wrote a book, with the ironic title *Two Terrorists Meet*, about the six hours he finally spent with Imelda at the Waldorf. At one point, according to notes he made immediately after the meeting, she had told him:

> Steve, the President [Marcos] has decided to lift martial law next month. He is very sincere about it, and he has already made an announcement. You know, last week I met with President-elect Reagan and Mr. Bush. They both expressed their friendship and support for the Philippines and for the President. They realize what an important ally we are to the U.S. and how important our country is to the security of the U.S. interests in the region. Reagan is quite different from Carter. I told Reagan—please, Steve, keep this to yourself—that the President plans to lift martial law next month and he told me not to act hastily. He said the stability and security of our country is

vital to the U.S., and we should not rush into any changes which might affect the stability of the Philippines. He practically told me not to lift martial law yet.

Neither Reagan nor his spokesmen ever denied that this was the gist of the initial face-to-face meeting between the incoming administration and the Marcos dictatorship. Psinakis summed up the fears of the opposition when he said, "I did not doubt Imelda was telling the truth about Reagan's comments on martial law. Reagan had made it clear during the campaign that he would support any tin-horn dictator who would claim to be pro-American and anti-Communist. Whether the dictator was in power illegally or whether he was staying in power by terrorizing his people and violating human rights would not be reason enough for Reagan to put some distance between such a dictator and the U.S. government."

Not only was Reagan placing himself and America closer to the Philippine dictator; soon some of the most powerful men in his new administration were journeying to Manila. By their actions there, they were showing the extent to which the opposition's fears about the Reagan-Marcos combination were coming true.

Just as Reagan's term began, Marcos announced that he was indeed ending martial law, but in the same breath he also announced that he was retaining all the powers he had given himself under martial law edicts, and issued a series of new edicts that permitted him to continue to rule by decree and to take personal political prisoners without bothering to use judicial procedures—in effect continuing martial law into the indefinite future. He announced he would hold what amounted to a Napoleonic plebiscite to give his country yet another in the bewildering array of constitutions it had had since his 1972 coup. He also announced a presidential election for a new six-year term under the new constitution.

The election was boycotted by all branches of the opposition, in the first joint action of moderates and Marxists. Marcos sent soldiers into villages all over the country; in some cases they left decapitated bodies in the village squares as a warning to get voters to go to the polls—even though no recognized opposition figures were running, only slates of unknowns designated by Marcos.

In June 1981, just as the election ended, Reagan dispatched the new secretary of state, Alexander Haig, to Manila. On June 18, Haig handed Marcos a personal letter from Reagan. Its theme, as reported in a UPI story datelined Manila, was that the "United States has agreed to help the Philippines fight terrorism by possibly prosecuting U.S.–based Filipino rebels. . . . President Ferdinand Marcos said visiting Secretary of State Alexander Haig gave him a letter from President Reagan that said Reagan's 'first concern really is fighting terrorism.

" 'The State Department is following up with the FBI and the Department of Justice the prosecution of terrorists operating in the Philippines and based in the United States,' the Reagan letter said.

"Marcos also said Haig requested the return to the United States of captured American terrorist Victor Burns Lovely to testify against Filipino exiles who allegedly plotted the bombings."

The story went on to describe how, according to the letter, various U.S. agencies, which sanctioned other exiles openly training to attack left-wing governments in the Caribbean and Central America, were cooperating in investigating the Philippine exiles. And Marcos also told the press, the story said, that "the Philippines and the United States are in the final stages of negotiations for an extradition treaty. Marcos did not say if the proposed treaty would include political crimes, but added, 'I think everyone should be covered. That is our position.' "

Almost instantly all moderate leaders of the exile opposition in America were visited simultaneously by FBI agents. Not a single opposition figure had accepted Imelda's offer to be permitted to join Marcos. Before long Psinakis's house would be searched in the middle of the night and his files taken away in a big FBI raid that included gunplay. And meanwhile the administration and the Marcos government initialed a radical extradition treaty.

If ever ratified by the U.S. Senate, where action was delayed, and upheld by the courts, extradition decisions concerning whether a crime committed in the Philippines was political or criminal would be transferred from the judiciary to the State Department.

Lovely was returned to America. Grand jury proceedings were begun against Psinakis. Lovely, though he would later begin alternately confirming and recanting his testimony, was placed under the Federal Witness Protection Program, which normally is used to protect informers in the domestic world of organized crime.

Although the new treaty seemed stalled, political asylum was practically eliminated for Filipinos; most of those already in America, such as Ninoy, would have their status revoked, left in limbo with neither Philippine passports nor American travel papers.

Nothing comparable had ever happened in America regarding the Philippines. But it was not so much the Haig visit to Manila that captured the imagination of Filipinos as the next official visit, which occurred some days later.

The occasion was Marcos's latest inauguration. The 1981 election had been farcical and characterized by overkill even though there had been no serious opposition. In addition to the killings to warn people against boycotting, the government had sent flying squads of voters from hamlet to hamlet to cast and recast ballots. Schoolteachers had been enlisted as poll watchers, and in the few cases in which they had refused to release results lopsidedly favorable to Marcos they had been forced to do so at gunpoint. The result was that the government announced Marcos had won with 88 percent of the vote.

It was not the first time such a thing had happened during martial law. It was but the latest in a long series of elections and plebiscites, some making use of ballots, some based on a show of hands in meetings held throughout the country. The results showing nearly unanimous acceptance of Marcos were always treated with universal skepticism. But the announced results of the 1981 election, if the subject of laughter everywhere in the islands, were good enough for Reagan's personal envoy to the elaborate inauguration festivities in Manila—Vice President George Bush.

On June 30, 1981, from a reviewing stand in the Luneta park near Manila Bay, Bush watched ceremonies that featured such trappings as a 1000-voice choir singing the words of Handel, "And he shall reign for ever and ever . . ."; a massive overfly of American-made jet fighters; and a guard of horsemen from the Manila Polo Club.

Then, back at Malacañang Palace, Bush joined the Marcoses in a post-inauguration celebration luncheon. He was in a peculiarly depreppyfied state, wearing the transparent embroidered shirt that is the Philippine male national dress, with tropical flowers draped from his neck to his knees. He stood and raised his glass, and looked in turn at his hostess and his host.

"We stand with the Philippines," he said, words that would be played and replayed by the state over radio and television. "We stand with you, sir. We love your adherence to democratic principles and to the democratic processes, and we will not leave you in isolation."

For one of the few times since martial law, the Philippines was suddenly the subject of editorials in most major American newspapers. Maybe it was a mistake, some of the editorialists said: it seemed impossible that a man of Bush's experience could say such a thing in a dictatorship that had so methodically dismantled the institutions of democratic government. But when Bush was approached by reporters in Hawaii on his way home, and later in Washington, he reiterated that he had meant what he said.

Now the rumor went out that the Marcoses would at long last get the official invitation to Washington they had so long coveted. Although their economic policies were falling apart and the Communist rebellion was on the rise, people who saw them on a day-to-day basis told us that from this point on a spirit of euphoria prevailed at Malacañang Palace.

There were other visits from Americans just below cabinet rank. On September 23, 1981, for example, U.S. Deputy Defense Secretary Frank Carlucci met in Manila with Marcos's old bodyguard, now Chief of Staff of the Armed Forces of the Philippines, Gen. Fabian Ver. According to the government press, Carlucci and Ver agreed the global significance of the big U.S. Air Force and Navy bases was an issue tied to control over internal subversion. They discussed plans for one of the next year's joint U.S.–Philippine military training exercises, which would use 3000 U.S. and Philippine troops in a mock invasion of Luzon, the Marcos press said.

Just before those war games, at the start of April of the following year, 1982, America's hard-line defense secretary, Caspar Weinberger, turned up in Manila. Marcos held a sumptuous luncheon for Weinberger that featured performances of native dances and an haute couture fashion show. Referring to Weinberger's service as a staff officer with Douglas MacArthur in World War II, Marcos hailed the defense secretary as "a son coming home." Marcos also produced yet another letter from President Reagan, this one brought by Weinberger, and read aloud from it: Reagan had promised that the United States would be a "steady and reliable partner" with the Philippine government in assuring military security. Weinberger spoke of the "deep nostalgia" he felt at returning to the Philippines, praised Marcos for attempts, which he did not detail, to improve his government's image, and gave the usual line about how the "road to peace is through strength."

Earlier, in a new secret "strategic guidance" that had been leaked to the *New York Times* and then made public, the Weinberger Defense Department had made clear just how seriously it took the role of the Philippines in America's overall world defense strategy. The strategic guidance claimed that America's Philippine bases had suddenly assumed new importance. With the Soviets getting established in Vietnam at Camranh Bay, the bases were needed, the document said, "to prevent the Soviet Union and Vietnam from expanding their influence in the region." And it said, "The biggest danger in Asia is the Soviet naval threat to American sea and air lines of communication that run from the West Coast through Hawaii, Guam and the Philippines to Diego Garcia and the American fleet in the Indian Ocean." This, and other documents that came out later, explained how the Reagan administration had determined that the Philippines was crucial to the Persian Gulf and even the Mediterranean.

And indeed the position of Subic and Clark bases, both less than sixty miles northeast of Manila and linked by a highly vulnerable forty-three-mile ten-inch oil pipeline, and of the various military and intelligence communications facilities spread about the islands, had not been exaggerated. Back in 1947, America's old colonial Fort Stotsenberg, a cavalry outpost that since 1917 had contained a landing strip called Clark Field, had been turned into Clark Air Base, which became, and remained, the headquarters of the U.S. Thirteenth Air Force. The old American naval station at Subic Bay, operational since 1907—and used to train most of the U.S. Marines who fought in World War I—was at the same time given the role it has kept through the years as the forward station for the U.S. Seventh Fleet. This first U.S.–Philippine Bases Agreement, signed in 1947, also allowed for operations by Americans outside the bases should internal unrest threaten these installations.

Over the years the importance of the bases increased. By

1983, Clark had all-weather runways that could service about 12,000 traffic movements a month, and it was serving as the communications hub for most U.S. Air Force traffic in the western Pacific and between the Pacific and the Indian Ocean. Seven or eight times a year U.S. Air Force units from all over the Pacific converged here for war games called "Cope Thunder," played out with Filipinos and sometimes other allies, which constituted the most extensive air combat training program regularly conducted outside America. Two-thirds of the air routes in the Philippines' flight pattern were permanently devoted to U.S. military use.

Subic, meanwhile, had evolved into the largest logistical support base in the western Pacific. Under Reagan it was serving as the home port for an American carrier task force designed for deployment to the Indian Ocean. It was being used for two-thirds of the support functions, including repair work, for the entire Seventh Fleet, which consisted of some 70,000 men, 550 aircraft and 90 ships.

Twenty-five miles north of Subic was the San Miguel communications station, which was the main communications center for the Seventh Fleet. And there were facilities at both San Miguel and Clark operated by the Pentagon and the CIA that were part of America's system of satellite surveillance of the Soviet Union.

Clark, serving as backup to the Australian Pine Gap CIA satellite surveillance system that covers the Soviet Union, had the only nonsatellite communications link from outside Australia to Pine Gap. Also, at the San Miguel station there was a radar installation aimed at detecting Soviet satellites, especially ASATs, antisatellite satellites that can disable the U.S. satellites. It was one of three such installations that the U.S. Air Force calls its "Pacific Barrier."

There was another surveillance system with a Philippine link, this one for detecting Soviet underground atomic tests. Clark was also a link in "Signal Scope," the worldwide communications system of the Strategic Air Command. And it was used by aircraft designed to provide instructions to America's nuclear submarines in case ground-based facilities were destroyed. Furthermore, P-3 Orion aircraft, apparently with "Lulu" nuclear depth charges, were based at Subic for purposes of hunting down Soviet missile submarines in the event of war. And at Clark and San Miguel the Pentagon and the CIA had strategic "C³I" systems—standing for "command, control, communication and intelligence"—for locating targets within the Soviet Union.

Filipino critics of the American bases naturally feared that they could draw nuclear retaliation against the Philippines in the event of a war between the superpowers. American critics said the bases should be moved elsewhere—to Guam, the Marianas, Palau, or even Singapore or South Korea—simply because the Philippines since 1972 had become one of the countries in the region most likely to be torn apart by internal conflict.

As if in recognition that the Philippines was so volatile that Americans might one day have to fight Filipinos outside the bases, Green Beret units from Okinawa had regularly been used in joint war games staged with Filipino forces. Now Subic was home to its own SEAL—"sea, land, air"—Navy commando team. And Clark had another counterinsurgency unit permanently based there, an Air Force Special Operations Squadron with MC-130E aircraft designed for antiguerrilla warfare.

The fact that the Pentagon saw the need for such units did more than underscore the dangers of linking the fate of its crucial Far Eastern bases and intelligence facilities to the fate of the Philippines. It was also another argument for moving the bases elsewhere.

Subic, located at the tip of a peninsula and protected by hills, was theoretically defensible. But Clark was another matter. It was located on a flat plain in what had been guerrilla territory in all Philippine wars, from the Philippine-American war to the anti-Japanese World War II campaigns to the 1950s Huk insurrection and the current nationwide New People's Army rebellion. In the event of a full uprising, the defense of Clark might require the conquest, at least, of most of Luzon.

And yet from the time he took charge in 1982, Reagan's ambassador to the Philippines, Michael H. Armacost, a former academic and government operative, had been saying publicly and privately that under no circumstances would the bases be relocated. No matter what happened to the Philippine nation, the American bases would stay right here.

Other U.S. ambassadors during martial law had taken care to keep the Marcoses at arm's length; but Armacost was being seen with them regularly, in televised receptions at Malacañang with the President or at televised ribbon-cutting ceremonies with the First Lady. As the negotiations to revise the current bases agreement, which would run out in 1984, drew close, Armacost again broke with his predecessors. They had all emphasized that the bases could easily be removed from the islands. Armacost was saying just the opposite. He was paving the way for shipping more military equipment to Marcos's security forces not in the name of military aid, which would surely run into trouble in the U.S. Congress, but as increased "base rental," which Congress had indicated in the past it would support.

The last bases negotiations, completed under President Carter, had taken years. But the forthcoming negotiations were receiving little attention from Malacañang. The issue was obscured by the official announcement, after Weinberger's trip, from both the White House and Malacañang Palace, that the most important visit yet on the newly active Washington-Manila axis would definitely take place before 1982 was over. The Marcoses' long-awaited official trip to Washington, denied them by Nixon, Ford and Carter, was announced for September.

By midsummer of 1982 Marcos, who had not been seen

in public for weeks, was appearing on television again. He was speaking, usually from Malacañang but sometimes from the safety of one of the military camps in the Manila area, about various plots he had uncovered. All sorts of people—rightists, leftists and moderates—were out to assassinate him and members of his family, he said.

He was ordering more crackdowns. They included mass arrests of people who had led the labor movements he had destroyed after imposing martial law. He was also lashing out at conservative members of the clergy who criticized him, as well as arresting the more radical priests and nuns who allied themselves with the Communists. And he showed he still had some surprises for any of his people who might get the idea he was faltering.

To put a stop to the rising crime in Manila, he said, he had sworn in a thousand plainclothes "marshals." He had told them to ride the brightly painted Jeepneys, the Jeep-like vehicles that serve as mini-buses. He had given them orders to shoot mere suspects on sight—shoot to kill. Just before he left for America, more and more political detainees were being brought in each day, and more and more people were vanishing, presumed executed. And in the marshals' first flurry of sidewalk justice, forty-eight men and women, half of them with no criminal records, were killed.

In America the preparations for the trip, though the emphasis was on public relations rather than open intimidation, were no less frantic; they were coordinated by Imelda's favorite brother, Benjamin "Kokoy" Romualdez, the governor of their home island of Leyte, who had been sent to Washington as ambassador specifically to pave the way for the visit. America's Filipino community, estimated at a million and a half including illegal aliens, was by now several times the size it had been when martial law began. Those who spoke out on Philippine politics invariably blasted Marcos, while most Filipino-Americans tried to remain apolitical, concerning themselves with pursuing their education and their professions and taking advantage of opportunities in America of the sort that had been drying up at home since the advent of martial law.

Throughout the summer of 1982, in the weeks just preceding the state visit of the Philippine dictator and his wife, the Philippine consulates in America staged celebrations to drum up good feelings towards the Marcoses. The islands' leading movie stars and starlets, MCs and comedians were sent to entertain at these bountiful affairs, widely attended by Filipinos, who came away loaded with food and souvenirs, such as T-shirts that proclaimed ominously in Tagalog, "ONE COUNTRY, ONE THOUGHT." In addition to the entertainers, batteries of PR men from the various government ministries had been dispatched to America, along with most of the top PR executives from the Philippines' major private businesses.

There were some negative aspects to the preparations. Although there were no face-to-face encounters with Marcos's exile opponents, most of the major opposition figures told of learning from friends that pairs of burly men—who seemed, as one said, like "boxers or bouncers"—were looking for them. But on the whole the big effort was to talk the nonpolitical Filipinos in America into pouring into the streets to welcome their leaders.

No spontaneous demonstrations of support for the Marcoses ever did break out in America, but in Manila spirits were high among the 700 people, including 200 members of the controlled press, who were making the trip for free with the presidential party on a 747 and a DC-10. One supposedly tame journalist, working for the government, said later, "There was a feeling before, during and after the trip that this was the last time we would all be together this way." He said that the atmosphere in the planes was that, with the President's health in question and most of his people against him, "this was the last hurrah."

Marcos and Imelda, however, treated the trip not as a last hurrah but as a new beginning, and seemingly with good reason. No matter that the press in America was having a heyday with such material as the $30 million spent on the trip and the 800 pieces of personal luggage that had accompanied the ruling twosome from the Philippines. No matter that all three networks, and editorials in most major newspapers, came down hard on them for their human rights violations and the rising numbers of murders that Malacañang condoned. They had proven during seventeen years in office that they understood power, and the most powerful man in America, Ronald Reagan, was behind them.

They made the most of it for the people at home. Upon their arrival on September 15, 1982, at Andrews Air Force Base, where George Shultz met them, they began a "private day," flying in separate helicopters to a welcome at the Washington Monument that the Philippine embassy had arranged. It was a ceremony that, as the *New York Times* said, "could have been scripted by Cecil B. DeMille." Several hundred Philippine-Americans, most of them bused in from Norfolk where they served with the U.S. Navy, were cheering and waving U.S. and Philippine flags they had been handed. There were military bands and native singers and dancers. They carried banners proclaiming, in Tagalog and other dialects understood at home but not in America, "LONG LIVE MARCOS AND REAGAN," "DOWN WITH FILIPINO COMMUNIST TERRORISTS IN THE U.S.," and "YOU ARE THE IDOL OF THE FILIPINOS."

The main point was the timing. Manila time is twelve hours ahead of Eastern Daylight Time. The reason the Washington Monument ceremony and other events in the thirteen-day tour of America were scheduled for the morning was so that they could be seen live, via satellite hookup, on evening television in the islands.

The camera angles used for Philippine TV had to be chosen

carefully, for the only spontaneous demonstrators on hand at this first and other appearances were anti-Marcos contingents with signs asking about his victims and comparing him to Hitler. The only demonstrators seen on the screen at home were the bused-in contingents.

The first day was devoted entirely to the home audience. And the next day's White House welcoming ceremony began at 10 A.M., which Rudolfo T. Reyes, the Philippine embassy's press counselor, noted, beaming, was "right smack in prime time."

Marcos and Imelda arrived in a black limousine at the side of the White House. As they got out, trumpeters ranged along the steps gave them a fanfare. The Reagans were there to greet them, Nancy kissing Imelda on the cheek. A twenty-one-gun salute boomed out, and men in wigs from the Old Guard Fife and Drum Corps marched slowly about playing "Yankee Doodle."

Reagan spoke of the Philippines' and America's "shared history and common ideals" and called the dictator "a voice for reason and moderation." Marcos spoke with a straight face of how Filipinos "stand for the ideals of democracy that is our legacy from the United States." They both recalled World War II when their countries had had a common foe. Marcos, either displaying a sense of humor he had never shown before or showing the results of sloppy briefing, spoke of how "you, yourself, Mr. President, played an unforgettable, heroic part in that conflict"—Reagan's only wartime role being the making of training films in Hollywood.

The two leaders then went off alone for an hour in the Oval Office. There, they said later, they exchanged stories about how they had both suffered assassination attempts and never did get around to discussing the human rights situation.

Marcos went on to a luncheon at the State Department. That evening he and Imelda were back for an outdoor, candle-lit, black tie dinner in the Rose Garden, where the pictures that would turn up in Manila's squatters' hovels were taken. Reagan told Marcos, "Our security relationship is an essential element in maintaining peace in the region. . . . Under your leadership, the Philippines stands out as a recognized force for peace and security in Southeast Asia." Marcos said America stands as the "trustee of modern civilization against the threat of a possible second Dark Ages." He told Reagan that Filipinos pray "your hand may be strong on the lever of power and save our humanity."

There was considerable comic interest to the other events of the visit. At one high-toned Washington reception Marcos was preceded by Filipino bodyguards with specially trained dogs to sniff for explosives. At times Marcos would disappear and Imelda would take over his schedule, including meetings with cabinet officials, so that, members of the party said, he could look into real estate she had purchased in the years he had been away from America. At most receptions and dinners she would stand up to sing before her husband's rambling speech began. Often, as in Los Angeles, the bused-in Filipino-Americans would walk out, carrying doggie bags of free food, long before he was through. When confronted by the American press he continually lied, as when he denied he held political prisoners or otherwise violated human rights. He also lied in saying that Amnesty International, which at this point issued a damning new report on the Philippines, had never contacted his government nor given him a chance to reply.

But what was being played up in the American media went unrecorded inside the Philippines. Each night there was live television from America. People we spoke with in Manila who had never been outside their country said they had the feeling during the time the Marcoses were abroad that all of America had stopped dead in its tracks to honor them. Actually, as was usually the case with Third World visitors, few Americans were even aware the Marcoses were in America. Their arrival itself got big play because it seemed so outrageous that Reagan, like Bush before him, should honor a right-wing dictator as a champion of democracy. But this was the time of a Beirut massacre, and besides there was little interest for Americans in the Marcoses' activities after the White House meeting. What stories there were about the Philippine leaders' appearances across the country were relegated to the back pages.

Still, the visit, because of the way it was played in the islands, had convinced many, maybe most, Filipinos that the Marcoses were creatures of America. As they paid homage to the Reagans, they looked more than ever like American puppets, leaders of a vassal state. And this was to the couple's advantage.

A circle had been completed. The Reaganites supported the Marcoses because they were in power. To Filipinos a more accurate version seemed to be that the Marcoses were in power because America supported them. Depending upon which mirror image you saw, the Marcoses could as well be the puppeteers as the puppets.

When we were in Manila in 1983 and one of us was talking with some of the country's principal ministers and military figures, everyone spoke of the euphoria from the 1982 trip that still lingered in Malacañang Palace. Even as the biggest campaigns yet were in progress against the Communist guerrillas, the government-controlled television was still replaying scenes from the Washington visit.

And now emphasis was being given for the first time to the opening of the base negotiations. The government newspapers and TV told of trips the top generals and the national defense minister, Juan Ponce Enrile, were making to Washington for the opening rounds. The story was treated as if these visits were mainly social affairs. Even here, in the preliminaries to what were supposed to be tough negotiations with national interests at stake, the euphoria predominated.

Then, before the negotiations even seemed to have gotten

past the feeler stage, it was announced in both capitals that they were over. America had agreed to raise the "base rental" from the $500 million in aid given for the 1979–84 period to $900 million for the next five years.

And so the euphoria continued, though in June there seemed reason for it to cease. Reagan announced he was going to make a swing through the Far East in November, and the Philippines was not on his itinerary. On June 25, Secretary of State George Shultz arrived in Manila. He heaped praise on the Philippines' "democracy," was photographed kissing Imelda on the lips, and called the ties between the two countries "very special." But then news stories appeared in America attributed to "senior officials" traveling on the Shultz plane, which in the conventions of the game almost certainly meant Shultz himself speaking. The so-called senior officials said, "The Marcos regime is entering its twilight and we don't want to find ourselves in the same position we did in Iran when the Shah was overthrown." Hence, it was reported, contacts would now be made with members of the opposition.

But in the nearly two months that elapsed between the Shultz visit and the Aquino assassination we were in constant touch with all major branches of the opposition. Every leader told us that no one had approached them from the State Department or any other branch of the American government. As if overruling Shultz, the White House added the Philippines to Reagan's itinerary.

It was weeks after the Aquino killing before the Manila visit was eliminated from Reagan's November Far Eastern trip. White House aides said privately that they could not let the President go to a place that had shown, at the very time sentiment was rising against America, that the life of even its own most popular politician could not be protected. They said Nancy Reagan had had the final say. Publicly, the scratching of Manila was done in a face-saving manner—after Marcos and Imelda had both threatened to go to the Russians

if Reagan should "insult" them by staying away. Visits scheduled for the same period to Thailand and Indonesia were can-
celled along with the Philippine visit, a White House press
handout said, since Reagan would need to hurry home from
the Far East to busy himself with Congressional business.

The Manila visit was revived as plans were laid for the
Reagan China trip of 1984; then it was eliminated again. By
now contact had been made with some of the more conservative Philippine opposition figures in the islands and in America. These conservatives put together a relatively small rally
in Manila to thank Reagan for backing out, although Reagan
had still not said a word against Marcos for the assassination—
or for anything else.

A counterpart demonstration to thank Reagan was held
in Washington by a middle-of-the-road exile group, the Movement for a Free Philippines, but it was lightly attended. One
officer in this group who stayed away said, "I can't stand the
thought of thanking Reagan for saving his own hide. He has
not done the Filipino people a favor."

By early 1984 the official American visitors Manila was
receiving—including the Reagan envoys Lt. Gen. Vernon Wal-
ters and John Monjo, deputy assistant secretary of state for
East Asia—were apparently urging Marcos to cease human
rights violations and restore democracy. They were respond-
ing to the political and economic chaos that followed the
Aquino killing. But White House spokesmen said Reagan did
not have the leverage to reform the regime. The opposition
leaders we spoke with said he did not have the heart to try.
Ambassador Armacost—in line now for a high post back in
Washington—did no more than make snide remarks in
speeches before luncheon groups about the dictatorship he
had supported. The regime, he said, seemed incapacitated
by the popular demonstrations, and by opposition from businessmen, who had brought commerce to a standstill and were
getting their capital out of the country.

Still, cynicism toward Reagan had not yet altered the pro-American bias that still seemed shared by the vast majority of Filipinos and Filipinas. Hope was not abandoned that America might one day do something about the dictatorship.

Whatever the state of the traffic between Washington and Manila, no matter how much Reagan might appear to be behind Marcos, Filipinos still widely believed that America was also their court of last resort. A good illustration came in our talks with one political prisoner in 1983, when the Reagan-Marcos connection seemed most firmly established.

Under the circumstances the tall, scholarly prisoner's words were surprising. Rather than dwell on the U.S.–Marcos dictatorship line that had become so familiar in the 1980s, he was saying that the anti-Marcos movement "is not against the Americans."

The conversation came during a lull in one of the sessions of the prisoner's hearings, still in progress in the sixth year after his capture, before a military tribunal in the basement of the Philippine Army Officers' Club at Fort Bonifacio. This Manila-area camp was where the most famous of what Amnesty International calls prisoners of conscience had been taken during the nearly eleven years since Marcos had staged his coup and introduced political detention. In February 1983 one of us had gotten into the seedy courtroom by calling the bluff that these hearings were legal and hence open. The guards, who had been insultingly thorough in the body search they conducted, now stood glaring with menace while plainclothes security men popped flash cameras, one shot after another, as the prisoner continued to speak.

What seemed to infuriate the soldiers most was the prisoner's cool lack of reciprocal hatred, and the way he made relaxed, joking small talk, as when he told about his brother, a medical doctor far from the action: "There are only three Filipinos in Beverly Hills and he's one of them. He loves acting and last year he got a small part in a Mel Brooks movie."

But though quick to smile, the prisoner as quickly became serious. Choosing his words with care, he described how, as he saw it, America held the key to the Philippines' future. "In fact," he said, "one of the big factors [in any alteration of government] will be the support of the American people. . . . If [America] someday would withdraw support, Marcos would change or go. Marcos is financially helpless. All he can do is what the United States tells him to do."

It was a refrain we had heard often from moderate and conservative figures of prominence whom Marcos had persecuted, men and women who felt betrayed by America yet had never quite abandoned hope that the dictatorship's demise could still be brought about by firm diplomatic pressure and threats from Washington, plus, perhaps, a little surreptitious help from the CIA. But the prisoner speaking now, although he was a nationalist who shared the consensus view of America's power over the Philippines, shared little else with moderate and conservative prisoners of conscience. It was, in fact, astounding how very far he was from being the sort of opposition leader you might expect to find taking a friendly position toward the United States.

His name, José Maria Sison, was known in the remotest hamlets, for by this time, at age forty-four, he had long been a legend. A former student organizer and university teacher and the most famous of the country's younger poets, he had gone underground in the late 1960s. He had become the leading theoretician, and Chairman of the Central Committee, of the newly regrouped Communist Party of the Philippines while it was still in an embryo state. He had been one of a band of some sixty guerrillas then operating just north of Manila who had founded the party's military arm, the New People's Army. He had moved about the country—inspiring "subversion and rebellion," according to the charges against him—until late 1977 when Marcos's armed forces flushed him out.

At the time he was operating in the President's own Ilocos provinces.

Since his capture, the party and the NPA had kept their leadership structure secret. But a number of knowledgeable people we talked with, including members of the National Democratic Front, the united front organization the party supported, would bring up Sison's name, despite the years he had been in military detention, when speculating about who the current Communist Party Chairman was.

If even the nation's most celebrated Communist was looking to America with affection and for relief from tyranny, there could be no doubt about how Filipinos in general saw their former colonizer. In the hall of mirrors that was the modern Philippines, the fate of the Marcoses was not only on the shoulders of Reagan; it had always depended upon the action or inaction of America, and in the eyes of many it always would.

After Reagan was elected, it had become widely respectable in nearly all circles in the Philippines, for the first time since the turn-of-the-century Philippine-American war, to be anti-American in matters of policy if not in regard to individual Americans. By now most opposition leaders, whether in jail, in exile, underground or enjoying limited freedom of movement, had called for the removal of the American bases. Still, some of the most potent opposition figures, including Ninoy Aquino, continued to talk of keeping up some version of the American tie after Marcos went—if only to give Filipinos an opening to the outside world or, more narrowly, if only as a matter of realpolitik. Shortly before his disastrous return home Aquino was still saying things to us like, "Anyone who thinks the Philippines can fight America's an idiot."

On the other hand, all, including Aquino, agreed there were serious questions about just how long the old American bond could survive Washington's support of the dictatorship. When we were in the provinces, one government official, a brave man who was actually an underground operative, spoke of how most college-educated young people, no matter what more sophisticated, older liberal and radical political figures might feel, had ceased already to see a difference between Americans in general and the specific Americans who were supporting the Filipinos' oppressors. "Americans are still popular in the *barangays*," he said, using the Malay word for the small rural villages or hamlets, also known by the Spanish word *barrios*, where two-thirds of the people live. But he also said he saw the day coming soon when "the people of the *barangays* join the voices saying 'Down with Americans!' When that happens you have lost the country. . . . The chances of that happening depend on how much longer the Marcos government will last and how long the United States goes on supporting it. . . . If the United States insisted we have fair elections, Marcos would have to listen. He could not afford not to."

Eventually we began to wonder just who the anti-Americans were. Despite the evidence of anti-Americanism, including graffiti and opposition proclamations, everyone we spoke with, even students who blasted Reagan's America, held out the hope that a change of American policy would set the old relationship right. In part this had to have been a matter of Oriental, specifically Filipino, courtesy. This is a society that considers it bad form to tell a foreigner something he might not want to hear. But it also had to do with the hall of mirrors, for the kind of democracy much of the opposition still wanted to see was the sort learned, if not always practiced perfectly, under American tutelage.

In part because America in this century put the Filipinos back on the road to democracy while defeating them militarily, but also because of the Filipinos' own actions, the creation of a military-backed dictatorship in the Philippines in 1972 was not the routine event it had so often been elsewhere in the Third World. In nearby countries such as Taiwan, South

Korea and Indonesia there was no modern history that entailed anything except autocratic rule and a politically powerful military. But when Marcos forced the Philippines into this mold, it meant a sharp break in the direction of the Philippines' political evolution.

Filipinos might be polite with Americans such as ourselves, but frequently during our 1983 visits we could detect an underlying fury even among the more conservative, older and most Americanized opposition figures. One such man was Dr. Salvador P. Lopez, who before breaking with Marcos had been president of the prestigious University of the Philippines. Lopez had served once as foreign secretary and had been an ambassador, including a stint as ambassador to the United Nations.

He spoke in high-pitched, often excited tones when we met him. He was sitting not in a makeshift military courtroom but rather amidst the marble and hardwood décor of the coffee shop at one of the regime's new luxury hotels. But despite the difference in the setting, Lopez was even more passionate than the Communist leader Sison in his denunciation of what Reagan was doing. To sacrifice the goodwill of an entire country for the sake of military bases that could be moved elsewhere was to him the ultimate absurdity. He said, "Your bases will go sometime, but in my judgment it is more important that you have one country in [Southeast Asia] that is on your side in your struggle of democracy against Communism." Then he turned to the broader question of American accountability for what Marcos had done:

> As a member of the same generation to which Marcos belongs, who was brought up under these principles, I consider it a tragedy that Marcos is being allowed to destroy the American labors here in setting up a democratic society, under the excuse of martial rule. You have invested fifty years of effort here. Your American teachers came here at the turn of the century and taught us. I am one of the products and I am

quite indignant. . . . Why is America allowing Marcos to do this, to destroy America's work?

By the time Salvador Lopez was speaking, the Marcos terror had entered its second phase. Both phases were in direct response to internal events in America. Phase one had been the period of political detention, torture and murder in what the rulers called the "New Society." Then came phase two, following Reagan's inauguration and Marcos's 1981 "election" when the New Society gave way to the New Republic, the gobbledegook name for the system after Marcos had proclaimed the end of martial law but kept all his old martial law powers. In phase one the response from America had often been weak, although Washington had continued to pay lip service to human rights and kept the Marcoses themselves at a distance. But in phase two, after the loudly heralded public embrace of the dictatorship by Reagan's men, the Philippines became more than ever before a place where government terror was the norm. All along, the new military had been using massacre as its response to armed guerrilla uprisings. Now the response to even verbal dissent was to put aside the legalities the government had used to attempt to show that it was following civilized procedures—the activities of its torturers to the contrary—and the method shifted to killing out in the open and to what Filipinos call "salvaging," which simply means that a suspect is kidnapped and killed and the body disposed of without a trace. Like the regimes of Central and South America that ran wild in their excesses after Reagan's election, Marcos too interpreted the new spirit of Washington as meaning that he had a license to kill, that no matter what he did now his protectors would look the other way.

But although Washington had tended even in the Carter years to ignore what was happening in the Philippines, and although the international press had most of the time focused its attention on other parts of the world, human rights observers and activists from both inside and outside the Philippines had been keeping score. Because they were watching, the true place of the dictatorship in history—as opposed to the place assigned it by the self-published books coming out of Malacañang Palace—was assured.

All along Marcos had shown that he felt confident that he could get away with what he was doing. Time and again he had been exposed, but he managed to move along in his usual pattern, confident the world would soon forget the exposés. Carter's protests may have held back the terror, but they did not stop the human rights abuses in the prisons. Most of the American press, which had been so indignant that Reagan would invite Marcos to Washington at the very time he was ordering new murders, had not followed up on the story of the new round of killings until editors' faces were rubbed in it by the Aquino assassination.

But although the foreign press had been looking elsewhere most of the time since the start of the Philippine dictatorship, too much was now on the record for Marcos to get away with his lies any longer. Maybe inside the Palace it was still believed he could rewrite history; but enough had been recorded about what he had done that no books from his Office of Media Affairs could alter how he would be remembered.

In some cases Americans, members of the nation upon which he risked his future, had been the ones who had held his true history up to the light.

6

THE U.S. AND THE TERROR YEARS

Questions of Accountability

IN ONE of the zanier episodes of the tragicomic times, three prominent American civil rights advocates, in town for, of all things, a human rights conference, drove across Manila on an August Monday in 1977. All of a sudden they appeared at a large military compound that was ringed with high walls and barbed wire.

They were met there by powerfully built, American-trained officers from an armed forces intelligence unit who must have had an inkling the Americans were headed their way. The visitors had announced as much at a news conference the previous day. But the officers still seemed taken by surprise when a heavy metal door at the back of the 30-acre compound burst open. To their consternation, in marched Ramsey Clark, the former U.S. Attorney General; Don Luce, who had exposed brutality toward political prisoners during the war years in South Vietnam; and Tom Miller, a California human rights lawyer. The three were playing hooky from a conference at the Philippine International Convention Center that was connected with what Marcos had proclaimed as "Human Rights

Week." They were off on their own, far from the comfortable, antiseptic royal enclosure on Manila Bay, looking into the true state of human rights in the conference's host country.

"What are you doing here?" barked one soldier, as others with pistols slapping their thighs ran and formed a ring around the three Americans.

"We have learned that people are interrogated and tortured here and we wish to determine if that is true," Clark said. Could he and his companions have a look around?

"No!" screamed a major as an aide grabbed for Luce's notes.

But the Americans, stressing that they were official government guests, finessed their way from one commander to another, including a lieutenant colonel who boasted of how he had been trained "in New York and Texas" and a full colonel trained at Fort Bragg, North Carolina, and Fort Benning, Georgia. After an hour-long delay, to give time for clearing away evidence, Clark, Luce and Miller, on orders issued from above, were shown into the rooms, located at the back of the big military enclosure of what they knew to be a "safehouse."

In the Orwellian newspeak that had become the regime's language, "safehouse" in the Philippines had lost its traditional meaning. It no longer designated a place of refuge for spies or robbers. A safehouse in the island dictatorship was, instead, a place for government soldiers to torture and kill, a place where records were never kept, so secluded that screams could never be heard. The government had spoken of safehouses but at the same time denied their existence. Yet here now was a delegation of foreign critics who had penetrated the heart of martial law darkness. Although during the delay the rooms of the safehouse had been cleared of prisoners and evidence, the Americans detected enough from the route they had followed, and the shape and placement of the rooms they were in, to know where they were. They had used a map drawn by a torture victim who had peeked under his blindfold as he was being taken away.

And despite the hour to clean up, "We found some evidence of torture," Luce said. It included "approximately eight 14-inch construction reinforcing rods next to a single-burner electric plate." A guard stammered that the rods were used to hold a pot on the burner. "All eight to hold one pot?" he was asked and made no reply.

In a small back room the Americans came upon, and Miller photographed, a number of automobile batteries attached to recharging devices. The use of electrodes wired to nipples and penises—as we would be told repeatedly by victims later—had been a favorite device since torture became acceptable with Marcos's 1972 martial law declaration. The 12-volt batteries that are used for vehicles had proved just right for creating pain that stopped short of death.

Later in that week in 1977 Clark, Luce and Miller, along with other American delegates, again slipped away from the proceedings at the Convention Center. They took to the streets and headed for what they had heard would be a "real human rights meeting" at a local Catholic college, St. Teresa's. There they found that the government had ordered the meeting canceled, but hundreds of young people were in the street to protest, hemmed in at both ends by riot police poised to charge. Luce and John Caughlan, a veteran of civil rights struggles in Mississippi and Harlem, spoke through bullhorns. Caughlan happened to mention that he had turned sixty-eight that day, and in typical Philippine fashion the protesters sang a lilting version of "Happy Birthday." The singing and speeches ended with a demand by a police commander for the crowd to disperse. Then water cannons opened up, scattering the protesters, flattening many to the sidewalk and walls. Next came a charge by the club-wielding riot police, bashing heads and bodies. Only the Americans were spared by the police, who, Miller said, "avoided our eyes as if in shame."

Somewhere in the melee a police officer demanded of Luce his justification for interfering "in our internal affairs." Luce's answer: "Because the guns and bullets used by *your* government to terrify your people come from *my* country."

The scene ended with policemen running down stragglers in alleys and beating them with truncheons as they fell to the ground. "All in all," Miller said later, "a fitting end to Marcos's Human Rights Week."

The dictator's Human Rights Week had been marked throughout by the usual low comedy that characterized the regime. That there should be such an event at all in a country Amnesty International had already labeled one of the world's worst human rights violators was theater of the absurd. Marcos, it was said, had actually outbid the Shah of Iran to get this gathering of international lawyers, judges and legal scholars for the week-long "World Peace Through Law Conference," organized by a former president of the American Bar Association, Charles Rhyne. Seven thousand foreign participants had been expected at the recently completed Convention Center, but only 600 showed up. This did not faze the rulers. Procedural rules forbade speakers to become "country-specific" when addressing human rights violations. In any case, the high points of the week did not entail human rights discussions. One outraged participant produced figures showing that more food was being consumed in seven days at the Convention Center than was eaten in a month by the quarter-million inhabitants of Manila's squalid Tondo slum. Van Cliburn, Margot Fonteyn and Rudolf Nureyev were flown in to perform for the delegates. A three-floor exhibit of dresses worn by Imelda Marcos had been set up in the Convention Center. Lithe models were brought in for fashion shows.

And there were other comic touches, straight out of the Keystone Kops. Twice Luce turned up unexpectedly at his hotel to find men going through his belongings; they explained they were "house painters." A cab driver tried to lure Tom

Miller into the back door of the National Police Headquarters, assuring him it was the Hilton Hotel.

But the members of the Ramsey Clark party, storming about town and taking advantage of their status as invited official guests, talked to many martial law victims and found that horror far outweighed comedy in the New Society. A typical story came from a woman journalism student in Manila who had been tortured during interrogation as a political detainee. "The current shot painfully through my body," Maria Elena Ang said. "I screamed and pleaded. . . . Several agents mashed my breasts while one contented himself by inserting his fingers into my vagina after failing to make me masturbate." They saw the medical report on another woman, Vilma Riopay, one of eighty parishioners arrested on the Visayan island of Cebu down in the central Philippines. The parishioners had been picked up in an effort to learn what their priest was up to. The hospital report said, "Patient lies in bed most of the time with eyes closed. She periodically whimpers, cries and mutters incoherently."

The Americans met with Trinidad Herrera, an organizer in the Tondo slum, who had been arrested in April 1977 and after weeks of electric-shock torture had emerged, they said, "able to merely sit and stare blankly with tears rolling down from her eyes." She still bore scars from the electrodes.

They were particularly interested in Mrs. Herrera's case because it was an instance in which the United States had become involved. Catholic church officials in the Philippines had prevailed upon the Carter administration to inquire into her fate. The then chargé d'affaires of the American embassy, Lee T. Stull, visited Mrs. Herrera in prison. Afterward he went to Marcos. He told Marcos what he knew of her summary arrest and her accounts of electric-shock torture inflicted through wires attached to her thumbs and a nipple. He asked Marcos what he would do about it.

The response had been immediate. Mrs. Herrera was ordered released and two Philippine Constabulary officers were charged with torturing her and sent before a military tribunal. But they were acquitted in proceedings so ludicrous that the defense counsel was permitted, without challenge, to suggest that Mrs. Herrera's torture scars were self-inflicted.

Yet at least the victim had been freed through American intervention. Years later the former president of the University of the Philippines, Salvador P. Lopez, who had turned against Marcos, would ask, "Why only this one, out of so many? We could never understand."

While it was true that after martial law was imposed no American president thoroughly embraced Marcos until Reagan came along, it was also true that none had shown much interest in his victims. When Nixon and Ford were in office, with Kissinger running America's foreign policy apparatus as a personal fiefdom, there was silence from America on the subject of Marcos's political detainees. When Carter came along there were at first extremely vocal protests to Marcos about his human rights record, and the Carter administration never stopped its pressure on Marcos to put aside the death sentence that a military court had passed on Ninoy Aquino. It was partly because of this articulated concern that the former senator was released to undergo heart surgery in Dallas in Carter's last year. But Salvador Lopez was right. After taking on the Herrera case, the Americans had seemed, in general, to lose interest.

In the summer of 1978 something curious happened. Vice President Walter Mondale went to Manila while the negotiations for renewal of the American bases agreement were in full swing. He was still talking in public about the Marcos human rights record, but he held lengthy conferences with the dictator in secret. After his visit there was a sudden lessening of pressure from Washington to stop the detentions and the torture—except for the periodic requests to release Aquino.

From then on, the raising of questions on behalf of other individual victims of the Marcos state terror was left to outside groups such as Amnesty International and to local people, especially Filipina nuns, who were able to keep track of many, though far from all, of the victims' stories.

Night and day since 1972 the nuns had been busy putting together what the survivors had reported—smuggling notes past guards in their prayer books during jail visits—in order to make certain that at least some of the horror was documented. The Association of Major Religious Superiors, the umbrella group of Catholic religious orders concerned with human rights, became the chief coordinator of the nuns' labors to get the story out. From that entity there eventually grew a far-flung corps of correspondents calling itself the Task Force [on] Detainees of the Philippines. The Task Force expanded to include more nuns, and also priests, civil rights lawyers and ex-prisoners. Their publications were routinely closed by the government, but they would appear again under other names. These crudely printed papers spread the word, under the editorship of their director, Sister Mariani Dimaranan, who worked at a decrepit typewriter, in a blue denim dress and nun's head covering, at a religious compound in Manila.

Although you would never have known it if you followed the government-controlled press, people throughout the Philippines had corroboration from the nuns of what they had heard or sometimes seen themselves. Thousands of cases were documented. When, on December 11, 1974, Marcos declared that "no one, but no one, had been tortured," the Task Force nuns went to work and quickly documented—by name, date, place, testimony of witnesses and medical reports on injuries— various instances of torture that had occurred the day before, December 10, and the day after, December 12. They told, for example, of how in Baguio City, the high-altitude resort town north of Manila, Eduardo Senense was "pistol-whipped, kicked, burned and left for dead" by soldiers the day before

Marcos spoke. And they told how in Manila, on the day after Marcos spoke, Charlie Palma was mauled with a gun barrel; electric current was shot through his body via wires attached to his thumb and penis. This bit of timely research, immediately giving the lie to Marcos's protestations of innocence, became a classic in the anti-Marcos literature circulated by opponents of the regime in the Philippines and in the exile communities in the United States.

The stories the nuns held up to the light at this time were unending. They told of how a young woman in southern Luzon, Flora Valencia Glor, was sexually tormented, force-marched for eight hours and denied assistance in delivering the baby she was carrying, which was born dead. They told of another woman, a Communist guerrilla named Perla Semonod, who was captured with her husband on the southern island of Mindanao in her second month of pregnancy. Taken to a military safehouse, she was made to lie on her back clasping a large block of ice on her chest until it melted. The remains of her dead child were later found inside her.

But it was not just the Task Force nuns and the local priests, lawyers and ex-detainees who were tracking the horrors that were euphemistically called human rights abuses. There were other church groups, both Protestant and Catholic, doing similar work, and also the International Commission of Jurists in Geneva and the UN Human Rights Commission. Various committees of the U.S. House and Senate also heard testimony. And Amnesty International, the most reliable of all sources working with political prisoners of conscience, had been issuing periodic reports on individual cases since the beginning. In the third year of martial law, Amnesty International sent a delegation to do research for a full-scale country report.

Thomas C. Jones, a lawyer Amnesty sent to the Philippines in 1975, afterward told a U.S. congressional subcommittee that the Philippines "has been transformed from a country with a remarkable constitutional tradition to a system where star chamber methods have been used on a wide scale literally to torture evidence into existence."

The Amnesty investigators in 1975 discovered that the implementation of state terror took place at eighty-four prisons set up specifically for political undesirables around the country as well as at the many secret safehouses, such as the one the Ramsey Clark party would burst in on. They became particularly interested in a sealed-off section of Manila's Camp Crame, which is national headquarters for the paramilitary Philippine Constabulary, the army's civil order branch. Here, the Amnesty investigators were told by the camp's victims of tongues being loosened in a ghoulish variety of ways: "fists, kicks, karate blows, beatings [with] rifle butts, heavy wooden clubs and family-sized soft drink bottles. . . . the pounding of heads against walls or furniture, the burning of genitals and pubic hair with the flame of a cigarette lighter, *falanga* (beating the soles of the feet), and the so-called 'lying-on-air' torture." This last involved making the victim lie rigid with his or her head on the edge of one bed and the feet on the edge of another. The body in the middle was beaten or kicked whenever exhaustion, weakness, injury or fatigue caused it to sag.

A particularly revealing name for the lying-on-air torture had been adopted by the soldiers. It related to the extravagance of the rulers. One year Ferdinand Marcos presented his wife on her birthday with one of the world's longest suspension bridges, linking her home island of Leyte to the island of Samar. In return she gave him for his birthday that year— all this out of state funds—a computer center. The name of the Leyte-Samar link is the San Juanico Bridge, and that is also the name that became common for the lying-on-air torture.

One of the prisoners Amnesty contacted in the Manila area was Benigno Carlos, a twenty-eight-year-old leftist who suffered from the tuberculosis that was rampant in the Philippines. Carlos told how members of the nation's top intelligence organization, the National Intelligence and Security Authority (NISA), amused themselves with him one night. The NISA men ganged up on him ten strong, beating him with fists and clubs for five and a half hours. Then they forced him to heft a stone almost too heavy to carry, and while he had it in his arms knocked him to the ground with 2-meter clubs. They formed a circle, bouncing him from one NISA man to another like a soccer ball. After that they entertained themselves by playing Russian roulette, using a service revolver they held against his head. Then they stripped him and continued the beatings in a lavatory while the colonel in charge looked on.

On the next day they beat him with the branch of a guava tree and played the San Juanico Bridge game. And there was one final ordeal. They released him when he signed a statement that he had not been maltreated: to get him to sign it, they had tortured him again.

Among many other stories Amnesty investigated which involved similar treatment of students, journalists, clergymen, moderates, leftists and frequently innocent bystanders were two we looked into separately and more thoroughly during our first 1983 visit. One is the story of Winifredo R. Hilao, a thirty-year-old civil engineer, who claimed no political allegiance but was arrested in October 1974. The other is the story of his twenty-one-year-old sister, Liliosa Hilao, who at the time of her arrest, a year and a half before his, was student-body president of her Manila college and about to graduate *summa cum laude*.

Winifredo Hilao was forced to sit on a block of ice while electric shock was administered to his penis and fingers. But his case was more than an example of sadistic torture; it also served as an example of what would happen to those who dared to appeal to higher authorities. When his family located him at Manila's Camp Aguinaldo, a family member managed to see National Defense Minister Juan Ponce Enrile, whose office is at the camp. At first, Hilao received a medical checkup at the prison hospital, where he was X-rayed and pronounced in satisfactory condition, though a later X-ray by civilian doctors would show tuberculosis. But two weeks later Hilao was transferred again, to his fourth place of detention and torture since his arrest. This time it was to the Constabulary's infamous Camp Crame and the same secret holding area where others had been tormented by the Fifth Constabulary Security Unit.

There the torture was resumed, at the hands of one of the same lieutenants who had punched, kicked and wired him for shock treatment at Camp Aguinaldo. Now, Hilao was told, the torture was not to force information from his past. The lieutenant, he said, "only wanted to know about the letter . . . which was sent to the Secretary of National Defense, Mr. Enrile, regarding brutal treatment against me."

This lieutenant beat him repeatedly with an empty bottle, shoved him into the commanding officer's office and made him stand, covered with sweat, against an air conditioner turned up to blow icy air on his body. Then the lieutenant pushed him into another room and beat him up again in front of a secretary. Afterward he was sent to yet another concentration camp.

Why the incredible cruelty toward Winifredo Hilao, against whom charges were never brought? Part of the answer was that his family had dared to go public with the case. Another part was that, as we were to learn in 1983 from Fluellen Ortigas, a fellow detainee who would flee the country following his imprisonment without trial, Hilao had the gall to torment his tormentors. "That guy had guts," Ortigas said. "As others were being tortured, he would call out to the guards, 'Hey, why don't you beat me instead? Your blows mean nothing to me.' "

And there was yet another reason. The Hilao family was, by its very existence, an embarrassment to the government because of the fate of Winifredo's sister, Liliosa, in April 1973.

She had been hauled in because prior to martial law she had been active in student demonstrations and was emerging as a leader through her position as editor of her college paper. The victim of an attempted rape before the raiding party so much as got her out of her house, Liliosa was taken to Camp Crame, and two days later the military prison guards told her family to come and get her body.

The family received it, they said, with the clothing bloodied and torn, her upper torso wrapped in bandages, and her face scorched with acid. Her internal organs had been removed, the family reported in documents smuggled out of the country after the Amnesty investigation, apparently to prevent an independent autopsy. The family reported receiving three versions from officials of how she died: heart attack, drug overdose and suicide.

By the time the government made its official reply to the 1975 Amnesty International report, it had settled on the latter version. Liliosa, the Philippine Solicitor General claimed, had gone to a prison toilet stall and swallowed a lethal amount of muriatic acid, a bathroom drain unstopper. He said another detainee had witnessed it, that Enrile had accepted the explanation by his soldiers, and therefore "the death of Liliosa Hilao has been satisfactorily looked into."

A fellow prisoner at the time, a well-known young woman author and journalist, Ninotchka Rosca, much later told us of the shock that ran through the camps when news came of Liliosa's death.

"You have to understand something about these soldiers," Ninotchka said. "The first time I was interrogated I was with a group of prisoners who were each questioned for twenty minutes. They kept me there for an hour. I asked them why and they said it was because I was the only one in the group wearing a miniskirt.

"These young soldiers suddenly had too much power. They were new, untrained, undisciplined. All they did was look at me, but they fooled around with a lot of the other girls. We knew what had happened to Liliosa. She was very pretty. The soldiers got too rough when they raped her. They hurt her badly. They panicked and forced muriatic acid down her throat. It was our most frightening time in prison. When this happened we knew that anyone could be hurt and killed without any political reason."

But the torture, if sometimes rooted in sexual sadism, more often was used to get information in order to crush the mounting opposition to the martial law regime. When the soldiers actually got hold of a real, live self-proclaimed Communist they were particularly harsh. The torture of José Maria Sison, the Communist Party Chairman, when he was first arrested after his capture in 1977, went on for seven months. It included something out of the nation's history, the "water cure," which had been the principal technique for getting guerrillas to talk back in the 1899–1902 Philippine-American war. This water cure involved pumping a prisoner full of water, then bouncing on his stomach as the water came back up, then repeating the process. At one point the water cure was practiced on Sison for six hours.

But, as the writer who had been a detainee at the same time as Liliosa Hilao said, the most frightening part was that the torture could be applied to anyone now that, with martial law, there were so few restraints on all those who wore a uniform. Meanwhile the members of the armed forces were becoming even more accustomed to brutality as they found themselves fighting actual wars. First the new military machine became bogged down in the south in a war, nearly hidden from the rest of the world, against the Moslem Filipinos known as Moros. Then the emphasis switched to a war of much greater national significance—that against the Communist guerrilla organization, the New People's Army, which was fanning out everywhere. With some 60,000 fatalities in the Moro war, and the number rapidly increasing in the NPA war by the time Reagan came in in 1981, it was no wonder that life in the camps, jails and safehouses remained precarious. By 1981 the Task Force nuns, who admitted they could keep track of only a fraction of the killings, had documented 1046 cases of murders of civilians. But by the second half of 1981 something else was in the air, and Amnesty International had decided it was time to send another mission to the Philippines to have a second look.

For 1981 was, according to all the human rights workers, a watershed year, marking as it did the change in emphasis from murder in the prisons to open murder and the practice called salvaging, the Philippine term used when someone is abducted and killed and his or her body disposed of in secret. The nuns' calculations showed that after the start of 1981 the number of victims killed by torture while under political detention actually decreased—"though not by much," one of their publications said. But the Task Force estimated that in 1981, disregarding salvaging cases, the number of civilians simply shot down in front of witnesses, never having been arrested—much less charged—suddenly tripled.

Ever since the beginning of martial law the police—like those special marshals Marcos swore in just before his trip to America—had been given great latitude. In the first years of martial law, the crime rate in the country went down as it became known that policemen and soldiers acting as policemen who shot suspects were usually exonerated. But these killings had to do with civil, not political, crimes.

Interestingly, by 1981, by the government's own figures, the rates for all major crimes were higher than they had been before martial law. As we examined the new military, we found that the reason for the rise in the crime rate was simply that there were so many new men in uniform, carrying guns, permitted to run wild. But what was most significant in 1981 was that the tactics that had been used by the police and the army against common criminals were now being used more and more against political enemies of the regime.

A part of it had to do with the presidential election in

the Philippines in 1981 and the decision to use state terror in an attempt to stop the voting boycott. But that year's key political development in America, the inauguration of a radical right-wing government friendly to the Marcoses, was by most accounts an even bigger factor.

It was not that anyone could point a finger at Reagan and say he had literally told Marcos to take off all restraints. But word was circulating that the American government was moving against opposition exile figures. And always in the background was the Haig visit, which put the opposition on notice that Reagan's government would work with Marcos's against opponents of the dictatorship, along with Bush's praise for the dictatorship and his assurance that "we will not leave you in isolation," the ballyhooed meetings between such officials as the U.S. Defense Department's Frank Carlucci and General Ver, the continuing visits of U.S. cabinet members to Manila, and then the presence at the Marcoses' side of Ambassador Armacost, and the Marcoses' visit to Washington.

Former Senator José W. Diokno, the one-time detainee who had split with Marcos before martial law and was now the nation's leading human rights lawyer, went over with us in detail the reports being sent in by lawyers' groups and church organizations that charted the sharp rise in open killing and salvaging from 1981 on. And it was not coincidence that whereas in its 1975 mission Amnesty International had tolled up primarily victims of torture, it found itself during its late 1981 mission—led by A. Whitney Ellsworth, publisher of the *New York Review of Books* tolling up victims who were killed outside the prisons.

The introduction to the report on the Amnesty International November 11–28, 1981, mission to the Philippines, released during the Marcoses' September 1982 trip to America, spoke directly to the differences in the findings of the two investigations: "While the pattern of violations noted by the 1975 mission delegates persisted, subsequent reports have given rise to new concerns. Although the number of people believed to be detained for political reasons fell . . . [the reports] indicated that more people were becoming victims of human rights violations of the utmost gravity, including 'disappearance' and extrajudicial execution."

Sometimes the incidents that got Amnesty's attention followed in the wake of strange acts of general carnage. For example, on Easter Sunday 1981, in Davao City on Mindanao, a grenade was hurled into San Pedro Cathedral while an evening mass was in progress. Just as a military squad arrived another explosion was heard. Witnesses told us that the soldiers panicked and began firing their weapons at random—at vehicles, into groups of bystanders, everywhere. Nineteen men and women fell dead on the spot and about 150 were wounded.

Like so many such acts during the Marcos period—following in the pattern of the Plaza Miranda bombing that had injured the entire slate of opposition Senate candidates ten years earlier—the San Pedro Cathedral incident went unsolved. At one point the New People's Army was blamed; at another point it was Moslem Moro guerrillas. But the only people who benefited from the San Pedro Cathedral bombing were the security forces, who were given a further excuse to clamp down.

By this time Davao City was entering a period of anarchy which would reach the point, when we went there in 1983, where assassinations had become routine matters, and no one was surprised when armed men for no apparent reason began firing at the obviously innocent, such as people waiting at bus stops. Like the cathedral affair, these violent acts usually went unsolved. But suspicions were always pointed in a single direction—as indicated by a typical sign we saw outside one downtown bank: "To All Military Personnel: Deposit Firearms When Conducting Business with This Bank."

Two days after the cathedral bombing, before dawn on

April 21, 1981, nine uniformed members of the Philippine Constabulary appeared at a poor barrio in Davao City. They surrounded the home of Avelina Osorio and said they had come for her son Margarito—whose case would be investigated and documented by Amnesty International, documentation we double-checked with survivors two years later in Davao City. Margarito, the soldiers said, was wanted for questioning; they told his mother he was a Communist New People's Army guerrilla and a suspect in the bombing. Hearing the commotion, Margarito's brother, Evilio, who lived nearby, came over with his wife, Felicissima. Then the soldiers, holding guns on the two brothers, marched them out of the barrio.

Instead of going to Constabulary headquarters, they were taken into a nearby cemetery. Margarito's mother and Evilio's wife tried to follow but were ordered away. Within an hour the women heard gunshots from the cemetery. They rushed to enter the grounds but the soldiers blocked their path. Felicissima waited outside the cemetery while her mother-in-law went to the local police and Constabulary offices, trying to learn what had happened. Three hours later the women were allowed to go to the cemetery. They arrived just in time to see the bodies of the brothers being carried away on wooden planks.

The official account of the Osorio brothers' killing stated that they were NPA guerrillas who had been "killed in an encounter." Meanwhile, authorities went on killing and arresting others, all for the cathedral bombing. In three separate operations connected with the bombing, one man was shot to death and nine people were arrested, some alleged to be NPA guerrillas, others alleged to be Moslem dissidents.

Filipino civil rights lawyers took up the Osorio case. They held unofficial public hearings at which other witnesses verified what the Osorio women said they had seen. They obtained the public coroner's report and found that it showed one of the brother's bodies contained eight bullet wounds, the other twenty-two, and that both of the brothers had been beaten. The lawyers said they would file formal charges against the Constabulary soldiers. In Manila the chief of the Constabulary, Lt. Gen. Fidel Ramos, a Marcos cousin, promised an investigation, but by the time we went to Davao in 1983 to talk with the witnesses, no investigation had been started.

Sometimes the soldiers seemed to have specific victims in mind, as with Margarito Osorio and the other cases Amnesty International looked into. Sometimes the killings seemed random, though the motivation might have been political. We spoke with a young woman who had been in the Cagayan Valley in northeastern Luzon in the period just before the June 1981 presidential election. In her area, the town of Baggao, the local Constabulary moved out and regular army units moved in at the start of May and announced they were there to see that people voted.

One evening in mid-May, in a barrio called Bulo, located in rice fields several miles outside town, a group of security men in civilian clothes suddenly appeared. They told the women and children to leave the barrio, tied up some of the men, and began shooting at the flimsy bamboo and nipa palm thatch houses. When they left, they took three men away into the fields.

In the morning the farmers saw their bodies. All three had been stabbed to death, and one had been decapitated. Until after the election, all 200 voting-age residents of the barrio and their children slept in town each night, walking three hours each morning out to work their fields. "The soldiers had accomplished their purpose," the girl said. "Now everyone was afraid not to vote, and now they were living in town right near the polling place."

The Amnesty International team found that sometimes it could not uncover the endings of the stories of victims in whom it was interested. This was because of the practice of salvaging, killing and disposing of bodies in secret. Amnesty was interested in the cases of two union organizers, a man named Antonio Santa Ana and a woman, Jemeliania Paguio. They had dared try to organize in a place Marcos had promised foreign businessmen would be free of labor trouble: the largest of the duty-free industrial zones for foreign-owned factories, located on Luzon's Bataan peninsula.

The two union organizers were taken from their homes by soldiers and jailed without charges in a Constabulary camp. After three weeks had gone by their families heard the kind of news that causes the greatest anxiety in the Philippines short of a direct death notice. Along with a man arrested for urging the boycott of the presidential election, the two labor leaders from the zone had "escaped."

Maybe they would turn up one day, but probably not. Well after their "escape," we could find no indication that anyone had heard from them. Their families assumed that the announcement of the escape was actually an announcement that they were dead, for this was the way things were from 1981 on in the Philippines.

The Amnesty investigators looked into a 1981 case on the island of Negros in the Visayas in which five men were arrested and tortured on the unsubstantiated report by a neighbor that they had had a hand in killing a member of the Civilian Home Defense Forces, an unpopular component of the armed forces. The investigators concluded that the real reason for the arrests was that the men were lay members of a Roman Catholic community service group that had tried to expose military brutality on the island.

The wife of one of these five men, Virginia del Carmen, saw her husband, Rudy, dragged from their house in Hinaoba-in. The next day she saw what the soldiers had done to him. His face and upper torso were a mass of bruises. Later she described what had happened: "First, he was stripped naked. Then the soldiers squeezed his testicles with pliers. They poured vinegar with pepper on his eyes. They poured gasoline on his feet and burned them. They forced him to drink two liters of water through his nose. He moved his bowels and vomited blood. In addition, they gave him electric shocks."

Three days after his arrest Rudy del Carmen was allowed out of detention to go home and tend to a sick child, but told to report back to the Constabulary camp the same day. Instead, he took his wife and child and fled to another town 30 kilometers away. There he was hunted down and shot by Constabulary troops who had surrounded a house he was in. This time it was not a matter of salvaging; his wife was permitted to see the body at a Constabulary camp.

The bishop in the area demanded a public meeting with the regional military commanders to look into del Carmen's death. Some 4000 residents of the hilly barrios of Negros attended. They told of constant molestation by military patrols and of numerous instances in which people had fled their homes out of fear they would be arrested and summarily executed. A Constabulary colonel ordered an investigation, then told a Rotary Club meeting that "Rudy del Carmen was not touched by the military." After that a Constabulary captain, notorious for acts of murder and torture, warned Virginia del Carmen that the entire family would be killed if she continued trying to implicate soldiers in her husband's death. The family dropped the case.

The Amnesty International report from the findings of its 1981 mission went on—name after name, page after page—recording in close detail how ordinary people were going to their deaths. A woman claiming her husband's body in Camarines Sur in southern Luzon was told by authorities that he was killed by soldiers along with a companion because they were "enemies of the government." The family of a nineteen-year-old food vendor found his body in a funeral parlor in Davao City two days after his arrest at a movie house; it was covered with marks from beatings; there were scald marks on the buttocks, fingers pointed askew from broken joints, the genitals swollen and bruised, an eye closed with stitches.

In another Mindanao province a man spent the night under police interrogation and the next day his body was dumped on a basketball court for all to see. And there were many other reports from around the islands of unsolved disappearances, and also of people fleeing their homes as mass arrests began, to find out later that those who stayed behind had been killed.

Some of the killings were military murders and massacres of villagers suspected of aiding the New People's Army. But as often as not there seemed no solid reasons for the individual murders that, at the time we went back in 1983, were on everyone's mind.

In February 1983 one of us sat in a bare lawyer's office in Davao City with Florita Alberga and her father, their gnarled farmers' hands drooping at their sides, as they spoke both of their fear and of their grief at the death of Florita's husband. The only apparent reason Eduardo Alberga, a farmer of no known political persuasion, had died was that a group of soldiers had gotten drunk.

Some time before the killing the Alberga family had been forced to leave their farm for a strategic hamlet, the idea being that if the people were herded into guarded areas the NPA guerrillas would be denied the food and shelter they needed. The Albergas and 260 other families were jammed into makeshift huts with nipa palm roofs and walls of scrap lumber and tin. Two months before we met Florita and her father, five drunken soldiers had entered this supposedly safe community, firing their weapons in the air. They ordered the nearest peasant, Wilson Sison, to fetch them a rooster trained for use in cockfights. When Sison and his aged father returned with the cock, the soldiers accused them of sullenness and began bludgeoning them with their rifle butts. The lieutenant in charge was well known in the strategic hamlet: Florita said he had already killed thirty-two people for the sport of it.

Eduardo Alberga had been selected by the 260 families to oversee security in the new community they were forced to live in. While the beating of the Sisons was in progress, the soldiers summoned him. They decided that Alberga, too, had the wrong attitude. The lieutenant ordered him to light a kerosene lantern. As he did, the gunfire began.

Florita told us she had found wounds where seven bullets had hit her husband's body, including one that had torn off the fingers of the hand he was using to light the lantern. The guns had also been turned on the Sisons. The younger was killed; the old man survived by spending the night playing dead next to the body of his son.

When asked to place blame for the murder of her husband, Florita first named the lieutenant, then said the soldiers as a whole "are the real enemy." She said that, because she was trying to press charges, she feared the lieutenant and his men might return any day to kill off the rest of the family. Meanwhile a local newspaper carried the official government version of what had happened: Eduardo Alberga, it said in a brief story, was a "subversive" who had been killed by military forces "in an encounter with NPA terrorists."

The killing had reached such a point by the time we returned to the Philippines in 1983 that virtually everyone we spoke with, with the exception of very high government officials, had a story they wanted to tell. It usually concerned a close friend or relative, sometimes an incident learned of from a neighbor. The story always had the same ending: someone being killed summarily by the rampaging military who in the past two years had been acting as if there were no longer any law that could touch them. The people told not only of political killings but of suspects in ordinary crimes such as robbery or narcotics offenses who were no longer being placed under arrest but were simply vanishing.

There were also, before the Aquino assassination, victims who were so prominent that they were on the verge of becoming national martyrs. One was a wealthy Jesuit-trained man named Edgar Jopson, who had once been voted "Young Man of the Year" by the Philippine Jaycees. At the time of his death he was only thirty-four years old, but he had spent most of the martial law years underground. He had been in prison, where he had been tortured. He had escaped and subsequently prepared widely circulated dossiers on his torturers. Marcos had put a price on his head. At the time Marcos was making his official visit to America, Jopson was shot dead by soldiers who found him in Davao City.

Jopson by this time was a member of the Communist Party and had been in the hills with the New People's Army, driven there when he found no recourse through any possible channels that existed after martial law. But there were others who had merely tried to do something to better the lot of the people, including two prominent physicians who had offered their services to the poor. In April 1982, Dr. Remberto "Bobby" de la Paz died when he was shot several times by soldiers who entered the free clinic he had financed and was running on Samar in the Visayas. A year later, a month after our first 1983 visit and five months before the Aquino killing, Dr. Juan "Johnny" Escandor was killed a day after he had been picked up in Manila. The familiar official version was that, although Escandor was already in custody, he had died "in an encounter."

De la Paz's friends speculated that he was murdered simply because he had become known on Samar Island as the "people's doctor," which in the military mind translated into "subversive." It was more difficult to explain Escandor's death since it had occurred right in the capital, not in a remote province where military brutality was less likely to come to light. But he was known to have spoken out about the government indifference to slum dwellers. When his family recovered the body they had a private autopsy performed; it was found that Escandor's skull cavity had been stuffed with dirty rags.

The opposition, including both the Communists and the

old moderates, tried to turn the murders of Jopson, de la Paz and Escandor into propaganda weapons. Literature was circulated identifying them and others as martyrs of the resistance to the dictatorship.

Aquino had commented on these killings. He had talked of how in the climate of martial law most people tried to put such matters out of mind, hoping that if they kept quiet, they themselves would be left alone.

There were no mass demonstrations following the killings of Jopson, de la Paz and Escandor. Aquino, who until the end said it was impossible to predict what would happen if he himself were killed upon his return, spoke with sadness of how Filipinos seemed to have forgotten the old conception, articulated in the various Malay languages, that "to be one nation, you must be like one body. The pain of the smallest finger should be the pain of the entire body."

During the colonial centuries, in order to survive, Filipinos had tended to play it safe when dealing with authority. This had changed when the Philippines became independent, but the colonial attitudes had returned under a dictatorship that was even more monolithic and severe than the colonial regimes. "When we start beginning to feel the pain of those who have been victimized by tyranny," Aquino said, "it's only then we can liberate ourselves. . . . The feeling right now is 'Fred was tortured, thank God it's Fred, not me.' That's the tragic part. Society is atomized. . . .

"Until the Filipino nation can feel the loss of one life as if it was their own we'll never liberate ourselves."

Soon banners did appear in the streets calling for revenge in the name of such martyrs as Jopson, de la Paz and Escandor. They appeared after the one murder that was so momentous in the minds of Filipinos that they would not keep quiet, and the dictatorship could not sweep it under the rug.

It was not just the millions who turned out to demonstrate at Ninoy's funeral procession. The demonstrations continued afterward. For the first time since Marcos had proclaimed martial law in 1972, the action in the streets equaled, then topped, what it had been toward the end of his last legal term in office. Sometimes he tried to ignore the demonstrators. Sometimes his security forces fired into the crowds. The crowds kept coming.

And the Americans of the Reagan regime in Washington were discovering something that their counterparts had learned at the end of the nineteenth century. No matter what the odds against them, no matter how compliant they might seem, there is a point beyond which Filipinos refuse to be pushed.

7

HALL OF MIRRORS INTERLUDE

Looking for a Leader in Manila

As THE STREET action mounted in late 1983 and the first months of 1984, Manila was crawling with foreign correspondents for the first time since the dictatorship began. At last, it seemed, the outside world saw that the official picture of the Philippines the rulers presented was not just flawed but cracked beyond repair.

People around the world had practically seen the Aquino assassination take place on their home television screens; then they had seen streets of Marcos's capital in flames. For the first time since his coup, Marcos appeared to have lost control; for the first time, his officials were speaking freely of the dire state of his health. Suddenly it seemed urgent to find out what had been going on during the dark years of the dictatorship. And the question was no longer just the behavior and fate of Marcos himself but rather what would come after him.

Some Americans reporting on the Philippines were determined not to make the mistake they had made five years earlier in Iran when they ignored every key political figure except the Shah. Officials of the American embassy were at last making contact, as Secretary of State Shultz had wanted, with the visible opposition and other alternatives to Marcos.

Diplomats and journalists alike were giving close scrutiny at last to the above-ground figures left over from the democratic politics of pre–martial law days, and also to the men and women who had been raised to great wealth and power by Marcos during the martial law years. These old opposition figures from before the dictatorship and the new figures of power who had come out of the dictatorship now shared center stage as the American foreign correspondents and the political and economic officers of the U.S. embassy got out to roam Manila.

Looking at Manila before, during and after the assassination, we found that the parallels to Iran were at the same time both stronger and weaker than was at first apparent. As in Iran, most above-ground opponents were by now not taken seriously; but the Philippines had had a tradition of open, adversary, democratic politics—a heritage that Iran had so notably lacked. In the Philippines there were people, some still only in early middle age, who had been wielding great power, or at least enjoying great influence and sometimes popularity, before Marcos killed democracy.

But there were other factors that were being ignored in the race to identify possible successors to Marcos. The tendency now was to view actual armed insurrection in the islands as what it had been in Iran—a mere annoyance rather than a central fact of life. Again, although there were similarities to Iran, there were great differences. The Shah had had to deal with some local ethnic uprisings; but almost since the day of Marcos's 1972 coup, virtually all units of his bloated military not assigned to guarding the palace had been bogged down in combating insurrection. Meanwhile, with freedom of expression quashed, a secret left-oriented network had grown up underground in the cities as well as the countryside. It took in much of the clergy, the university world, organizations of lawyers and workers, and all the nationalistic groups that Marcos had tried to suppress. Large parts of these factions were by now operating under circumstances of such secrecy that most of the foreign correspondents, as well as the U.S. embassy officials, seemed unaware of their presence. Although many Filipinos saw the underground left of today as the government of tomorrow, it often seemed to outsiders that the images of the left had somehow been deflected out of sight in the hall of mirrors.

Our own view, based on an extensive network of contacts with the left, was that the forces that were operating underground were more interested in organizing for the future than in seizing power immediately. But there was always the chance that chaos would thrust power upon them in spite of their timetable.

As a result of our trips to Manila in 1983, and our continuing contact with both the open and the underground opposition, we became convinced that it was the men and women of the underground who would ultimately triumph. But we also came to believe that there would be at least one stage of government, and probably two stages, before that happened.

Almost certainly there would be a period of even harsher dictatorship, led by the rapacious new oligarchs and military strongmen whom Marcos himself had created. And before or after that dictatorship, probably because of outside intervention, there would be a period when old opposition leaders from before 1972 would hold sway, or give the appearance of holding sway—simply because they were acceptable to the U.S. government.

We continued to follow up on the various peasant, worker, student, radical clergy and human rights groups that, operating underground and scarcely noticed by the foreign press, were responsible for much of the street action after the assassination. But we did not underrate the open opposition figures. Because of the strength of the tradition these old-guard oppositionists came from, they, just like the Marcos generals and cronies, were still forces to be reckoned with in Manila.

At the top of the list of above-ground opposition leaders was a flamboyant, princely former senator named Salvador "Doy" Laurel. He headed the largest open opposition grouping, a combination of political parties and factions called UNIDO.

The stylish pipe-smoking scion of a politically powerful and economically potent clan based in Batangas Province south of Manila, Doy Laurel was hardly the popular leader Aquino had been. Aquino had moved easily among the people, speaking their language, giving away large parts of an inheritance that was minuscule compared to Doy's. Doy traveled with a retinue, not with the ostentation of Imelda but clearly as an aristocrat. He had completed his education at Yale, from which he held a law degree and a doctorate. He owned and managed vast holdings, including land in his province, one of the major banks in Manila, and even that elite beach resort we had seen so incongruously advertised on a billboard set in a Manila slum. He was known for his extravagant playboy escapades, and counted among his accomplishments the wooing and winning of famed Filipina beauties. He was widely traveled, perfectly at home in sophisticated world capitals. He had never been forced into exile or incarcerated in a political prison.

Yet although his background was hardly that of a rough and tumble political in-fighter, after having decided to oppose Marcos Doy Laurel had in recent years become something of a fire-eating orator. More important, he had won the trust of Aquino, with whom he had continued to meet regularly abroad. They had planned to stump the country together if Ninoy was permitted back and given his freedom. Doy was the man who broke the news to the crowd outside the airport on August 21, 1983, that Ninoy had been shot.

At the time Laurel was the right age, fifty-four, for a run at the presidency should some semblance of democracy return. He was backstopped by his more politically hardened

brother, sixteen years his senior, José Laurel, Jr., a tough former Speaker of the House who in pre–martial law days had
a power base rivaling Marcos's own, holding court late at night
while seated at a nightclub table surrounded by Sten-gun-
toting bodyguards.

As the Marcos regime started to fall apart, such private
retinues of bodyguards were appearing again; Doy always had
armed men around him now. He spent much of his time rally-
ing supporters in the financial district, where after the assassination businessmen, middle-class office employees and even
government bureaucrats were taking to the streets to demand
that Marcos step down. But Doy was now also going out among
the people, speaking even in the more dangerous slums, in
a way he never had before. In February 1984 Marcos inadvertently raised Doy's stock by having him held briefly on a
trumped-up charge that would have carried a life sentence.

Doy Laurel thus seemed in a strong position; in the months
after the assassination he became the darling of the foreign
press. And yet the very fact that he was neither in jail nor
in exile made him, in the minds of many potential followers,
a compromised figure. He had not come out categorically in
opposition to Marcos until the dictatorship was eight years
old; he had at one point been a member of the New Society
Movement political party Marcos created; he did not resign
his seat in the widely ridiculed rubber-stamp National Assembly Marcos set up until after Ninoy was murdered.

This man who was being touted as the prime alternative
to Marcos was a uniquely Filipino figure. Most men of comparable power had been destroyed by the 1972 coup. Doy,
however, had been allowed to hold on to his properties and
to continue to do business because of a principle that goes
deep into the Malay past and tends to override any national
laws. It is based on a concept called, in Tagalog, *utang na
loob*, which translates roughly as "debt of gratitude" or "debt
of honor." It is so deeply rooted in Philippine tradition that

even Marcos, seemingly willing to break any law, had so far taken a kid-gloves approach with the Laurel clan.

Back in 1935 a man named Julio Nalundasan beat out Marcos's father, who had strived in vain all his life for high elective office, for a congressional seat from the Marcoses' home province of Ilocos Norte. Three days later Nalundasan was shot and killed by an unseen assassin. The rifle used in the murder was traced to an ROTC arsenal at the University of the Philippines, to which young Ferdinand Marcos, then a law student, had access. This and other strong circumstantial evidence had led to Ferdinand Marcos's conviction for murder.

The young Marcos defended himself—meanwhile taking, and getting the year's top grade on, the national bar exams— and then handled his own appeal before the Supreme Court. The chief justice happened to be Doy's father, José Laurel, Sr. As Ninoy Aquino, whose own father had been a close associate of the elder Laurel's, used to tell it, the chief justice sympathized with the bright young convicted murderer because Laurel himself had been through something similar, gotten away with it, and gone on to have a useful and productive career. It was Laurel who persuaded the rest of the court to acquit Marcos on a technicality, thus saving his life, and thus binding him forever to all members of the Laurel clan through *utang na loob*.

Later José Laurel, Sr., a longtime admirer of Japanese civilization and recipient of an honorary degree from the University of Tokyo, had agreed to work, along with Ninoy's father, Senator Benigno S. Aquino, Sr., with the soldiers who occupied the Philippines in World War II. Because, he said, he could lessen the harshness of the occupation, Laurel became president of the Philippines in a wartime puppet regime. Ferdinand Marcos became an anti-Japanese guerrilla, but there were gaps of years that were never adequately accounted for by Marcos's official biographers. Whether or not it was true, many Filipinos believed that Marcos had spent much of the war not in the mountains of the Ilocos provinces but in a Manila hospital, allowed to live because he was under the personal protection of President Laurel.

There was no question that Doy had benefited financially, and stayed out of jail, because of Marcos's obligation to his family. There was also no doubt that he had eventually moved to burn his bridges to the regime and had become a serious opponent. But personal matters tend to play a role in all political events in the Philippines. No matter what he did now, some Filipinos continued to believe that while Marcos had been destroying Philippine democracy and the Philippine economy, Doy had been, on balance, a beneficiary of the dictatorship.

We had met with Doy often, in America and in the Philippines, in the two and a half years before the assassination. We continued to see him in the aftermath. He used to say that, because it was the leftists who had carried on the armed struggle against Marcos, he and other old-guard politicians had become "irrelevant" to Philippine political life. He used to worry that "our best young men are going to the hills," and said that although the non-Communist opposition was in the majority, it was a "silent majority" and he could not figure a way to give it a voice. After the assassination we heard no more talk about irrelevancy from Doy. Instead, he focused on his acceptability to America. He let it be known he was not in accord with those calling for immediate removal of the bases. And, as he had all along, he kept up his personal ties to such old Yale men as Eugene Rostow, a key planner of the Vietnam war, and the conservative former U.S. senator James Buckley.

The majority he claimed to represent became less silent after the assassination as demonstrations broke out in the financial district. And it was, indeed, hard to think of a candidate more acceptable to America than Doy Laurel, one of the few opposition leaders of any stature who never picked up on the "U.S.–Marcos dictatorship" line. The Laurel name was a part of Philippine history, familiar to every schoolchild. But we had to wonder if he had not been right the first time when he spoke of himself as a figure of the past.

The outside observers who suddenly got interested in the Philippines after the Aquino murder found it extremely hard to identify just who could be effective as an alternative to Marcos. William Sullivan, who much earlier had been an architect of America's secret war in Laos, was one such interested party. Ambassador to the Philippines under Ford and Carter, he had been ambassador to Iran at the time the Shah fell. After the Aquino assassination Sullivan began talking about avoiding making the mistakes in the Philippines that had been made in Iran. He wrote an article making the case that it was time for America to hook up with the Philippine opposition, and he advocated that the U.S. send a political operative, such as Reagan's old public relations man Lyn Nofziger, to set up a "government of national reconciliation" to bring back democracy in the islands. He singled out as a Filipino who would have to be involved in such an undertaking a man who because of his calling had actually already ruled himself out as a direct participant in government—the owlish, brilliant and often outspoken archbishop of Manila, Cardinal Jaime Sin.

That the comically named Cardinal Sin was even considered by a man like Sullivan to be a key player in the politics of the Philippines was an indication of just how thoroughly silenced, and thus humiliated, Marcos's temporal opponents had been during the years of strongman rule. Sin did issue challenges to the dictatorship. When one of us met with him in 1983 he described the situation: in most parts of the country the only authority was either the military, which seemed to be out of control, or the sophisticated apparatus of the insurgent Communists' own military arm, the New People's Army. The church had to move into this vacuum in the provinces and defend the people's rights, because "we are the only ones left there," he said. "We always speak out and that is why we are branded as subversives."

It was true that the rulers branded even conservative churchmen like the cardinal with the catchall "subversive" charge. Actually Sin deplored, just as the government did, the fact that more and more priests and nuns were joining the underground, even taking to the hills and carrying and using arms. More than one observer pointed out that the Marcoses had managed to make the Philippines the only Latin American country in Asia, and one aspect of this was the wide appeal Marxist ideas and liberation theology had for the clergy. But the government had long since gone too far even for conservatives like Sin. In February 1983, shortly after we first talked with him, Sin issued a pastoral letter, which he had gotten every bishop in the country to sign, that was read from every pulpit in the islands and passed out in mimeographed form for parishioners to study. This document condemned the human rights atrocities of the regime and its neglect of the poor, its internal corruption and its suppression of dissent. A few weeks later he issued an appeal to the United States to stop supplying the government with arms. "It would be an insult to the Christian morality of [Americans] if their generosity were translated into weapons that enable Filipinos to kill Filipinos with greater dispatch," he said.

Sin still kept his lines out to Malacañang Palace, although he kept up his criticism. At a birthday mass for Marcos shortly after the Aquino murder, this usually controlled man broke into tears as he pleaded that the Filipino people be spared further terror. Sometimes he told jokes about the Marcoses and sometimes he got involved in unintentionally humorous situations, such as the time he stopped a project of the First Lady's to build a basilica on the scale of St. Peter's and dedicate it to herself and her husband. But his was essentially a moral, and conservative, voice.

Outsiders found him appealing. After all, there was a tradition of church involvement; at the turn of the century Filipino priests had fought in the hills against the American conquerors. But Sin had placed himself in the Church's older mainstream, disassociating himself from insurrectionists and also always pressing for continuation of American-style separation of church and state in the Philippines. He intrigued outsiders who were looking for new political leaders, but he continued to speak of himself as a nonpolitical churchman.

After the Aquino murder there was, however, one aboveground opposition figure who maintained credibility in all opposition circles and who had never been tainted by association with the dictatorship. This was José W. Diokno, the gaunt, chain-smoking ex-senator who had been jailed by Marcos and after his release dedicated himself, with obvious risk to his person, to fighting human rights abuses.

Diokno did not write off the underground. Although he had never spoken as a Marxist himself, he had—like Aquino and unlike other open oppositionists—kept lines out to everyone opposing the dictatorship. Unlike Laurel, he had not come from a powerful clan but rather had risen on his own from ordinary circumstances. He was by far the most popular of the well-known open opposition figures. In the aftermath of the assassination he sometimes acted as adviser to the Aquino family.

Diokno's relatively modest home in Manila was open to everyone, night or day. He shared with Aquino the insistence that every member of his family treat any Filipino or Filipina with courtesy and respect, whatever their social standing. Anyone wanting his help concerning government abuses was welcomed through his front door. As he coordinated the activities of the lawyers and nuns working to record past acts of government terror and to prevent future ones, he became probably the most widely liked, even loved, single individual in the country.

Diokno earlier had ruled himself out as a presidential contender. He said he did not see how anyone in his lifetime
would be able to govern a democratic Philippines without
at least tacit U.S. backing, and he said he would not get such
support since he remained adamant that the big U.S. bases
must go. He said he recognized that this attitude ultimately
would also make him unacceptable to large numbers of Filipinos, since many had a stake in the American connection. The
bases pumped vast sums into the economy each year, and
moreover, vast numbers of Filipinos were living off either
American military pensions or the U.S. Social Security checks
of family members who had gone to America to work. Yet
perhaps they, and the Americans, would eventually come to
see Diokno as at least a lesser evil: by 1984 Diokno was playing
down the unacceptability question just as Laurel played down
the irrelevancy factor.

There were other well-liked figures from the past who
also counted themselves out because of the anti-American position they had developed during the martial law years, or
because of their age and health. Everyone looked up to the
former independent senator Lorenzo Tañada, who had been
a mentor to both Diokno and Aquino, but Tañada was well
into his eighties now. Marcos's old Vice President, Fernando
Lopez, also opted out on grounds of age. Others who had
been credible opponents of Marcos had been incapacitated
by wounds from the bombing at the opposition rally in Plaza
Miranda the year before the coup. Doy Laurel was the only
previously high-level political figure who was now speaking
as if he were a presidential contender.

A handful of old-style, aristocratic political figures had managed to win local offices as opposition candidates in the otherwise rigged martial law elections. The most prominent of these
politicians who had come up after the coup was Aquilino Pimentel, the mayor of the medium-size Mindanao city of Cagayan de Oro. Pimentel had gained added prominence when

Marcos jailed him on the charge that he had donated about $10 to the New People's Army; at the time of Aquino's assassination he was still under house arrest on Mindanao. But neither he nor any other local opposition figures had had the opportunity to test themselves in national elections. Such was also the case with members of Aquino's immediate family— especially his widow, Corazon, and his younger brother, Agapito—who began leading demonstrations after his murder.

The only new figures who gained national prominence and power during martial law were people personally chosen by Marcos. Some were simply apolitical technocrats, such as the Wharton-trained minister of finance, Cesar Virata, who was liked by businessmen but had never been in politics. After the adoption of the 1981 constitution, which vested all power—legislative and judicial as well as executive—in the office of the presidency, Virata had been named prime minister as well, but this title carried no added responsibilities.

At one moment Marcos would be saying Virata was his designated successor. At another he would be anointing a former Chief Justice, Querube Makalintal, the Speaker of Marcos's National Assembly. But they had in common the lack of a political base, so such announcements were taken as postponing the succession question.

The most powerful civilians inside or allied with the government were not the technocrats; they were the men always referred to as the "cronies," who owed their power to the fact that they were engaged in private businesses with the Marcoses. Often the national defense minister, Juan Ponce Enrile, who had started out as Marcos's personal lawyer, was spoken of as his successor. Before martial law Marcos had appointed Enrile to such posts as customs commissioner and chairman of the Philippines National Bank. Shortly before the coup he had been given the defense portfolio. He had made a fortune after martial law by taking over land in his home province of Isabela, which was also a guerrilla stronghold. He had made another fortune as the head of a private law firm that handled all the business from the various conglomerates that Marcos and the cronies put together after the coup. Among his fortune-making deals had been a scheme to corner the coconut market. Before martial law Enrile had run for high office only once, when he had made a bid in 1971 for a Senate seat under the old system in which all senators were elected by the country at large. He had been defeated badly. His power rested not on a popular following but on his ability to hold on as a Palace favorite.

Other civilians around Marcos were mentioned as possible successors. There was Edgardo Angara, a law partner of Enrile's, whom Marcos had given an aura of respectability by making him president of the University of the Philippines. There was the Annapolis graduate Alejandro Melchor, Marcos's former executive secretary and now the Philippines' delegate to the Asian Development Bank, a man taken seriously probably more for his old ties to America than for his ties to Marcos. And naturally everyone was watching the woman whom the CIA had long ago labeled the "presidential understudy," his wife, Imelda, who remained his chief foreign affairs troubleshooter, governor of Manila and the head of the catchall Ministry of Human Settlements. After the Aquino assassination she announced, as she often had in the past, that she was retiring from public life; but early in 1984 she was back in the spotlight, even handling foreign affairs, while her husband remained cooped up in the palace.

A year before he established martial law, when his legal two-term tenure in office was drawing to an end, Marcos had proposed running Imelda for president as his proxy, much in the manner of some colorful American western and southern governors. But no grass-roots movement had ever built up for Imelda. She was a product of what Aquino said his Harvard colleagues called "Marcos's Professor Higgins complex"—a poorly educated beauty queen whom Marcos had decided to make into a leader.

Her lack of a political base did not stop the speculation

that Imelda would head a post-Marcos government, however. She carefully cultivated ties to the military, particularly to the most powerful military man of all, Gen. Fabian Ver. In the minds of many of the above-ground and underground opposition leaders, the most likely post-Marcos scenarios had Imelda fronting a government controlled and operated by military men, prior to a direct military takeover.

Marcos, having introduced the coup d'état to the Philippines, had frequently rotated major commands so that no one could get in a position to stage another one. There was constant talk of plots among the new military, but only two officers had held major national commands all through the period of the dictatorship. Both were relatives of Marcos. One was his very respectable first cousin, Lieut. Gen. Fidel Ramos, the chief of the Constabulary and vice-chief of staff of the armed forces. The other was the shadowy Gen. Fabian Ver, the man the Aquino family believed was as responsible as Marcos himself for Ninoy's murder. Those who began looking for future leaders in the period after the assassination usually, after seeking out members of the old guard opposition and trying to get a fix on Imelda, found themselves concentrating on Ramos and Ver.

One of Marcos's chief acts in preparation for martial law had been to promote Ramos, then forty-four, to brigadier general in March 1971; the following January he gave him command of the Constabulary. Ramos had already had a brilliant career unrelated to Marcos's patronage. A star pupil in his home province of Pangasinan, to the south of Marcos's home province, he had graduated from the prestigious high school in Manila that was attached to the University of the Philippines and then won appointment to America's West Point, where he graduated in 1950. He had served overseas with the Twentieth Battalion Combat Team of the Philippine Expeditionary Force to Korea in 1952, and with the Philippine Civic Action Group in Vietnam in 1966 and 1967. He had kept his close ties to the U.S. and had gone back there on various training courses, including training with the Green Berets at Fort Bragg.

The American connection was considered a strong point in Ramos's favor. An even stronger point was the fact that he was seen by the people as the only important general of the martial law era who had not taken advantage of his position to accumulate a personal fortune. Meanwhile, he had been a key figure in the drastic expansion of the armed forces under Marcos, presiding not just over the Constabulary but also over a new military force called the Integrated National Police, which brought all local police forces under central military control.

One of us talked with Ramos at length when we first went to Manila in 1983. He was, in fact, the only high-ranking official who had actually requested to see us before we arrived. It was a friendly and low-keyed session. He spoke of the difficulties of waging war against one's own people and of his hopes that the government would be able to win the guerrillas over to its side through social and economic development. He told a few lies, claiming that the counterinsurgency practice of strategic hamleting of rural citizens hardly existed and that soldiers guilty of atrocities were invariably punished. He arranged for one of us to see José Crisol, the deputy national defense minister, who had been Magsaysay's old psychological warfare chief and now held considerable power in the omnipresent intelligence community.

In spite of his lies, Ramos gave the impression of being one of the few voices of reason left in official Manila in 1983. We did get to see most other officials who interested us, but we did it in spite of obvious attempts by the Information Ministry to block our way. There was such chaos by 1983 that communications between ministries, preoccupied with their personal intrigues, were breaking down. Word was clearly coming from Malacañang not to see us, but usually we had already been seen before it arrived, invited in after drawing on personal introductions and contacts.

But although Ramos was forthcoming compared to the more secretive figures of martial law, we hardly felt the session with him gave us any insight into the workings of real power. For by that time the name on everyone's lips was not Ramos but Ver. And shortly before the Aquino assassination Ramos was in effect demoted by Marcos, who said that henceforth there would be a break in the chain of command and Constabulary officers were to act as if they were personally and directly responsible not to their chief, Ramos, but to Ramos's superior, Chief of Staff Fabian Ver.

Before the end of our first 1983 visit, one of us was getting anonymous threatening phone calls in Manila—something that would recur in America after the Aquino assassination. The threats, we determined, had probably originated with certain individuals in the Information Ministry who wanted us out of town, but the callers, knowing who was weak and who was strong, did not say they were calling in behalf of the diminutive information minister, Gregorio S. Cendaña, but rather that they were speaking for General Ver.

By now—as became evident to outsiders after the assassination—it was clear that Ver was the most feared man in the Philippines after Marcos himself. Even Enrile had complained openly that he was probably the only defense minister in the world whose subordinates reported directly to his chief commander, Ver, rather than to himself. But Ver, though he seemed to be everywhere in the background, was an extremely mysterious figure. Very little had ever been written about him by either his supporters or his detractors.

Some of our fanciest footwork while trying to get a fix on the government was for purposes of trying to find out something about Ver. We cultivated not just underground opposition sources and local government sources but also secret sources within the overseas intelligence community in our effort to put together a picture of the man.

Nobody we talked with, including officers who had sat at the desk next to his for extended periods, would give details of Ver's family background. He was born in Marcos's small hometown, Sarrat. He used his mother's maiden name. In 1983 Imelda had had the modest Ver family home rebuilt and made into a museum, to give the impression that he had come from the landed gentry, but no one took such claims any more seriously than they took Imelda's own pretentions to aristocratic roots.

One officer who had served with him told us that since Ver was only about two years younger than Marcos, "It is almost a certainty they were boyhood friends." He also said, "Certainly they were related because that's the way things are in small towns." But this officer, who for some years had a desk in the same office as Ver, claimed not to know Ver and Marcos's exact relationship—even though it is virtually impossible to know any Filipino personally and not know at once about his family background. We could find no verification for the widespread rumor that Ver was Marcos's illegitimate half brother. We did hear frequently that he was Marcos's uncle by marriage.

Although nobody took seriously Imelda's claim that Ver was an aristocrat, he probably did come from the middle class; he was affluent enough to leave his province in the 1930s to become a pre-law student at the University of the Philippines.

He graduated in 1941, having finished basic and advanced ROTC programs. And then comes a typically mysterious blank in his life. According to his official biography he was commissioned in the Constabulary in 1945, *after* the war. It seemed inconceivable that brother officers who served with him could not know how he spent the war years, but that was what they claimed. They did agree that he was never, like Marcos, an anti-Japanese guerrilla. And what *was* known was that 80 percent of the Constabulary served the Japanese during the war.

There was also nothing in the official biographical material coming out of Ver's office, or written up anywhere, that explained precisely what he was doing at the time of the Huk guerrilla insurrection in the early 1950s. It was known that at some point he was Constabulary commander in the area of Cavite on Manila Bay. One fellow officer told of an incident when a unit Ver commanded against the Huks had become encircled and had to be rescued by other soldiers. And there was a Tagalog-language adventure movie that depicted a Constabulary commander leading a sort of Dirty Dozen commando unit, made up of convicts, against the Huks—the sort of untamed paramilitary unit that would be typical of the Philippine military after martial law. Movie-goers believed this commander was Ver, but loyal fellow officers said the movie was fiction.

What was known for certain was that, before Marcos became President, Ver was more of a policeman than a soldier. He was in the Constabulary's Criminal Records Service and its Police Intelligence Branch. He was also, for a time, a prison warden. He moved up in rank slowly, to second lieutenant in 1946, first lieutenant in 1953, and captain in 1955, a rank he stayed in until after Marcos was sworn in as President in 1966.

But his career was set before then. In 1963 he was suddenly detailed to the then president of the Senate, Ferdinand Marcos, and stayed with him from then on except for an interlude between late 1963 and early 1965 when he was in America; there he trained at the Police Chiefs Academy in Washington, the VIP Protection School run by the Secret Service, a drug enforcement program at the Treasury Department, and the Police Administration School at the University of Louisville. According to one associate, Marcos had sent Ver abroad to get him "out of harm's way" in the no-holds-barred political fighting that began as Marcos went after the 1965 presidential nomination. In another version he was sent away by Marcos's opponents so that he would not be able to help in the campaign. In any case he was back well before the November 1965 election. He served as Marcos's chief of security during the campaign, taking on the position of chief bodyguard himself, and was seen frequently serving as Marcos's driver.

In published photographs, Ver, tall for a Filipino, invariably had a threatening grimace on his face. He was more steely-jawed in these portraits than in life. Some military subordinates described him a cultured man, but a former superior, who had played a key role in creating the Constabulary's intelligence branch after World War II, said one reason he was not promoted faster was that he was guilty of "anomalies," which in the Philippines means stealing. This superior also said that Ver had hired himself out as a security officer to private businesses.

Whether or not he was guilty of anomalies before joining Marcos, he became wealthy afterward. By the 1980s he was maintaining a second family on a Long Island estate in New York.

His office described him as having been the "father of police intelligence" in the pre-Marcos era when he was an aging captain. One officer told us that in those days Ver had become an intense admirer of J. Edgar Hoover. The officer said Ver had the attitude that Hoover was "a man who can hold on to his office. Oh, boy. There's a man who knows what he's doing."

This officer, a friend and admirer of Ver's, told us that Ver saw how Hoover "had the goods" on American congressmen, and used his secret dossiers to protect his own position. Ver followed Hoover's example and put together dossiers on Philippine congressmen after Marcos's election, the officer said. From then on it was risky for any one congressman to exercise the old constitutional prerogative of Congress to challenge a President trying to promote a favorite officer to a higher rank. Ver himself, stuck at the rank of captain for eleven years, had later complained of civilian interference in his career. "In those days, military promotions were politically motivated, and I was always at the wrong side of the political fence," he told a magazine interviewer.

After Marcos was sworn in, Ver became head of the Presidential Guard Battalion, the military unit charged with guarding Malacañang Palace, and also of the civilian Presidential Security Unit. He then presided over the fusion of these two groups into something called the Presidential Security Agency. The battalion became three battalions, each with about 1200 men, which rotated, one always at Malacañang while the other two, one officer told us without cracking a smile, "were doing field work like hunting down Communists—in the same manner as the guards at Buckingham Palace."

Less than six months after Marcos's inauguration in 1966 Ver had at last been made a major, and by the end of Marcos's first year he was a lieutenant colonel. His Presidential Security Agency now began getting armored cars, helicopters, even Navy vessels. Ver became a full colonel. Not long before the coup he, like Ramos, became a general officer. After the coup, the various units he controlled were combined with new components from the Air Force, the Constabulary and the Marines—all brought together under a new entity called the Presidential Security Command.

By the 1980s the Presidential Security Command was responsible not just for guarding Marcos but also for protecting the various private business interests, such as logging concessions, that the Marcos family and their friends took over. Most estimates of its pre–Aquino killing strength were in the vicinity of 15,000 men, and when demonstrations broke out after the killing additional battalions were withdrawn from the field and added to the Presidential Security Command.

Ver's other major assignment right after martial law was imposed was to head up a new national, military-dominated intelligence apparatus, controlled by a new agency called

NISA, the National Intelligence and Security Authority. Marcos credited Ver with foiling a series of assassination plots. Ver's personal agents were said to be found in every government office, in every major business, on every college campus, and in every large military unit. NISA men were sent as attachés to foreign embassies and to consulates in the United States, where the largest overseas Filipino community was located.

One reason there was talk of Cardinal Sin taking a direct political role after Marcos's departure was that, as Sin pointed out, only the church and the New People's Army rivaled in scope the organization under Ver. By 1983, after beating out Ramos for chief of staff and then taking on Ramos's main Constabulary responsibilities, Ver seemed by far the strongest figure in the archipelago.

But this was the view from the hotel rooms of the more recently arrived foreign correspondents and from the American embassy; this was the view from official Manila. Ver might look more powerful than any of the above-ground politicians, more powerful even than other martial law figures such as Defense Minister Juan Ponce Enrile and Imelda Marcos. Yet not everyone agreed that his authority was beyond challenge.

Compared to other figures of power examined by the press and by American officials after the assassination, Ver did look omnipotent. However, if the underground was even close in its estimates of its support, Fabian Ver would need all the firepower at his command to survive, much less rule, in the Philippines.

8

COMMUNIST GUERRILLAS AND THE UNDERGROUND

Insurgency: The National Tradition

IN 1896, as the Spanish empire was drawing to a close, there was one popular and respected Filipino leader who stood out from all the rest: the young novelist, physician and political thinker José Rizal. Rizal, whose words had been read by or read to nearly everyone in the archipelago, had been calling for reform within the system and for greater participation by Filipinos in the Spanish colonial government. Although he wanted change, he had disavowed the forces of armed insurrection that were already turning much of Luzon into a battleground and were spreading through the rest of the islands. His main goal was to arrange a peaceful solution between the people and their overlords.

But in December of 1896 Spanish soldiers took Rizal, who had been exiled to Spain and then had returned, to Manila's great open green, the Luneta. In a place that would later be called Rizal Park, they executed him by firing squad. His death meant the immediate collapse of attempts at peaceful reconciliation. This man who had never been an armed insurrectionist himself became the symbol of a long, violent revolution.

In the twentieth century, monuments were erected to Rizal in the Luneta and in squares throughout the nation. Presented still as a man of peace even though the revolutionaries had spoken in his name, he had become the Philippines' national hero.

To draw parallels between Rizal and Ninoy Aquino was irresistible. After Rizal's execution, the fight was carried on not by people who sought compromise but by men and women who planned the violent overthrow of first the Spanish and then the American colonial regimes. An organization called the Katipunan, a Tagalog contraction standing for "Highest and Most Respectable Association of the Sons of the People," led by Emilio Aguinaldo, a middle-class municipal officer still in his twenties, henceforth dominated the cause. General Aguinaldo and his men fought the Spaniards to a standstill, then accepted a truce whereby in exchange for a general amnesty in the islands they would exile themselves to Hong Kong.

But when the Spaniards refused to carry out the amnesty, Filipino and Filipina guerrillas who had stayed behind resumed the insurrection. And Aguinaldo and his fellow exiles spent their days in Hong Kong and other Asian cities arranging arms purchases and shipments. After Dewey's victory in Manila Bay in May of 1898, they returned on an American ship. While Dewey waited on his flagship for the American ground troops steaming out from San Francisco, a full-scale uprising by Filipinos against the Spanish broke out.

The Americans at first did not take Aguinaldo and the Katipunan very seriously. They thought his was essentially a local, even tribal, revolution among the people, living in the Manila area, who called themselves Tagalogs. Although all of Luzon, which has many ethnic groups in addition to the Tagalogs, quickly fell to Aguinaldo's rebels, the Americans continued to treat them as an unimportant force. It was the American flag, not the Katipunan's, that flew from Manila's fortifications after the formal Spanish surrender. The Americans refused to let any Filipino troops follow them inside the city's walls.

The Americans, who admitted they had little prior knowledge of the Philippines, quickly learned how thoroughly they had miscalculated the aspirations of its people. When war broke out between Americans and Filipinos in the year after Dewey's victory, the fighting spread all through Luzon, then down into the Visayas and eventually farther south to Mindanao and the Sulu islands. It took more than 150,000 American soldiers, fighting for three and a half years, to quell Aguinaldo's forces. More than 4000 Americans were killed in combat; there are no very precise histories of the war and so the estimates of Filipino deaths vary from as low as 100,000 to as high as 1 million, out of a population that had probably been somewhere between 7 and 8 million.

After the Filipinos discovered they could not beat the Americans in pitched battles, they decentralized, forming into small hit-and-run guerrilla units that staged ambushes, set booby traps, cut off communications, killed rather than take prisoners, and nearly always disappeared long before massed American forces could arrive at the scene. The Americans were as harsh as the guerrillas and sometimes harsher. They were led primarily by officers whose experience was in what used to be called "Injun warfare" on America's Western frontier. Some American units did not hesitate to massacre civilians believed to have given aid to the rebels. Crops were torched along with villages, leading to hunger and starvation. As in Vietnam much later—and again in the Philippines under Marcos—zones were set up in which commanders ordered that anything that moved would be killed. The Americans also herded people into the equivalent of strategic hamlets. On both sides torture was routine, and so was the mutilation of bodies, including the practice that would be resumed in Vietnam of cutting the ears off corpses as souvenirs.

When Marcos proclaimed martial law in 1972, he at first

made the very same miscalculations the Americans had made more than seven decades earlier. He too assumed that he faced nothing more than an isolated outlaw uprising. He proceeded confidently against the recently formed Communist-led New People's Army as if the NPA represented nothing more than a localized threat.

Marcos's approach to the Communists revealed the contradictory conceptions and perceptions that characterized the Philippines under martial law. Although in 1972 Marcos belittled the rural guerrilla forces of the New People's Army and said they were nothing his "New Society" should fear, he was also quick to call anyone who opposed him a Communist. And although the NPA did at that time seem weak and cut off from the mainstream of political life, he nonetheless decided to attack it in force.

At the same time he touched off a major local rebellion among the people known as Moros, Philippine Moslems who live in the far south, mainly along and near the western and southern coasts of Mindanao and in the Sulu chain. The minority Moros feared that with all forms of legal redress eliminated by martial law, and with no recourse to change via elections, they would be overrun by northerners who coveted their lands. At the beginning of martial law they looked more formidable than did the New People's Army. But Marcos's war against the Moros, although it resulted in tens of thousands of deaths and left perhaps millions of people as refugees, was still a local affair. By the time we went back to the Philippines in 1983 it was the New People's Army that was on everyone's mind.

Only two years earlier, in 1981, the talk you heard in the islands tended to center on the economic hardships, the rising crime rate, and how the criminals were usually men wearing government uniforms. But by 1983 what you heard most was how the NPA guerrillas had proved during the martial law years to be the only national force that had effectively fought

Marcos's uniformed terrorists, and how New People's Army members had become the people's agents to bring the perpetrators of atrocities to justice.

Back in 1972, when Marcos overturned the constitution, neither the NPA's supporters nor its opponents claimed that it had more than a few hundred men and women under arms. Furthermore, in what the NPA leadership would later admit had been a major mistake, most of these guerrillas were concentrated in a single area, which made them sitting ducks. Although a few were elsewhere in Luzon, most had moved from their original bases in central Luzon north of Manila up to Isabela Province in Luzon's northeast. Isabela contains the Sierra Madre mountains, which run north and south, bounded on the east by the Pacific and on the west by the fertile rice-growing Cagayan River valley.

This was precisely the same part of Luzon where General Aguinaldo had wound up establishing his headquarters in 1900. He had gone there because it was inaccessible. It was still relatively isolated in 1972, although since Aguinaldo's day roads along which troops could be marched had been built leading into parts of Isabela. Also, man had learned to fly, and Marcos now had American fighters with rocket bombs and helicopter gunships.

In addition, Marcos's martial law decrees had just eliminated all institutions that would have restrained him from harming civilians. And so, using heavy air cover, he promptly dispatched 7000 crack troops to Isabela. The devastating search-and-destroy missions they carried out, the bombing and strafing, and the hamleting of civilians constituted the largest such operations conducted in the islands for a generation, since the height of the central Luzon Huk Communist insurgency of the early 1950s.

On the one hand Marcos was saying that the NPA was so small and alien to the people as to be of no consequence. On the other hand he was implying by his massive reaction to these guerrillas that they actually posed a threat to the regime. As was usual all through the Marcos years, the people did not know which of his statements to believe, and so believed none of them.

This credibility gap was also increased by the nature of the first martial law arrests. Although Marcos claimed he could wipe out Communism with one big sweep in Isabela, he was also justifying the establishment of dictatorship as being essential to free him to go after "Communist subversives," who he said were everywhere. The gap became wider still when he failed to present anything except the most sketchy evidence that there was then a formidable Communist conspiracy against the government. And it became a credibility chasm when the only people he detained after his coup who had any wide popular following turned out to be liberal anti-Communist politicians and journalists who had been exposing the corruption of his regime and calling for reform within the democratic system.

There were certainly Marxists among the people swept up by the military and placed in political prisons in 1972, but they were hardly noticed. It was years before the list of political detainees, which would grow to contain well over 70,000 names, would include a single man or woman Marcos would or could claim was a top, or even middle-level, figure of the Philippine Communist Party; or of the National Democratic Front, formed in 1973, which later united Party members with radical and reformist church and labor groups; or of the Party's New People's Army.

Meanwhile, the NPA's forces continued to grow. They held on to early bases in Isabela and other parts of Luzon despite the major onslaught. Before 1973 was over there were also New People's Army units operating in the Visayan Islands of the central Philippines and on Mindanao in the south. By 1975 they were in the provinces surrounding Manila. And before 1976 was over they were also operating in the Cordillera, the huge mountain chain that runs north up the spine of Luzon, its western slopes leading into Marcos's Ilocos provinces along the South China Sea coast.

But right to the end, when Marcos was sick and brooding on his place in history, the view from Manila often bore little resemblance to the view from the countryside. Marcos continued to push against the Communists with his armed forces; but the instincts of an old pol that had served him so well much earlier in his scramble to the top now seemed to blind him to what was going on underground in his nation.

At the time we were first back in the Philippines in February and March of 1983, at the start of the island's hot, dry season, six months before Aquino's death, what seemed to rile Marcos the most was still the activities of the peaceful reformers. One after another, Presidential Commitment Orders listing these politicians, including many in exile, were being issued from Malacañang. Meanwhile the New People's Army, according to reliable foreign diplomatic and intelligence sources, had established fronts in fifty-six of the country's seventy-odd provinces, actually controlled some 20 percent of its barrios, had some 10,000 full-time fighting men— as opposed to farmers who sometimes fought—using mainly American weapons captured or purchased from government soldiers, and was supported by tens of thousands of armed political cadres and other full-time organizers, plus millions of people ready to feed and shelter NPA members and hide them from government agents.

And now, in February and March 1983, the government was conducting its most massive offensive ever against the NPA—indicating that perhaps Marcos's stated fears about the open opposition were not in fact his gravest fears. Under the personal direction of Marcos, National Defense Minister Enrile and generals Ver and Ramos, the armed forces were, Marcos announced, about to wipe out the NPA once and for all. At this moment, military men told us, 50 to 60 percent of all the armed forces' regular combat units were on Mindanao, sweeping the big southern island from east to west. American embassy officials who went down to see the action were amazed. As one of them put it, "This is exactly like Vietnam."

But it was Vietnam with a difference. There was military movement everywhere, but the diplomats did not see a single engagement. The NPA units were refusing, as usual, to be drawn into pitched battles, although out of sight of the diplomats they continued to keep pressure on the government soldiers. What the regime said it was staging quickly turned out to be but another of those false final battles that are so often announced by governments in the course of counterinsurgency wars.

Furthermore, an estimated 80 to 90 percent of the NPA's armed men were not on Mindanao at all but on other islands, most of them hundreds of miles away, which made nonsense of Marcos's claim that he could wipe out the NPA altogether by destroying it on one particular island. And meanwhile the NPA, as if to underscore how helpless it had made Marcos, picked this particular time for what appeared to be a coordinated, nationwide show of strength. On Mindanao itself, despite the government reinforcements sent in, and all through the other islands, the NPA was staging a series of hit-and-run actions, assassinations and ambushes.

Most of the guerrillas on Mindanao at this time were operating in two typical kinds of units: there were highly mobile patrol-size units, and there were two-person teams they called "sparrow" units, whose specialty was killing government men or informers whom the NPA would identify in its propaganda as responsible for abuses of the populace. As NPA soldiers explained it to us, the assassins would attack like sparrows, which dive in pairs for food, one after the other, so that if the first one misses the second one does not.

Although the guerrilla war was still being waged primarily by these small units, the NPA on Mindanao had for months felt confident enough to operate also in company-size units of a hundred or more guerrillas. And now, as fresh government troops swarmed in from the north, the NPA had recently begun attacking in units that were even larger. Two hundred guerrillas at a time, some full-time soldiers with M16s and some local farmers with pitchforks and machetes, would rush into Mindanao villages, easily taking the lightly manned police and Constabulary posts and disarming, sometimes killing, the defenders.

A month before the big government sweep was started, one of these 200-strong units had captured the town of Mabini, north of Mindanao's Davao City, and held it for a full day just to demonstrate the NPA's growing power. Shortly afterward a general in charge of intelligence operations in the area, Ignacio de la Paz, suffered a heart seizure and died. The story going around Manila was that Marcos had called de la Paz on the carpet at Malacañang and the President's furor over the rebel achievement had caused the heart attack.

Meanwhile, as the government sweep of Mindanao was in progress, the NPA continued to hold organizational meetings in many parts of the island; NPA soldiers continued to collect taxes, as they had for several years now, from Mindanao's plantation owners; and at night the NPA's armed propaganda units openly conducted what they called, in 1960s American phraseology, "teach-ins" in the villages and even on the plantations. One such teach-in featured color slides showing Imelda Marcos and her retinue of hundreds in the new royal enclosure on Manila Bay, and also Imelda alone fingering a diamond rosary.

We were able to document certain of the hit-and-run attacks that occurred on Mindanao during this time. Our starting point was not the government but rather the underground news bulletins the NPA issued, which listed the government units that had been attacked and the names of government officers and men who had been killed, always with such specific detail that the information could be checked with their families.

For example, at Maco on northern Mindanao twenty-three regular army soldiers of the Forty-first Infantry Battalion were killed in ambush, and the NPA added new M16s to its arsenal. At barrio Bonifacio in Magsaysay in Misamis Oriental Province, Col. Adolfo Areoloa, commanding officer of the 534th Infantry and Construction Battalion, was killed in ambush with three of his soldiers. In adjoining Misamis Occidental Province Lt. Col. Jaime Somora, commanding the Ninth Infantry Battalion, was killed.

As the fruitless government sweep of Mindanao continued, it seemed a particularly good time to look around the whole archipelago to get an idea of what the NPA was doing. There was always disagreement between the government and journalists, foreign diplomats and other outsiders about the exact strength of the NPA. But what was important was not the numbers of men and women claiming allegiance to the New People's Army but rather the scope of its operations. In order to paint a picture of what was going on in the underground we decided, as an exercise, to put together a bird's-eye view of some of what the NPA was doing at a time we were both in the country. One of us traveled to many of the provincial areas where the guerrillas were operating. And we both talked with a variety of travelers, Communist and non-Communist, Filipinos and foreigners, who were in other provincial areas at this time.

North of Mindanao, in the central part of the country, the Visayan island of Samar was a scene of great rebel activity, as it had been since the year after Marcos's coup. It was also, like parts of Luzon, a place that had a strong tradition of guerrilla warfare. Back in the Philippine-American war a former Indian fighter, Brig. Gen. Jacob Smith, who was in charge of operations in the area, had been so infuriated by Samar guerrillas that he announced his intention of turning the entire island into "a howling wilderness" and had gone a long way toward reaching his goal before he was pulled out at the instigation of angry American civilians.

During the Marcos era Samar had become an area of such obvious government neglect that tropical vegetation was closing in on the villages and there were no longer any passable roads connecting many major towns. The NPA organizers who came in early in the martial law period were widely welcomed, and in government retaliation the people of Samar had been the victims of some of the worst atrocities committed by Marcos's armed forces. At this time in 1983 there were ten battalions of government troops living in garrisons on Samar, but the NPA controlled virtually all of the nongarrisoned parts of the island.

And at this time government soldiers were being killed on Samar just as they were on Mindanao. For example, on the northern part of the island, Lt. Mario Ty, a company commander of the Nineteenth Infantry Battalion, and four of his men died in a highway ambush in San José. To the west on Samar, near the town of Wright, fifty NPA soldiers ambushed a team of army engineers from a Vietnam-style civic action unit, leaving five government men dead.

Throughout much of the rest of the Visayas, such as on the island of Panay, the government soldiers kept to their garrisons most of the time as they did on Samar, leaving the NPA free to organize and indoctrinate in the countryside. On the southern part of the Visayas' Leyte, Imelda's home island, the commander of the Fifty-fifth Constabulary Battalion, Lt. Col. Ruperto Legarda, was killed in an ambush. On the depressed sugar-growing island of Negros, NPA men disguised as government soldiers raided the Candoni town hall, killed two members of the hated paramilitary Civilian Home Defense Forces, and took away seven rifles, five .38 revolvers, a .45 automatic and 1000 rounds of ammunition.

At this point one of us went to the long southern Luzon

peninsula called the Bicol that stretches into the Visayan region. It is a dramatic, mountainous area famed for the 8000-foot-high Mount Mayon, perhaps the world's most symmetrical volcano, which erupts every ten years or so and in times of peace is one of the Philippines' prime tourist attractions. But Bicol was now known not so much for its beauty as for its role in the rebellion, a place penetrated by the NPA even before martial law.

The current activities in Bicol illustrated the personal nature of many of the NPA's operations, showing how the NPA adapted to local circumstances by getting involved in the life of the people who lived in an area. Ideology played little or no part in many of the encounters with government forces. Instead, the violence often seemed mainly to be a matter of getting personal revenge for past grievances, frequently ignited by some mindless military killing. The activities of government soldiers often meant blood debts had to be paid, and it was the NPA that assured they were.

An example was the story of a series of killings one of us heard from participants in Naga City in Bicol. The story concerned what happened after a young man named Jeffry Maceda, Jr., whose only offense was that he was the brother of an NPA commander, had been shot and killed by Julian Medallada, who was the brother of a policeman. In retaliation, the NPA killed a Civilian Home Defense Forces member. Then the NPA ambushed a bus in which twelve military men were going to the victim's funeral. All twelve died, as did seven civilians, in one of the still relatively rare cases of bystanders being caught in NPA actions.

When we were back in Manila between trips to Mindanao and Bicol, we talked with an American, a man who had dedicated his life to helping Filipinos do something about the tyranny. He had recently gone out on an NPA patrol in central Luzon in an area less than two hours' drive from the capital. The patrol was attacked by a band of former Huk guerrillas, now one of the many irregular mercenary units that were paid by the government. The American and the members of the patrol escaped, taking their wounded with them, by making an all-night march through submerged rice fields, pausing to rest at the huts of NPA sympathizers.

At one point, bleeding from insect bites, their feet swollen, trudging through the paddies in what seemed to the American a remote area, he heard a familiar noise. It was the sound of jet aircraft engines warming up. The guerrillas showed no surprise. They were used to the sound and knew exactly where they were. They were passing the outer perimeter of Clark Air Base.

At this time ordinary travelers moving around just outside Manila, as in the adjoining Quezon Province, were continually being stopped at roadblocks. The guards who manned them explained that they were necessary because of NPA movement in the area. While the government claimed it was on the verge of defeating the NPA by sweeping Mindanao, its soldiers knew that NPA units were up here, hundreds of miles north, near the capital and the bases. And in addition they controlled enormous stretches of territory in the more rugged terrain farther north, which happened, to the government's embarrassment, to be the home territory of leading members of the ruling martial law elite.

The NPA was so firmly entrenched in Isabela Province in the northeast, where Aguinaldo had once been headquartered and where martial law had made Defense Minister Enrile the principal landowner, that the guerrillas were acting in many parts of the Cagayan Valley as if they were the effective government. Over the years, after surviving the post-coup attack in Isabela, they had managed to force landlords and their agents to drastically reduce rents in the valley. And in the valley and in the Sierra Madre mountains, as elsewhere in the rugged north, the NPA was providing many of the services that would normally be expected of a government.

NPA members acted as impartial judges to settle local disputes. NPA medical teams, carrying complete card index files on their patients, journeyed from village to village, barrio to barrio, to tend the sick.

It was satisfying to the NPA to be operating here on Enrile's home ground in northeastern Luzon, but even more satisfying to be operating in the Ilocos provinces of northwestern Luzon. The NPA had recently been moving about Ilocos country, including Marcos's and Ver's home province of Ilocos Norte. As in other regions, it had built its strength gradually, capitalizing on government abuses. The starting point had come in 1976, when NPA units had entered the wild mountains of the Cordillera—that chain that runs north to south, with the Cagayan Valley, the Sierre Madre and the Pacific to the east, and the Ilocos provinces and the South China Sea to the west.

The NPA had first come in when the government had threatened to push some 100,000 members of animist mountain tribes, the Kalinga and the Bontoc, off their ancestral lands and burial grounds, which were to be flooded by a dam that was part of a hydroelectric project on the Chico River in the Cordillera. The NPA members had won the trust of the tribespeople to the point where NPA leaders and Kalinga tribal leaders were taking oaths of loyalty that entailed the ritual mixing of each other's blood. The government, despite the protests of Marcos's business friends who would have profited from the new electric power source, had had to abandon the dam project. By then the Kalingas and Bontocs were so well organized that they decided to stay with the NPA, and so the fight went on.

The action was dramatic in this part of the Cordillera, where there are rice terraces, first built long before colonial days; they rise layer upon layer, held in by 8-foot-high stone walls, scaled up the 5000- to 8000-foot mountains. At about the time of the sweep of Mindanao, a Constabulary patrol spotted an NPA unit holding a teach-in on the top of one such terraced mountain and thought they had the makings of an easy attack.

The patrol crept partway up the mountain to get within range and began lobbing mortar shells at the summit. The Kalinga NPA fighters grabbed their weapons and began bounding down the mountain, leaping from the eight-foot terrace walls, taking a couple of steps and then leaping again. The members of the government patrol also pulled out and headed down the mountain, but they had hardly begun their descent when they found themselves outflanked from below by the guerrillas they had spotted above them. As they came off the mountain they were caught and cut to pieces by the tribesmen they thought they had trapped. An American with experience in Vietnam who saw this piece of action said the NPA soldiers in the Cordillera were "every bit as good at what they did as the Viet Cong."

Further into the Cordillera, and stretching west into the Ilocos provinces, there was another government project that had caused a reaction similar to that caused by the Chico River Dam. And this one stood also as a clear example of how Marcos had used his absolute control over the government to enrich his associates and himself. It had to do with one Herminio Disini, a cousin of Imelda's, who put together a billion-dollar business conglomerate after martial law was declared.

Shortly after the coup Marcos granted Disini a concession to open up a half-million acres of previously public forest land in the Cordillera and, along with Japanese partners, build a large pulp paper plant to process the timber. It was known as the Cellophil project, the name coming from one of two new Disini companies set up to exploit the concession—the Cellophil Resources Corporation and the Cellulose Processing Corporation—which covered parts of three mountain provinces as well as parts of the lowland provinces of Ilocos Norte and Ilocos Sur.

The Cellophil project meant the devastation of mountain meadows that another tribal group, the Tingguian, used for raising cattle. It also meant that they and lowland Filipinos would lose the wood they required for fuel and building, the game and honey they got from the forest, and the fish they took from forest streams, which constituted their main source of protein.

When the Tingguian, and also many nontribal people, resisted, troops were moved in to protect the interests of Disini and his Japanese partners. Among the units was the Sixtieth Constabulary Battalion, which was particularly notorious because of its tradition of staging public beheadings and taking ears and otherwise mutilating bodies.

The people living in the area were ordered to stop cutting trees for their own use. Mayors and governors in the region were replaced by new officials, sometimes from the Constabulary and the army, who had shown special personal loyalty to Marcos. As if to underscore the dictator's personal interest, soldiers from Ver's Presidential Security Command escorted Cellophil executives when they came up to look over their holdings in 1977. When logging operations finally got underway in 1979 there were Constabulary units throughout the concession, and periodically more troops were brought in.

The Cellophil approach to logging so blatantly ignored all principles of conservation that Marcos's sister, Elizabeth, whom he had made governor of Ilocos Norte, complained that Disini's people were "lawn-mowing" the forest away in her province. The new pulp paper mill filled the sky with smoke for miles around. The Abra River, which flows through the mountains and into the Ilocos provinces in the concession, clouded up with wastes from the mill. Four species of fish disappeared altogether; livestock dependent upon river water died, and so did some of the people who were accustomed to using the water.

Four Roman Catholic priests were among the NPA forces

that began moving into the Cellophil lands in 1980. One, Father Zacarias Agatep, was killed in late 1982 and immediately afterward two informers were shown in a picture on the front page of a government-controlled Manila newspaper receiving checks as a reward. In 1983 another of the priests, Father Conrado Balweg, also with a price on his head, was taunting the government, daring Marcos's men to "come and get me if you can." He appeared in a BBC documentary on political oppression in the Philippines that brought angry threats from Marcos and his Information Minister Greg Cendaña—in part because it was narrated by the popular former senator and current civil rights champion José Diokno.

In 1983, still in the same period when the government was trying in vain to sweep the NPA off Mindanao in the south, Father Balweg in the far north sent an open letter to the regime hailing "opposition to the present evil system." He said, "I assure you that in the NPA, the issue is not whether one believes in God. The moral imperative of our times is to be a true Filipino fighting for national independence and democracy."

Father Balweg's version of the "moral imperative" explained much of what had been motivating the guerrillas in the period of only a few weeks in 1983 when we put together a partial picture of the nationwide insurgency actions going on against the government. Although far from complete, our picture confirmed that the above-ground opposition figures the foreign correspondents were soon seeking out in Manila probably constituted the least serious of the threats faced by the military dictatorship.

All within a few weeks in 1983, there had been an NPA priest taunting the government from Marcos's home territory; tribespeople defying the authorities in a way that was creating guerrilla warfare legends; Communist soldiers setting rents in the vicinity of estates belonging to the national defense minister; NPA bands operating just outside Manila and, perhaps more ominously, just outside the big American bases; and NPA men and women taking on the role held before 1972 by the local judiciary and also playing Robin Hood, acting as if they were the true police, judges and often also the only true government, all through Luzon and down through the Visayas and all through Mindanao where the regime was trying in vain to fight a final battle.

By the time Aquino came back and was killed, the regime had tried nearly everything against the guerrillas. Officers had been authorized to dispense bribes, using both cash and offers of resettlement with free land. There had been civic action military development projects such as America had attempted seventy years earlier in the Philippines and more recently in Vietnam. There had also been the harshest sort of counterinsurgency measures including, in addition to the torture that Marcos had made standard procedure, hamleting and the setting up of free-fire zones. The regime had done nearly everything it could militarily, with the exception of saturation bombing in every part of the archipelago, and genocide, to bring the guerrillas to their knees. And yet at no time since the start of martial law had the New People's Army failed to grow and expand its geographical area of operations.

In the months after that February and March period in 1983 when we were in the islands and the sweep of Mindanao was on, the NPA continued with the sort of actions we had noted. And at least twice more in the months that followed before the Aquino assassination, Marcos announced from Malacañang Palace that the NPA had been annihilated. But the NPA activities never ceased.

There was a seeming lull in the countryside immediately following the August 21 Aquino assassination, as the action shifted for the moment to the city streets. But less than a month had passed after the assassination when word came out of the southern Mindanao city of Zamboanga of a large ambush that had taken place in a rural area near that usually relatively peaceful city. On September 20, a day before the wildest street riots yet up north in Manila, some seventy guerrillas attacked forty-nine government soldiers who had crammed themselves into an armored vehicle northwest of Zamboanga City.

Thirty-nine soldiers, including the lieutenant in command, were killed, along with seven civilians who had hitched a ride on the vehicle. Local authorities said the NPA men who surprised the soldiers were dressed to look like Philippine Army members. The NPA, whose casualties were not known, had fled after taking American rifles from the bodies.

The guerrillas were able to operate around Zamboanga now, as earlier, because the repressive policies of the regime had made them popular. Down here Marcos-backed Japanese and American agribusiness firms used moonlighting government soldiers as private security guards, making the soldiers perfect targets. The NPA still found that martial law excesses were helping it win an ever wider base of support. As in the past, leading Filipino Marxists spoke to ever-wider audiences each time the repression got worse.

They said they hoped that Marcos would remain alive and that he, Ver and Imelda would stay in power, because these rulers had so thoroughly, and for so many years, been creating precisely the sort of climate in which Communism flourished. Underground figures told us they had actually been pleased when Reagan had embraced Marcos and become the dictator's main support, for it seemed to confirm what they had been saying all along about American imperialism. It was believed that the Marxists were the only Filipinos outside the government who hoped Reagan would visit Manila despite the assassination. Such a visit could win further converts among members of the opposition who still thought the American influence on the Philippines was benign.

Time was more clearly than ever on their side now, they were convinced. Right after the assassination the most visible remaining student leaders had gone underground. Many of the speakers at the Aquino memorial rallies were wanted men, members of the National Democratic Front. The open opposition leader Doy Laurel may have been the prime organizer in the financial district demonstrations, and he may have been increasing his base of support, but it seemed clear that there were other forces at work in many of the bigger crowds that materialized in other parts of the city during and after Aquino's funeral.

Should the demonstrations get so large that the people would march in the millions on Malacañang, the Communists felt they were ready, through their network of underground organizations, to provide leadership for the mobs. If the military men should take charge of the country, directly or through Imelda or someone else fronting for them, in the event of Marcos's death, the far left would still be in place all over the country as the only active opponent of the armed forces. Should there be an American-backed successor government of old-line politicians from big landowning families and the military men and business cronies whom Marcos had elevated, then the Communists would still stick to their old strategy of gradually taking control of the countryside.

Philippine Marxists had, by a long and often tortuous road, come to a form of Communism that they considered uniquely Filipino, a movement that could play on the glorious past of armed resistance to oppression. Unlike earlier Communists in the Philippines, those who called the shots now seemed to speak as Filipino nationalists first, international Marxists second. The earlier Communists, whose activities dated back to the formation of the first Philippine Communist Party in 1930, had made certain mistakes that had prevented them from seizing power, the present-day Communists said. The members of the new Party and its armed branch and affiliated underground mass organizations were determined not to make those mistakes again.

The old Communist Party, which made no secret of its close ties to Moscow, had made a certain amount of headway before World War II by defending peasants against the security forces of the big landowners in central Luzon. When the war came, these fighters became the nucleus of the Hukbalahap, a contraction for the Tagalog words that mean "Anti-Japanese People's Army." Guerrilla units fought in various parts of the islands, many of them working with a few American officers who had been left behind when MacArthur departed or were later brought in by submarine. Their activities were coordinated by radio contact with MacArthur's various headquarters outside the country. But the Hukbalahap, usually known simply as Huks, of central Luzon operated independent of, and on a larger scale than, the American-controlled guerrillas elsewhere.

The war gave them, like Mao's bands in China, wide support among the peasantry. Not only were they fighting the hated Japanese, they were also still taking on the big landowners of central Luzon. And meanwhile Filipinos who had been members of the Philippine Constabulary before the war joined up with the Japanese Battalion of Constabulary. In addition to aiding the Japanese, they also hired out, as was their tradition already, as security guards to the big landowners.

It was a strange war: by common agreement the Huks and the Battalion of Constabulary members avoided direct conflict, for both knew they would suffer more if the Japanese disbanded the Constabulary and sent in their own police forces. But what was clear after the war was that the guerrillas were identified by the people as their armed protectors, the Constabulary members as servants of foreign oppressors.

At first the Huks, seeing the powerful position they were in, tried to gain power in the postwar Philippines peacefully through the democratic process. But MacArthur refused to recognize them, which meant that their members, unlike the other Philippine guerrillas, qualified for neither back pay for their efforts in the war years nor for future U.S. Army pensions. And when a group of candidates won election to the Philippine House of Representatives with Huk backing from central Luzon, the Congress refused to seat them. The Huks then changed tactics, prepared now to triumph not through the ballot but by resuming their guerrilla lives, fighting the government military forces that were being formed in the 1940s with American arms, organization and training.

Following the Moscow, rather than the Peking, version of how to operate an insurrection, they tried for a fast seizure of power. With all the arms in circulation in the islands following World War II it was not difficult for them to get guns. By the late 1940s they had an army of perhaps 40,000 soldiers, primarily people who had come from the peasantry of central Luzon. They staged massed attacks, and frequently won, against the new postwar national military forces. In 1950 their leader, Luis Taruc, known as "El Supremo," announced their timetable: they would control Manila within two years.

Many people believed them. There was a sudden flight of capital out of the country. Harry Truman announced that the threat was so great that an additional half-billion dollars in military aid was being set aside for the Philippines.

In retrospect it is not difficult to see why the Huks failed. In their confidence they did not bother much with peaceful persuasion to convert people to their side, but rather attacked villages that refused to support them. In their haste they abandoned the guerrilla tactics that had been so effective against the Japanese and fought the better-armed Philippine government forces in massive, head-on engagements. They hardly bothered with organizing outside central Luzon, and hence were considered an alien force by many poor people in other parts of the country.

And then they came up against the popular leader—really the only truly charismatic national leader besides Ninoy Aquino to arise in the Philippines in modern times—Ramón

Magsaysay. At the urging of the Americans, particularly a CIA man on the scene, Col. Edward Lansdale, Magsaysay was made secretary of national defense. He played as much upon his efforts to better the lot of the people as he did upon the vastly superior firepower he had at his command.

"I, too, had been a guerrilla—against the Japanese," he said later, after his election to the presidency in 1953. "I knew you cannot beat guerrillas except by unorthodox tactics. So I launched an unorthodox campaign. Where they used terrorism, I used kindness—plus pesos. Anyone who brought me information I rewarded liberally. Also, I promised to give any Huk who deserted exactly what he claimed he was fighting for—land, house, rice."

In the meanwhile, a reform movement had begun in the colleges and universities, and Magsaysay brought in young graduates, in a domestic organization much like the later American Peace Corps, to help develop the barrios of central Luzon. The Huk threat was over by 1952 when Magsaysay's young assistant Ninoy Aquino took El Supremo Luis Taruc's surrender. From then on most of the remaining Huks, thoroughly demoralized, turned to banditry and the sort of activities they had fought against; some of them eventually hired out as strikebreakers to contractors who supplied labor for the American bases at Clark Field and Subic Bay.

Yet Magsaysay, who died in a midnight plane crash in the Visayas on March 17, 1957, and his successors never quite made good on their promises. And after Magsaysay, political life gradually returned to normal, which often meant government support of the wealthy against the poor. National politics became characterized by infighting between the old-style, often corrupt practitioners of the politics of the past—the most successful of whom proved to be Ferdinand Marcos.

While the people were organizing themselves into new groups to promote the aspirations of workers and laborers, many intellectuals were coming to the view that the Huks had been so clumsy that Communism had not yet been fairly tested in the country. The debate about what went wrong with the peasant Huks and what should be done to achieve their goals in the future began to come to a head at the University of the Philippines in the early 1960s. The dialogue about what to do next involved not just students and teachers but also survivors of the Huk campaigns who had disassociated themselves from other Huks who became mercenaries, bandits and racketeers.

The pivotal figure in these discussions was the young poet and professor of literature José Maria Sison, who like Marcos was an Ilocano but was unlike Marcos in nearly every other way. He had long since rejected the sort of politics Marcos represented. Sison had started out at Manila's exclusive Jesuit-run Ateneo University, which was at the forefront of the reform politics Magsaysay had preached. He came to reject the Jesuits' approach as too mild to achieve the solutions he felt his country needed. He moved to the University of the Philippines, where at first he became a supporter of the old Moscow-oriented Party of the Huks. Soon, however, Sison and other intellectuals were looking to Mao's China for inspiration.

In 1964 Sison founded a student organization called the Kabataang Makabayan, or Nationalist Youth, known thereafter as the KM. Membership quickly rose to the thousands on college and university campuses. It became a mass organization, rooted not in the peasantry, as were the Huks, but in the intelligentsia. The KM tended to take a Maoist line, advocating the careful building of a rural base in order eventually to encircle and take the cities—as opposed to the rapid uprising and seizure of power advocated by the Huks.

Leftist leaders we spoke with years later, including Sison himself and associates who were currently in exile, in jail or underground, described how Marcos, during the constitutional phase of his presidency from 1966 to 1972, had unwittingly made their work easier. Marcos spoke of sweeping land reform but failed to carry it out. There was little he even pretended he would do for the nation's rural and urban poor. He became the most vocal supporter in Asia for Lyndon Johnson's Vietnam War.

A reconstituted Communist Party of the Philippines, completely separate from the old, enfeebled, Moscow-leaning party, was formally established on the day after Christmas, 1968. Then the intellectuals of the KM joined up formally with the people they wanted to help. On March 29, 1969, Sison and his associates rendezvoused in the mountains of central Luzon with a band of Huks who had kept their faith in Communism under the leadership of Bernabe Buscayno, who had become celebrated under the *nom de guerre* Commander Dante. There they formed the New People's Army. Official Party literature speaks of this new force as a group with enough stolen guns to "arm nine undersized squads of seven fighters."

In the 1940s and early 1950s the Huks had insisted upon rigid adherence to a precise ideological line. After a day of fighting, they would gather around campfires and individuals would be forced to make formal confessions about how during the day they had done this or that which was not in precise conformity with correct Marxist-Leninist thinking. Sison's new Communist Party of the Philippines had at first been rigid, too, in this case in its adherence to Communist principles as written down by Mao. But the new Party came to see in the years after martial law that it could not expand its base if it did not play down ideology. Adherence to Communism was not even a prerequisite to membership in the New People's Army. And the first chairman of the National Democratic Front was a radical, but non-Communist, priest, Father Edicio de la Torre, who joined with a group he had formed called Christians for National Liberation.

With plans to move very slowly in building up support in the countryside, the new Party first drew attention in the cities. In the first round of massive street demonstrations against Marcos, which occurred in 1970, leftist student organizations, some of them Communist, were able to mass crowds of 50,000. In the next round, in 1972, the crowds were reaching 100,000. There was a certain amount of violence, which according to the then free press was usually instigated by government provocateurs who insinuated themselves into the crowds and threw homemade bombs in order to change the nonviolent character of the demonstrations. These demonstrations, though much smaller than some of those after the Aquino killing, meant, Marcos claimed, that the "Communists were at the very gates of Malacañang." The demonstrations were one of the reasons Marcos gave for declaring martial law.

At first martial law had a seemingly devastating effect on the Communists. With a nightly curfew for five years and patrols always in the streets, the big demonstrations in Manila came to an end. And with most of the fledgling NPA forces holed up in the Cagayan Valley, many, no one knows just how many, were picked off by the infantry, artillery and air force units that invaded Isabela Province.

Starting in the year after the coup, however, the Communists began to regroup. They admitted they had followed Mao too literally in trying to set up one major base area; such could never be accomplished in an island nation. Declaring there would be "no more Yenans," referring to Mao's old base area in northwestern China, they rapidly dispersed to other parts of Luzon and also to the other islands. In 1974 they decided to give up precisely fixed headquarters altogether. Meanwhile, in 1973 they had announced the formation of a preparatory committee to establish what they called the National Democratic Front, which looked very much like the old united front approach that had been used with success in Eastern Europe and China. At first the organizations that came into the National Democratic Front, the NDF, were primarily Marxist groups. But from about 1975 on the NDF grew more rapidly, taking in a wide range of antigovernment activists who were, probably more often than not, not Communists themselves. This new catchall underground organization came to include, in addition to the Party and its front organizations, an impressive range of worker, farmer, human rights and church groups.

Martial law had been announced as a temporary measure. But as it became apparent that Marcos would hold on to his new powers indefinitely, more and more people became convinced that there would be no quick peaceful restoration of democracy. The only way they could be effective, they decided, was to become underground, often armed, operatives.

By the time of the Aquino assassination the NDF included organizations that had never before been associated with insurrection against the government. It had, for example, a branch that was recruited from the country's half-million traditionally conservative public and private school teachers. It had a group called the Nationalist Health Association that took in thousands of medical professionals.

One of the men who founded the Communist Party of the Philippines in 1968 said much later, "We know about Mao Tse-tung and Ho Chi Minh, but we are above all Filipino revolutionaries. The most important thing is to broaden our base as the seeds of a coalition government." This was a far cry from suddenly overwhelming the capital. But he said the decision to move this way was "not only out of expediency but a positive development in itself."

One guerrilla said, "We are very patient. We are not like the [Huks] who thought after two years of struggle they could walk into Malacañang." Sison himself wrote: "I suppose this party will always integrate the universal theory of Marxism-Leninism with the concrete conditions of the Philippines. . . . But I will venture to say that under certain conditions it is desirable to achieve some *modus vivendi* between the [Communist Party] and the Philippine Government—not necessarily the Marcos Government . . ."

Although the emphasis was on a uniquely Philippine version of Communism, the Party and the National Democratic Front kept lines out to both liberal and Communist European nations through a permanent office the NDF maintained in Western Europe. Its representatives in America, meanwhile, worked with exile members of the formerly wealthy political families who were opposed to Marcos, and who in the late 1970s and early 1980s were believed to be directing bombings and arson aimed at destabilizing the regime in Manila—a tactic the Communists themselves, for the time being at least, rejected.

The titular leader of the above-ground opposition in Manila, former Senator Doy Laurel, was not alone in his fears that the best and the brightest in the nation had by now irrevocably linked their lives with the radical left. Aquino too had believed that, because of Marcos, the far left had become the most potent force in the country. During his exile he kept in contact with both the NDF and the NPA even as he spoke against Communism. Like the leftists, he had said he would be willing to serve in some sort of post-Marcos coalition government—moderates and leftists each apparently assuming they would wind up on top in the end.

Shortly before Aquino went back he held negotiations, to which we were privy, with NDF representatives, trying to persuade the leftists to rally in the streets upon his return. The reply to his request had been that the left would not come out for any individual politician. But after Aquino was killed NDF members were seen not only speaking at many of the bigger rallies, but also marshaling the funeral crowds and leading demonstrations, even in the U.S. sailors' town of Olongapo outside the Subic Bay base.

Still, few of the foreign correspondents who rushed into Manila after the assassination seemed to have an inkling of the left's strength. Having neglected the Philippines for years, and unaware of the berserk nature of the changes that had occurred as Marcos reestablished a colonial economy while his wife went on an imperial building and spending spree, these journalists were trying to treat the Philippines as if it were a normal country. In a normal country, you go to see the head of the loyal opposition, and so they went to see Doy Laurel, and sometimes José Diokno. If they had asked Diokno the right questions, he could have put them on to the left, but they treated him like an establishment opposition senator, not like the almost saintly human rights activist that circumstances had forced him to become.

There were a few traveling correspondents, and a few more resident ones, who knew exactly what was going on, but many seemed more comfortable with the opposition that could be seen above-ground—Laurel, Diokno, other ex-senators, a few local officials, and Archbishop Cardinal Sin. Still, the left had been strong enough, and the underground secure enough, that for several years now, if they wanted, visiting reporters could, like visiting clergymen and human rights activists, be put in touch with NDF officials and even be taken safely into the hills, into NPA guerrilla areas. Enough outsiders had seen the underground at work that accounts of NPA activity—such as the activity we found when we decided to look around the country during one brief period in 1983—could be verified by many disinterested, as well as interested, parties.

The first thing outsiders who took the trouble would learn was that the NPA was operating virtually on its own, primarily with stolen American arms, as it conducted what was now the only growing Communist rebellion in Asia. There had been a brief period much earlier when China, which had never been known for giving strong material support to revolutions in other countries, had sent in some arms. But even the government did not claim there had been any arms shipments from China since 1973.

That year a ship linked to China and bearing arms for

the NPA had gone aground off Isabela Province. The event was still being played up heavily a decade later in the Marcos books coming out of Malacañang. It was much on the mind of Constabulary Chief Ramos when one of us talked with him. But Deputy Defense Minister Crisol boasted that the regime had undercut the NPA by sending Imelda to be photographed embracing Mao shortly before his death. NDF officials pointed out that after Mao's death China had been taken over by men who had no sympathy with overseas "Maoist" revolutionaries. But whatever the reason, no one, either in the government or in the Communist Party, claimed that there was any substantial outside aid coming to the NPA.

A few Russian weapons were used, since there were still plenty of Russian arms circulating in Southeast Asia from the time of the Vietnam war—in fact they were seen openly on sale in the black market in the provinces. But the NPA had opposed the Russian version of Communism from the start, and no one claimed that the NPA by now was armed to any significant extent by any outside power. The government, in fact, claimed this was one of its weaknesses. NPA members called the lack of outside support a positive advantage because it meant that the guerrillas had to make the rebellion purely indigenous, a factor that strengthened their movement.

An example of how the movement had become Filipinized was the decision early in martial law to decentralize in order to turn the island terrain of the Philippines into an advantage rather than an obstacle. In 1983 a thirty-year-old NPA guerrilla called Ka Rita—*ka* being a short version of "comrade" in Tagalog— told a church reporter visiting an NPA front in southern Luzon of how until 1974 "we established what we now call 'artificial base areas' here. We even built our own villages in the mountains and brought the masses there." But since then the emphasis had switched to mobile units operating on wide fronts, which usually took in three provinces, always able to keep on the move, a step ahead of the government forces.

A former priest who joined the NDF and watched the

development of the NPA at first hand explained how "it was a disadvantage initially to operate on separate islands, but as soon as you set up fighting fronts, the disadvantage becomes an advantage. A fighting front means a unit is intact, in place. The NPA is not forced out any longer when they are attacked. They simply move to one side or the other."

The Party leadership tried neither to escape into impenetrable mountains nor to remain in any one specific area. But although the leaders kept on the move, they also kept within easy distance of Manila, risking capture, a National Democratic Front official told us, so as to be able to communicate with men and women from the various fronts. Because they took such risks, some top leaders were arrested, including Buscayno, still known as Commander Dante, who was captured in 1976, and José Maria Sison, captured the following year. But other leaders always appeared in their place.

Splitting with the practice of other Communist movements, the Party in the Philippines went so far to avoid reliance on any one indispensable individual that the names of officials of the Party and of the NPA were not even made public. There was never an El Supremo. Nearly everyone believed that the man who spoke as chairman, using the name Amado Guerrero, was Sison. Nearly everyone believed that the man operating as chairman after Sison's capture was a younger University of the Philippines activist, Rodolfo Salas. But because the Party leaders' identities were formally kept secret, it was easier than it might have been for a new leader to slip into the shoes of whomever the government arrested or killed. And because no one man was considered indispensable, the Party and NDF leaders and the NPA commanders felt freer than they might have otherwise to take great risks.

The risks for most members of the NPA were minimized by the uniquely Filipino Communist practice of capitalizing on ties of family, friendship and ethnic origin, rather than trying to overcome such potentially divisive factors. The government armed forces command continued its practice of sending units from any given area into an area far away where different dialects were spoken. The military wanted to be sure its men would not hesitate to kill because of matters of friendship or blood ties. The NPA did just the opposite. There were the extreme cases of forming new blood ties with tribal peoples, and wherever the NPA sent its fighters it tried to assure that most of them would already have ties through extended families among the people with whom they were operating. Outsiders learned the local dialects. And the NPA encouraged establishing new family ties through marriage.

Correspondents who visited NPA areas generally found that about a third of the armed guerrillas were college and university graduates who had studied in Manila; the rest were people who had spent their lives in the areas in which they were now operating. But this was far from the only reason why the NPA had never stopped expanding after martial law.

"Why are they growing?" asked José Diokno. His reply to his own rhetorical question was an echo of what Cardinal Sin had said. "Look, there is effectively no government in the countryside except the soldiers—and they are bandits. The NPA are at least honest, and they provide a measure of justice to people who never had any."

It was for purposes of better positioning themselves to win the people's trust that the NPA members worked so hard at becoming a part of the social fabric. In the Philippines of the 1980s you never saw those ideological confession sessions that you saw in Huk days. Guerrilla action in villages often consisted of young people strumming guitars and singing songs for the villagers' enjoyment, or conducting health classes, or leading propaganda sessions that were entertaining because of the ways the excesses of the rulers were depicted, or conferring until late at night with village elders.

The usual technique was for NPA members to start visiting a village on a seemingly informal basis, making friends, exchanging gossip, slowly building up awareness of the possibilities for opposing the government. A farmer in central Luzon told a reporter of how "when the New People's Army came to our barrio and explained their ideas, we joined with them. On a day-to-day basis we fight the landlords and the [Constabulary]. In this barrio we have reduced the land rents and improved the lives of our families.

"In the old days the landlord used to walk through the barrio to collect his rents—[well] over 50 percent of our crop. As the struggle heated up, he only came with a [Constabulary] patrol. Then the NPA ambushed the [Constabulary] and killed eight of their men. At that point he decided to lower the land rent. He won't come into the barrio at all."

A visitor to Luzon's mountains described how, "unlike the government troops, the NPA always seems to be busy, helping villagers with their problems, training, studying and above all building up human relationships. Every village I entered, it seemed like the NPA was greeted like long-lost relatives. . . . In this region NPA projects include support for setting up cooperative shops when the rice supply runs out, health programs, literacy campaigns, the prevention of tribal wars, mobilization against multinationals exploiting the mineral wealth, and the extension of peace pacts to develop solidarity between both tribal and lowland Filipinos against the Marcos regime."

In order to continue with such activities, the NPA had to police the areas in which it worked, but it avoided the excesses of the Huks in maintaining order. Rather than imposing harsh military justice, the NPA members were acting more as if they were ordinary local judges and policemen.

When dealing with local bullies and people who regularly committed minor crimes, the NPA would first issue warnings, then drive the offenders away. It was common to deal with adulterers by hitting them on the palms with pieces of bamboo, a form of mild corporal punishment used in Philippine schoolrooms. Drunks who disrupted village fiestas were strapped to coconut trees until they sobered up.

"We are not the Khmer Rouge," one guerrilla emphasized. Sometimes after a victory blood debts would be settled, but, he said, "There may not be as many as you think." Informers were often killed, as were perpetrators of atrocities against civilians, but government soldiers who fought but did not go after civilians and did not torture were usually left alone.

The guerrillas themselves held to a stricter code than they expected of others. They were under orders not to drink. They knew they could expect execution if they raped or looted.

One guerrilla we talked with in northern Mindanao, a plainly dressed twenty-six-year-old woman named Ka Lerma, said that the lives of guerrillas were so carefully controlled that their local NPA organizations had to "approve NPA marriages and the birth of children." A year's waiting period was required after announcing the intention to wed but, she added, matter-of-factly, "that rule is often broken." She spoke from experience, she said, for she at the time was engaged to a fellow guerrilla. What was adhered to, she said, was the code of conduct the NPA insisted upon of never abusing civilians. Then she went on to talk, in the same unemotional tones, of an ambush in which she had recently taken part in Lapla barrio in the municipality of Sulu in Davao del Sur Province.

The mayor of the town had started a racket. He had decreed that all able-bodied males must take a karate course in order to be prepared to fight on the government side in paramilitary units. He had hired, Ka Lerma said, a notorious Constabulary informer as the sole instructor, and the instructor had then kicked back to the mayor a part of the approximately $1.50 monthly fee that was charged each student for the compulsory course. The NPA had sent in a sparrow unit, which executed the crooked instructor. The angry mayor jumped into a jeep, followed by two vehicles with Constabulary troopers, to hunt down the assassins. Meanwhile a local thirty-five-member NPA unit prepared an ambush with the full knowledge of the villagers. Seventeen government soldiers and civilian officials, including the mayor, were killed; the NPA unit lost only one life, that of its commander, who was shot through the forehead. The NPA soldiers collected all of the government soldiers' M16s before disappearing.

Ka Lerma, who was killing government soldiers at the same time as she was planning her wedding, was a local woman in many ways typical of the NPA. But equally typical were the young men and women who had been born with silver spoons in their mouths and seemed to have brilliant careers before them, but gave it all up because they could not stomach doing work for the benefit of the dictatorship.

The NPA now had such nationwide support that it was more comparable to the forces of General Aguinaldo's Katipunan than to the localized Huks. And the New People's Army and National Democratic Front membership, as the government inadvertently made clear whenever it captured a prominent underground figure, included people who already had wide credibility as potential top officials in some future national government.

One of the most celebrated National Democratic Front members was Horacio "Boy" Morales, who had headed up a government think-tank, and been hailed by the regime as the principal planner in establishing Imelda's Ministry of Human Settlements. Like the eventually martyred Edgar Jopson, he had been voted one of the ten outstanding young men of the year. But in 1977, just before the Jaycees were to present him with his award, he defected.

He issued statements from the underground, speaking, many people believed, as the chairman of the NDF. As a one-time government insider, he exposed the achievements the Marcoses claimed. He showed how the regime's land reform program "actually favors the big landlords and gives them the right to exact such a high price for the lands tilled by the peasants for years." He described how, although some wealthier farmers had benefited from martial law, "the heavy amortizations, burdens and risks imposed on the peasants only worsen their condition, particularly those who have barely enough to meet their basic needs." He further detailed how the regime's development programs had "turned into a 'development industry'" of which the Marcos cronies and their American and Japanese partners were prime beneficiaries, with the "most rapacious among them . . . the dictator himself and his closest relatives."

"It became very clear to me that the system can never be reformed from within," Morales said in his first statement from underground. "Thus, I have decided to join the National Democratic Front and take part in the armed revolution against the Marcos dictatorship and all that it serves."

Shortly before his capture in 1982 Boy Morales said, "We are Filipino revolutionaries. Some of us are Communists but the majority are not. The Communist members of the NDF resent being called Maoists because of the derogatory connotation that they are subservient to a foreign power. They prefer to be known as Filipino Communists."

Whether the Communist Party would wind up taking control in the Philippines, or whether it would eventually become but one of many factions as in France and Italy, Morales was under no illusions that the movement he joined had been started by anyone except the Communists. But with Marcos having killed off, jailed, corrupted or exiled non-Communist politicians whenever they seemed to challenge him, establishment dissidents like Boy Morales found they were out of other choices.

And thus the Communist-led movement in the Philippines was something quite different from the urban worker-based movement of the Soviets or the peasant-based movement of the Chinese. By the time of the Aquino killing it contained representatives of all parts of Philippine society.

This had been true, too, of the guerrilla insurrection the

Americans faced at the turn of the century. The Katipunan then, like the NDF and NPA now, cut straight through society, embracing virtually all of what then made up the Philippine intelligentsia, a large number of the islands' businessmen, most of the native clergy, and Filipino officials who had served in the Spanish government.

One of the things that worried José Diokno most about the Philippine-American bases agreement was its clauses that would permit Americans to get involved in putting down any domestic uprising that might threaten their installations. They had done it before: the war against the Huks had to a large extent been directed by American advisers. Most key officers of the current Armed Forces of the Philippines had received training in America. And meanwhile there were the 15,000 American servicemen who were physically present in the islands.

What would be the response, Diokno wondered, should American troops get caught in a cross fire between the NPA and the dictatorship's military? Would America feel compelled to come in and try to put down the Philippine guerrillas?

Diokno, with his intimate knowledge of the NDF, knew how wrong the foreign correspondents were to give all their attention to the above-ground opposition. He knew well where the best and brightest of a generation had gone during the years of martial law. And he saw the parallels with the situation in the islands at the time of Dewey's victory. He fervently hoped, he said, that Americans would remember their history. Far too many seemed to have forgotten what had happened the last time the United States got involved in a truly national insurrection in the Philippines.

9

AMERICA'S FORGOTTEN WAR

Intervention the First Time Around

IT HAD BEEN a sequence of events of the sort that would become familiar to Americans again in the Vietnam era and also the era of Reagan. As the nineteenth century wound down, far-off people were moving to take control of their own national affairs. As they did so, self-righteous statements and threats were coming out of Washington to the effect that whatever these people did should be done in what one particular American administration said was the American way.

On June 12, 1898—two months before American soldiers who followed Dewey to the Philippines entered Manila—the government of Gen. Emilio Aguinaldo proclaimed Philippine independence from Spain. On January 23, 1899, after months of meetings in the town of Malolos north of the American-occupied capital, Aguinaldo and his associates formally proclaimed the establishment of the First Philippine Republic.

This new republic promptly promulgated a sophisticated constitution that included a Bill of Rights and provided for an executive composed of a President and seven ministers to govern along with a popularly elected legislative assembly. Within two weeks, however, the officials of the Malolos republic had been branded outlaws by new colonizers. And the islands had become the scene of America's first major overseas war.

The period between Aguinaldo's declaration of independence and the outbreak of war was a time of uncertainty both in the Philippines and in America. Still formally talking as allies, the Americans and the Filipinos both reinforced their own separate lines as shipload after shipload of American troops arrived in the islands. In Washington, President William McKinley, who had first said that America wanted nothing more than a refueling and repair station on Manila Bay, now expressed fears that some other colonial power would take over where the Spanish had been forced to leave off. But he had religious matters on his mind too. Speaking in moral certainties, he raised the stakes. As McKinley related it later, he went down on his knees "for light and guidance from the 'ruler of nations'" and found "plainly written the high command" from God that America had a duty "to educate the Filipinos, and uplift and Christianize them"—apparently unaware yet that they had been largely Christian for centuries. On December 10, 1898, with American soldiers dug in outside as well as inside the walls of Manila, American and Spanish negotiators signed the Treaty of Paris, which officially ended the Spanish-American War, and agreed that all of the Philippine islands would be ceded to the United States for $20 million.

While the treaty was being debated in the U.S. Senate, tensions naturally continued to rise in the area around Manila as it seemed increasingly likely there would be war between the foreigners and President Aguinaldo's new republic. American ships were moving to various other parts of the islands. Near Manila both the Americans and the Filipinos were still reinforcing their positions.

In January 1899, at about the time the new republic came into being, McKinley's military commander in the Philippines, Maj. Gen. Elwell S. Otis, a civil war hero who had later developed the reputation of being a desk-bound officer, ordered that his men get ready. They were told to exchange their "dress whites" for "fighting khaki." Then on February 2 he told all native employees of the American military to leave, and placed his troops on full alert.

Back in America a debate was raging between people who frankly called themselves imperialists, advocating territorial expansion, and anti-imperialists, who said America should never become a colonial power. The split in the Senate was such that it seemed a toss-up whether or not annexation would be ratified. When the Senate voted, on February 6, it turned out that the pro-imperialist Vice President and President Pro Tem of the Senate had to cast the deciding vote for the required two-thirds majority. It was that close even though cables had already reached Washington describing how, starting February 4, American boys had been dying for the sake of holding these islands.

It looked suspiciously as if the war had been started without reference to Congress—one of the many striking parallels between the McKinley and Reagan eras. Commanders in the islands knew February 4 was a particularly good day to get a war underway since the top Filipino officers had gone to Malolos to attend a big ceremony to be followed by a formal ball.

At a regimental outpost near Manila, manned by the First Nebraska Volunteers, orders had been received that day to fire on any intruders. Pvt. William Grayson, who was standing guard with an old Civil War .45 Springfield rifle, later recalled what happened after he and his fellow sentry, a Private Miller, shouted "Halt!" at one of four approaching Filipino soldiers, whom historians now believe were drunk and unarmed.

"I challenged with another 'Halt,'" Grayson wrote afterward. "Then he immediately shouted 'Halto' to me. Well, I thought the best thing to do was to shoot him. He dropped. Then two Filipinos sprang out of the gateway about 15 feet from us. I called halt and Miller fired and dropped one. I saw that another was left. Well, I think I got my second Filipino that time. We retreated to where six other fellows were and I said, 'Line up fellows; the niggers are here all through these yards.' "

For six hours the American soldiers blasted away, with Springfields, Mausers, and Krag-Jorgensens, at Filipino positions. They were firing long after sundown, when they were unable to see any targets.

The official version of what had happened was rather different from Grayson's. In Washington, Secretary of War Elihu Root said, "On the night of February 4th, two days before the U.S. Senate approved the treaty, an army of Tagalogs, a tribe inhabiting the central part of Luzon, under the leadership of Aguinaldo, a Chinese half-breed, attacked in vastly superior numbers, our little army in the possession of Manila, and after a desperate and bloody fight was repulsed in every direction." But later testimony, including that of Gen. Arthur MacArthur, who was commanding the sector where the fighting started, made it clear the Americans fired first, continued to do most of the shooting, and received little return fire from Filipinos.

In any event the situation between American and Filipino troops had been fast approaching flash point. The few American officers who had had any recent fighting experience had gotten it mainly in Indian campaigns, and the Americans felt themselves surrounded by savages. The Filipinos, for their part, felt they were being cheated of the fruits of their victory over Spain and moreover did not like the day-to-day treatment they were receiving. The American troops, some of them regulars but most of them state militia volunteers right off the farm, commonly addressed the Filipinos to their faces as "niggers" or "gugus," the latter epithet a precursor of the American label "gook" that would be attached to Koreans and Vietnamese.

Part of the nastiness of the three-and-a-half-year war that followed the events of February 4, 1899, had to do with racism. In typical letters home, the American boys wrote of how the Filipino fighting men—whose numbers have been variously estimated at from 40,000 to 100,000—and Filipino civilians could only understand the kind of warfare that had been used against American Indians.

The literature on the war is slim, as if the academic community and popular writers were aware from the start that it was a period Americans would prefer to forget. This was something very different from the heroic engagements that would come in the two world wars; here a big nation that considered itself the most advanced in the world was taking on a nation so remote and apparently insignificant that most Americans had never heard of it. But recently, following the Vietnam experience, there has been a resurgence in academic interest in East Asia. There are still gigantic gaps to be filled in concerning the Philippine-American war, but some headway was made in 1982 with the university press publication of a book by Stuart Creighton Miller of San Francisco State University. The title, *Benevolent Assimilation,* is an ironic use of the euphemism employed by McKinley to describe what was being done to the Filipinos.

Miller located a letter one American soldier wrote home early in the war telling of how he and his comrades in the Philippines planned "to blow every nigger into a nigger heaven." Another soldier wrote home of how the islands "won't be pacified until the niggers are killed off like Indians." Lt. F. Sladen, a West Pointer, recorded in his diary how his unit caught enemy troops wading through a river in a cross fire. "From then on the fun was fast and furious," he said, as a pile of corpses rose up "thicker than buffalo chips." An enlisted man sent a letter to his father telling how "picking off niggers in the water" was "more fun than a turkey shoot."

The war was only a month old when the first recorded

reprisal against civilians was ordered. Gen. Lloyd Wheaton was leading a thrust southeast of Manila. To Wheaton what was happening to his men—being impaled on the bamboo prongs of booby traps, sometimes having their throats slit while they slept, constantly getting caught in ambushes by an enemy that quickly disappeared—had no place in civilized warfare. After two of his companies fell into an ambush, he ordered that every town and village for twelve miles around be burned. In a letter published without comment by a Boston paper, one of the men who participated in this action described the "people's shrieks and torments."

General Otis—like Marcos much later—was soon giving the press details of a "brilliant victory" he expected through a "master stroke of war" that would prove to be the "final battle." But each time Otis—now settled in Malacañang Palace as Governor-General—sent out mass expeditions, the enemy would evade the Americans. At one point the Americans did manage to engage 5000 enemy soldiers, but the Filipinos got away along the Luzon coast. A U.S. Navy warship followed, barely too late to catch the fleeing combatants; instead, its guns destroyed each coastal village it passed. In his frustration, Otis ordered the use of a new secret weapon, a steam-driven fire engine that was filled with petroleum which it sprayed on villages before they were put to the torch.

There were efforts to "Filipinize" the war, letting Asians fight Asians—another harbinger of future wars in Southeast Asia. But for the time all this meant was the recruitment of about 5000 Macabebes, traditional mercenaries from the village of Macabebe in the central Luzon province of Pampanga, northwest of Manila—which is where Clark and Subic bases were later located. For centuries the Macabebes had served the Spaniards. They had been at the heart of the Guardia Civil, established to put down growing insurrection in the nineteenth century. Now they formed the ranks of the American-officered Philippine Scouts. But the Macabebes were already outcasts all through the islands, and hence in Philippine eyes the fighting still constituted resistance to a white man's colonial war.

Letters home from the Americans continued to detail atrocities in what was typically referred as "the nigger fighting business." A soldier from Kingston, New York, wrote about an engagement in which a town surrendered and was occupied by two companies of Americans: "Last night one of our boys was found shot and his stomach cut open. Immediately orders were received from General Wheaton to burn the town and kill every native in sight; which was done to a finish. About 1,000 men, women and children were reported killed. I am probably growing hard-hearted, for I am in my glory when I can sight my gun on some dark skin and pull the trigger." A Californian in another town wrote, "We make everyone get into his house by seven P.M., and we only tell a man once. If he refuses we shoot him. We killed over 300 natives the first night. . . . If they fire a shot from a house we burn the house down and every house near it, and shoot the natives, so they are pretty quiet in town now."

Both sides commonly killed prisoners. Mutilation of bodies was the norm. And both Filipinos and Americans soon started cutting the ears off corpses.

The war continued to expand, through Luzon and down to the Visayas in the central Philippines, where American navy ships arrived with troops that took the principal cities on Negros and Cebu. In their frustration in failing to track the enemy's movements in the countryside, much less corner him, the Americans began routinely to use torture in seeking information from prisoners. A specialty was the infamous water cure, which would be reintroduced in the 1970s and 1980s by the military men serving the dictatorship created by Marcos's 1972 coup. It was described by contemporary observers as a combination of American know-how and Spanish sadism. One soldier, who had himself frequently applied the water cure, described how four or five gallons of water, sometimes salt water, would be forced down a prisoner's throat or through his nose so that his "body becomes an object frightful to contemplate." Then the torturers would kneel on the prisoner's stomach, bouncing up and down, forcing the water out; they would repeat the process until they lost patience or, as was more usual, the prisoner either informed or died. Death in most instances was attributed to heart failure.

Toward the end of 1899, as the action picked up after the rainy season, the International Red Cross sent a representative, F. A. Blake, to Manila at the request of Aguinaldo. The Americans let Blake land. They restricted his movements to behind American lines, but he managed to see many villages whose flimsy bamboo and nipa palm houses had been burnt to the ground. He also saw, he said, "horribly mutilated Filipino bodies, with stomachs slit open and occasionally decapitated." Back in San Francisco he told a journalist, "American soldiers are determined to kill every Filipino in sight."

By now it had become clear to the hardest-liners in the field that what they were fighting was a movement that had broad-based, nationwide popular support. General MacArthur told a reporter that "after having come this far, after having occupied several towns and cities in succession, and having been brought much into contact with both *insurrectos* [Aguinaldo's soldiers] and *amigos* [Filipino businessmen in Manila who worked with the American administration there], I have been reluctantly compelled to believe that the Filipino masses are loyal to Aguinaldo and the government which he heads."

Another general said it looked as though the Americans would have to kill off half the Philippine population if they were ever to bring "perfect justice," meaning military victory, to the islands. A veteran of Wounded Knee, Col. Jacob Smith, who would gain infamy in the Visayas later in the war, said he had already adopted on Luzon the tactics he had learned in the American West because fighting Filipinos was "worse than fighting Indians."

In the first months of 1900 the war entered its pure guerrilla phase. Aguinaldo moved up to mountain headquarters
in Isabela Province in Northeastern Luzon and directed that
his troops henceforth avoid pitched battles in favor of the
hit-and-run guerrilla methods that had proved far more successful. The Filipinos were now abandoning major towns and
cities to the occupation of the Americans on Luzon, in the
Visayas, and in parts of Mindanao. But before departing they
ordered local officials to act as if they were going along with
the American soldiers but meanwhile gather information for
the guerrillas on the Americans' plans and movements. The
American troops were stretched thin now. The guerrillas
would come in behind the units sent out to occupy the towns
and cities they had vacated. They would cut telegraph wires,
stage carefully worked-out attacks on supply wagons, and pick
off straggling infantrymen. When the Americans pursued their
tormentors they fell into well-planned ambushes.

With the guerrilla phase of the war in full swing, the atrocities committed by both sides increased. A town official told
members of an American unit that he would lead them to a
spot where arms were hidden. Instead he led them into an
ambush in which they were butchered with bolo knives, the
large single-edged knives that are used both as machetelike
cutting tools and as weapons in the Philippines. In reprisal
for the ambush, twenty-four Filipino prisoners were executed.

And now, with the war at its peak, an announcement came
that the war was over. The announcement was intended to
provide a graceful exit for Otis, who on May 2, 1900, after
twenty-one months in the islands, was replaced in Malacañang
Palace by a new commander and Governor-General, Arthur
MacArthur. On the day of the change of command a reporter
asked Otis if he thought the war was finished. "I have held
that opinion for some time that the thing is entirely over,"
Otis said. "I cannot see where it is possible for the guerrillas
to effect any reorganization, concentrate any force or accomplish anything serious." But the day before, May 1, the Forty-

third Volunteer Infantry had lost nineteen men on Luzon when they fell into what their captain called a well-planned trap. The day after Otis spoke, May 3, a similar fate befell regulars from the Twenty-sixth Infantry down on Panay in the Visayan Islands.

During Otis's time a civilian commission, which had concluded that Filipinos wanted and should have self-government, had been on hand in Manila. No one paid it much attention. But now McKinley, since 1900 was an election year and the press was making fun of the military's false claims of victory, decided to send out a much more powerful Second Philippine Commission. Its five members were charged with working out the first moves toward self-government. Unlike the first commission, it did not have to report to the military. It included two academics, a former chief justice of the United States Court in Samoa, and the former vice governor of Tennessee. Its chairman was a rotund young Ohio judge named William Howard Taft. As the military was fond of pointing out, the average weight of these new commissioners was 228 pounds.

They were on their way by steamship before May of 1900 was over. Almost immediately after their arrival in June a rift began to open between MacArthur and Taft. Unlike Otis, MacArthur had recognized the popular nature of what was officially called the Philippine Insurrection. But MacArthur's response to this discovery was not to meet the Filipinos' demands but rather to face up to the fact that it would be harder to defeat them than was first thought. He persuaded Washington to send him more troops and pressed harder in the field than Otis had. Taft, on the other hand, thought compromise was in order. He began issuing proclamations of amnesty. But MacArthur was refusing to carry these proclamations out.

It was not that Taft was liberal in modern terms, but he was extremely liberal in comparison to the insulated American military establishment that was attempting to run the Philippines in mid-1900. Taft thought Filipinos should be started at once on the road to full independence, although he also thought full independence would necessitate "fifty or one hundred years" of careful tutelage "to develop anything resembling Anglo-Saxon political principles and skills." Still, Americans and Filipinos would, together, eventually build a new independent nation in Asia, he said. To the chagrin of the military, who still talked of niggers and gugus, he began referring to the Filipinos as "our little brown brothers."

A new song, heard wherever in the islands American troops went, ran:

> *I'm only a common soldier in the blasted Philippines.*
> *They say I've got brown brothers here, but I dunno what it*
> *   means.*
> *I like the word fraternity, but still I draw the line.*
> *He may be a brother of Big Bill Taft,*
> *But he ain't no brother of mine!*

Soon men who had supported the imperialist cause were saying it was time to simply pull out of the islands. John Foreman, an Englishman who had been attached to the American delegation to Paris at the end of the Spanish-American War and had advised holding on to the Philippines, now said American soldiers had so mistreated the population that to conquer the islands would involve costs higher than they were worth. The well-known pro-imperialist American journalist George Kennan said he had finally come to the conclusion that the "deep-seated and implacable resentment" of American conduct in the Philippines made it unlikely America could ever effectively govern the islands. "We have offered them many verbal assurances of benevolent intentions," he said, "but at the same time we have killed their unresisting wounded . . . and we are resorting directly or indirectly to the Spanish inquisitional methods. . . . [That] the present generation of Filipinos will forget these things is hardly to be expected."

MacArthur held fast. During the second half of 1900 he

said over and over that the situation was getting so out of hand that still harsher tactics were called for. He spoke with disgust of how the enemy fighters were not conventional army men but rather "criminals" and "murderers" who "make intermittent returns to their homes and vocations" and thus "divest themselves of the character of soldiers and if captured are not entitled to privileges of prisoners of war." He had Filipino prisoners executed on grounds that by choosing to fight as guerrillas they had removed themselves "from the pale of the law."

MacArthur's reports, like Otis's, claimed that fifteen Filipinos were killed for every American. A report on three towns in Batangas, the province that would later be led by the Laurel political clan, showed that their total population had dropped from 41,306 in 1896 to 11,560 in 1900, and the surrounding land under cultivation had dropped from about 49,000 acres to less than 1600.

A War Department report in 1900 said that 14,643 Filipinos had been killed in action and another 3,297 wounded thus far. It was a good indication of how prisoners were being treated. In America's Civil War, and in the Boer War then going on in South Africa, five men were wounded to each one killed. In the Philippines the ratio was reversed. Five Filipinos were killed for each one wounded, indicating that those captured were more often killed than made prisoners. MacArthur's rejoinder: "It arises from the fact that our soldiers are trained in what we call 'fire discipline'; that is, target practice. In other words, they know how to shoot." Later he said Anglo-Saxons do not die from wounds so readily as do members of "inferior races."

Back home much of the press still railed against the war. Anti-imperialist groups held meetings throughout the country protesting what America was doing in the Philippines. But the appointment of the Taft commission had defused the opposition, and anyway McKinley's opponent in the election, William Jennings Bryan, had lost much support by his past vacillating on Philippine policy. McKinley easily won reelection. With no further need to protect himself with the imperialist wing, he now sided with Taft against MacArthur, speaking of self-determination for the little brown brothers.

In the summer of 1901 MacArthur was relieved of his command. Taft moved into Malacañang as the first American civilian Governor-General. Before the year was over, boatloads of American schoolteachers were arriving to start the first classes, given in English and following an American curriculum, in the towns and cities that were under occupation.

But still the war went on. MacArthur's command was given to Lt. Gen. Adna Chaffee, a rough-and-tough cavalry officer who had come up through the ranks during the Civil War and, like so many others who wound up in the Philippines, had spent most of his adult life fighting American Indians.

Despite the McKinley-Taft stated policy of benevolent assimilation, Chaffee was soon clamping down harder than ever before, using especially brutal tactics in Batangas and on the Visayan island of Samar. He was also expanding the scope of the fighting, sending large detachments all over the Visayas, and also moving in force into Mindanao.

Until now Mindanao had hardly figured in the war. Its people were mainly Moslems, known to other Filipinos as Moros, the name given to them by the early Spanish colonizers who, having recently at last driven the Moors of North Africa out of Spain, found to their horror that there was a big island full of Moslems in their new Far Eastern domain. Christian Filipinos, like the Spaniards, tended to look upon the Moros not as brothers but as alien heretics. Before Chaffee arrived, most of the fighting on Mindanao had been between rival Moro groups loyal to various sultans and other chiefs. The Spanish had from time to time controlled Mindanao coastal towns as they tried to subdue the Moros, but in general they had left the Moros alone, not having the armed strength to fight the major war that would be needed to conquer them. Chaffee, however, added the conquest of the Moros to America's goals. And his act of sending soldiers in force into Moro territory caused the Moros to put aside their internal squabbles and unite for the first time.

Meanwhile, on Luzon, Chaffee applied an extreme form of the policy that would later be called hamleting to the battered inhabitants of Batangas. In all cities in the province the people were driven from their homes, which were destroyed, and placed in what were called "reconcentration," or *reconcentrado*, camps. Areas surrounding the camps were designated "dead lines," the equivalent of the later free-fire zones. Crops and food stores as well as homes outside the camps were destroyed, and so too was anything found living, whether it be a farm animal or a human.

The anti-imperialist outcry at home had softened as McKinley sent out teachers and entrusted Taft to take the first steps toward leading the Filipinos to self-government. But the outrage was revived as news reached America of what Chaffee was doing. He unintentionally contributed to the outrage by lifting the heavy press censorship that had been imposed by Otis and MacArthur. An example was a story, which the previous commanders almost certainly would have killed, that Chaffee allowed to be filed by a correspondent covering the campaigns in Batangas:

> The present war is no bloodless, fake, opera bouffe engagement. Our men have been relentless; have killed to exterminate men, women, children, prisoners and captives, active insurgents and suspected people, from lads of ten and up, an idea prevailing that the Filipino, as such, was little better than a dog, noisome reptile in some instances, whose best disposition was the rubbish heap. Our soldiers have pumped salt water into men to "make them talk," have taken prisoner people who held up their hands and peacefully surrendered, and an hour later, without an atom of evidence to show that they were even *insurrectos*, stood them on a bridge and shot them down one by one, to drop into the water below and float down as an example to those who found their bullet riddled corpses.

Soon witnesses were going public with the story of an operation in Batangas in which 1300 prisoners had been methodically executed. A Filipino priest was called in to hear the prisoners' final confessions, which lasted for several days. Then the priest was hanged on a gallows in full view of the condemned men. Finally the prisoners, in groups of twenty at a time, were forced to dig mass graves. When a grave was ready, the twenty would be gunned down before it. The whole operation took weeks.

A corporal told of an incident which, fellow soldiers said, was typical of what went on in Batangas. His company, he reported, had shot and killed a large group of civilians waving white flags, because they had received orders "to take no prisoners." The only civilian in this group not killed, he said, was a beautiful young mother, spared so that the officers and men could take turns raping her.

Many tales were related about the concentration, or reconcentration, camps. An early army public relations man, Col. Arthur L. Wagner, told U.S. senators how 8000 Filipinos were put together in a camp "about two miles long and one wide," which would have given them each an area to live and roam in of 12 by 6 feet. Wagner said a small church inside the camp held 127 women, a single house 270 men, and a one-family nipa hut 40 people. Around the camp was the dead line, where anyone appearing would be shot on sight. Wagner said the point of the camp was "to protect friendly natives from the insurgents" so as "to assure them an adequate food supply," and also to instruct them in "proper sanitary standards." It was suggested, with irony Wagner missed, that since the purpose of the camp was to protect our friends, the dead line should be called a "life line." He said he thought that would be a fine idea.

A letter from the commander of another Batangas camp called such places "suburbs of hell." "What a farce it all is," the commander said, "this little spot of black sogginess in a *reconcentrado* pen, with a dead line outside, beyond which everything living is shot. . . . Upon arrival, I found 30 cases of smallpox, and average fresh ones of five a day, which practically have to be turned out to die. At nightfall crowds of huge vampire bats softly swirl out of their orgies over the dead. Mosquitos work in relays. This corpse-carcass stench wafts in and combined with some lovely municipal odors besides makes it slightly unpleasant here."

Much of the story of Batangas, such as the army PR man's version, came out in hearings before a special Senate committee. In September 1901, two months after Chaffee took command and Taft became Governor-General, McKinley was assassinated and his Vice President, Theodore Roosevelt, became President. As a long-standing advocate of imperial expansion—who as assistant secretary of the Navy had given the first orders that Dewey head toward the Philippines—Roosevelt at first urged Chaffee on in applying to the Filipinos tactics he had used on the Indians. But at the end of 1901 a chance encounter occurred between a reporter and Jacob Smith, the Wounded Knee veteran, now a general, who had said early in the war that he found it worse to fight Filipinos than to fight Indians. Smith had later been responsible for much of the slaughter in Batangas. Now, he told the reporter, he planned to set every house on the Visayan island of Samar on fire, and he said he expected he would wind up killing off most of Samar's people.

Word of what Smith was planning set off such a furor in the Senate that even leading imperialists agreed it was time to investigate reports of atrocities. It was through newspaper accounts of the special Senate committee's hearings that most Americans first learned of the killing of prisoners, the common use of the water cure and other tortures, the reprisals against civilians, the burning of villages, the reconcentration camps, and the dead lines. But nothing else the committee heard got the press attention given to what Smith was doing on Samar.

The people of Samar, the third-largest island in the country, then as today had the reputation for being wildly contemptuous of authority. It was said that men on the island frequently ran amok, a Malay term that passed into the English language during the Philippine-American War: it means to suddenly, without necessarily any apparent reason, go into a murderous frenzy and start killing anyone around. The term was most often applied to the wild Moro warriors of the far south, but it was in currency on Samar too. When American infantrymen first landed there they were met on the beaches by members of a Christian sect, calling themselves the Dios-Dios, who dressed in red and believed they could not be harmed by bullets. Bolo-waving members of the sect ran up to the invading Americans in suicidal charges.

In August 1901 Company C of the Ninth United States Infantry landed at the port town of Balangiga at Samar's southern end. There were no Dios-Dios around, and the initial occupation took place smoothly. But what the men of Company C did not know was that from the start the inhabitants of the town—including a Filipino priest, police chief and mayor—were plotting their slaughter.

Early on the soldiers' first Sunday morning in Balangiga, all the inhabitants of the town turned on them all at once, some with guns, most with bolo knives. Although the Americans, with their rifles, inflicted heavier casualties than they took, Company C was decimated in the melee. Some of the Americans escaped in a boat to a headquarters post at a port town to the north, Basey; but of the eighty-eight men in the company, fifty-nine were either killed outright or died later of their wounds, twenty-three more were wounded, and only six escaped the massacre unharmed.

Fifty-five volunteers, including the six unwounded survivors, promptly returned from Basey to Balangiga on a gunboat. Using Gatling guns and cannons, they killed every human being they saw as they steamed down the Samar coast. When they stormed ashore at Balangiga, they found a funeral in progress for 250 Filipinos who had been killed by members of Company C. The Americans captured twenty gravediggers and ordered them to remove the Filipino bodies from a trench that had been dug and replace them with American bodies. Then they had the gravediggers pour gasoline over the Filipino bodies and set them on fire. Next they executed the gravediggers. And before departing they, as had become near standard procedure, set the town on fire.

Chaffee had already made it clear he was ready to let his men take drastic reprisals. In one such reprisal, shortly after he took command, a Filipino captain on the island of Bohol killed an American corporal who had raped his girlfriend. In retaliation, the Americans burned the towns of both the captain and the girl. Similar incidents had also taken place during the summer on Cebu and on Marinduque. And in the devastated province of Batangas on Luzon, Chaffee had sanctioned written orders that for each American killed his comrades should "by lot select a P.O.W.—preferably one from the village in which the assassination took place—and execute him."

Zeroing in on Samar now, Chaffee stayed in character. He turned complete responsibility for the island over to Jacob Smith, promoting him on the spot to brigadier general. To a battalion of 300 Marines headed for Samar Smith gave very precise orders: "I want no prisoners. . . . I want all persons killed who are capable of bearing arms in actual hostilities against the United States." When the Marines' commander asked Smith to be specific about just where the cutoff line should be regarding these potential bolomen, Smith said "ten years of age." The commander asked for clarification, and Smith repeated the ten-year age designation a second time. Later he shouted, "Kill and burn! The more you kill and burn the better you will please me." And then he sent out a handwritten message concerning his desire to make Samar "a howling wilderness."

But despite the wave of killing that followed on Samar, the war was by now drawing to a close. In the spring of 1901 Aguinaldo had been captured; before long he agreed that his cause was hopeless and offered to work with the Americans. Gradually the leading commanders were coming over to the American side. And Filipinos were impressed that Smith was court-martialed for unleashing atrocities on Samar, even though he escaped imprisonment and was merely put on the inactive list.

Somewhat grudgingly Roosevelt took note of what had been revealed in the Senate committee testimony. On Memorial Day of 1902 he acknowledged that there had been "a few acts of cruelty . . . committed in retaliation" for atrocities committed by Filipinos. But in any case the fighting by now was only sporadic except in Moro country. On July 4th of 1902 Roosevelt declared that the war was over, adding that he considered it the most glorious war Americans had ever fought.

It may have been a harbinger of similar statements Reagan would make about Vietnam, but in any case the Americans had by now taken two-thirds of the Philippines. Yet while on Luzon and in the Visayas the business of nation building now got underway, the Americans had one last ordeal ahead of them: the pacification of the Moros.

On Mindanao and in the Sulu islands the Americans, joined by enlarged Philippine Scout contingents and then by the new Philippine Constabulary—the enlisted men of both organizations being Christian Filipinos—came up against the Moros' belief in what they call *juramentado*. It means that a Moro who kills a Christian will be rewarded by going to paradise. Because they did not fear death, the Moros would keep coming at the Americans and their Filipino allies, waving bolos and screaming even after suffering mortal gunshot wounds. It was specifically because of the Moros that the U.S. Army replaced the .38-caliber service revolver with the .45-caliber automatic as standard issue. And the new invaders took a leaf from the Moros' book by playing on superstitions. A dead Moro would be burned with the carcass of a pig, which the Moros believed would prevent the warrior from reaching paradise.

In the Moro fighting, which dragged on until late 1913, the killing tended to be wanton and indiscriminate, just as it had been in the war against the Filipino Christians. The Americans, with the Scouts and Constabulary, rarely took prisoners and neither did the Moros. Nothing approaching a definitive history of this war against the Moros has yet been attempted, but there are documented glimpses that give an indication of how harsh it was—and why the resentments of the Moros would continue to seethe beneath the surface, to come into the open again when they faced a new wave of repression after the 1972 coup.

In 1906 when Gen. Leonard Wood staged an assault at Mindanao's Mount Dajo, some 600 Moros, including women and children, took refuge in the crater of an extinct volcano. For a day and a half American troops and their Christian Filipino allies, having encircled the crater rim, shot rifles and artillery down at the people massed in the crater, all of whom were killed.

Shortly before the final peace pact with the Moros in 1913, troops led by Gen. John "Black Jack" Pershing engaged in five days of fighting at Bagsak on Mindanao. The official U.S. communiqué said that between "300 and 400 hopeless fanatics and cattle thieves" were killed. A San Francisco newspaper, which had a correspondent in the Philippines, reported that the number of deaths was more like 2000, and included 196 women and 340 children.

After 1913 the emphasis in the Moros' territory, as in the northern and central parts of the country, was on education, self-government, and progress through public works. In addition, as a kind of final solution to the Moro problem, the U.S.

administration of the Philippines encouraged, and financially aided, Christian settlement in Mindanao, which became the Philippines' frontier. The Commonwealth, and then the independent government of the Philippines, continued this policy—which some called resettlement and others called land-grabbing—to the point where by the time Marcos came along the Moros were a 40 percent minority in the area they had controlled when the Americans first attacked.

After Marcos staged his coup, he soon had more men in the field than the Americans had had at the turn of the century. And they were far better armed, some of them better trained, than their earlier American counterparts. Also, with continuing American economic as well as military aid, Marcos was announcing greater expenditures to counter guerrilla action through peaceful means than there had been in either the Philippine-American War or the Huk rebellion.

And Marcos had already gone to some lengths to try to make his military popular and expand its role. While still a legal President he had started using soldiers, for the first time, as workers in such basic infrastructure projects as putting up schools and building roads.

But his armed forces, though its officers and men were all Filipinos, could never escape their mercenary heritage. They were still seen as direct descendants of the Guardia Civil, the Philippine Scouts, and the American Philippine Constabulary that in World War II had chosen to serve the Japanese. Although on paper Marcos's plans looked plausible, causing a good part of the middle class to favor martial law when it first began, these plans were never implemented. The people wound up losing not just their rights but also money and property to the new soldiers and officials favored by Malacañang.

Even at Malacañang, deep in the hall of mirrors, it became clear that the people increasingly saw antigovernment guerrillas as being in the tradition of the armed forces who had fought for Filipinos, with uniformed government soldiers still seen as the enemy. When Marcos suddenly announced that he was taking the people's constitutional rights away and setting up a military government, the guerrillas got moving. And while the New People's Army was slowly building up national strength, another war broke out in the far south in Mindanao provinces and on small islands where the Moros still predominated. In late 1972 the Moros, because of the looming oppression of the dictatorship, picked up where they had left off in 1913.

10

MARCOS'S HIDDEN WAR

Prelude to the National Struggle

AT THE time martial law was declared in 1972, life in the Moro part of the islands had recently become more perilous than at any time since the early American colonial days. And then, with their region in tumult, the Marcos coup itself provided the spark for a fresh uprising of the descendants of those same Philippine Moslems who had warded off Spanish occupation for centuries and prolonged the Philippine-American War.

This new Moro war, fought with even greater brutality than the first one, turned out to provide a testing ground for the enlarged armed forces Marcos was putting together. During their years in the south the government troops became precisely the sort of ruthless military machine that Marcos and his Ilocano generals believed they needed if the dictatorship was to endure. Later, as campaigns were stepped up against the wider New People's Army insurgency, it was troops who had gained their experience by killing Moros who were turned against NPA soldiers, and also civilians, in all parts of the country.

Government lack of concern for the welfare of the Moros had been so great by 1972 that officials in Manila could not say for sure if the Moslem population was 2.5 or 4 million. Most who were involved in the war that followed, whether as observers or combatants, agreed a dozen years later that at least half of the Moro civilians not killed after martial law had been turned into refugees. By low estimates, such as those given by some military officers in the field, Marcos's Moro War had left more than 60,000 people dead; but others, including some foreign diplomats, suspected the figure could have reached into the hundreds of thousands. And even in 1984, after the Aquino assassination and with the new turmoil in Manila, the Moros were still fighting—despite the fact that entire towns and cities, large lush stretches on the southern and western coasts of Mindanao, and entire small islands off Mindanao had been turned into what looked like a moonscape.

It was a war that received little attention from the outside world, and not very much in the Philippines, since it was fought in a small area far away from Manila among people about whom most Filipinos knew little. By the time it started, most of the Moro population had been pushed into parts of the far south that comprised only 17 percent of the land they had controlled at the turn of the century, and 80 percent of them were landless tenants. Few Filipinos seemed particularly concerned about the fate of these non-Christians. With press censorship at home, and the foreign press most of the time ignoring the war altogether, Marcos effectively kept his near-genocidal campaigns against the Moros a nasty little Palace secret.

One American free-lance correspondent, a twenty-seven-year-old Midwesterner named Frank Gould, traveled extensively in the war zones of the south when the fighting was at a peak in 1974. He collected numerous firsthand accounts of the horrors. And then one day he disappeared, never to be heard from again. Carefully piecing his story together in the course of the next decade, his family reached the conclusion that Gould had been a victim of General Ver's intelligence organizations.

Before the 1972 coup touched off the Moros' fierce fight for survival, Marcos had already become a hated figure in the areas that make up what Filipinos call Moroland. It had started with the 1968 operation, which Aquino exposed, known as *Jabidah,* when Marcos had recruited Moros to fight as commandos to press his claims to territory in the Malaysian part of Borneo. No one could forget how sixty-eight of these commandos had been executed at their training camp on Corregidor Island in Manila Bay in order to keep them from talking.

But this attempt to cover up his plans for waging covert war in Malaysia was only one of the events that had turned the Moros against Marcos in the years just before martial law. Since Marcos did not attempt to curb corruption among his followers, so many people from Luzon and the Visayas rushed in to lay illegal claims to land, timber and minerals on Mindanao that its frontier period came to an end. There was nothing left to be stolen. The emphasis now was on intimidating local residents who resisted the greedy outsiders.

By this time there were roaming bands of fanatic private Christian militiamen, calling themselves *Ilagas,* which means "rats," in the pay of carpet-bagging planters, loggers and entrepreneurs from Luzon and the Visayas. They were fighting regularly against various private Moslem militias, which took names such as "The Barracudas" and "The Black Shirts" and could be equally fanatic. There was also fighting between the armed guards of the various feudal, landowning Moro clan leaders, plus battles between these guards and other guards of wealthy Christians.

In the local elections of 1971, just as during the presidential election year of 1969, Marcos dug deep into state funds to try to defeat anyone who did not support him. He also ordered the intimidation of voters. Since he did not feel he could trust traditional Moro politicians to support his plans to centralize the economy and the corruption in the hands of his family, Moros were among those who suffered most during the 1971 political campaign.

In June of 1971, a group of *Ilagas* went to the small barrio of Manili in Carmen in the province of North Cotabato on Mindanao's western coast. They asked the people there to come to a peace conference. About 200 Moros, including women and children, entered Manili's nipa thatch mosque and waited for the conference to start.

A group of *Ilagas* arrived along with a contingent of government soldiers. A grenade was hurled into the mosque, killing about seventy people instantly, and then the soldiers and *Ilagas* started firing into the houses of the barrio. As in all such massacres in Moroland, there were few survivors among the Moro civilians. The men's heads were cut off. Pregnant women were disemboweled. The ears were cut from the heads of children. Hundreds fled Manili and surrounding barrios. From Malacañang came an announcement that the area was being placed under "Constabulary control" to protect the residents. But the Constabulary never arrived.

One particularly vicious massacre aimed at intimidating Moro voters in 1971 took place in Lanao del Norte province in southern Mindanao. Like other such events before the days of martial law, the incident was documented in detail in the press. Voters in the municipality of Kauswagan had decided to stay away from the polls because the area was controlled by *Ilagas*. The local Constabulary, however, guaranteed their safety and offered them transport. But a truck carrying voters returning from the polls was stopped by government soldiers at the barrio of Tacub. The soldiers ordered the voters to get out and lie face down on the ground. Then they shot them.

Up to now most Moros, although some had been working to form a Moro independence movement that would cut through all factional lines, had not seen the need to unify on a large scale in the face of the terror. They had assumed the terror would go away when Marcos's second and last legal term in office came to an end. Hence their violent, concerted reaction to the 1972 coup.

The end of democracy meant there would be no reform president—whom everyone had assumed would be Aquino—who would get rid of offending military officers from the north. It meant the commanders assigned to Moroland by Marcos's cousin, the Constabulary chief Fidel Ramos, would stay in place indefinitely. It also meant that the pro-Marcos Christian mayors and governors, who had beaten Moslem incumbents in the wild 1971 elections, could no longer be turned out at the polls. Land-grabbers could no longer be taken to court since Marcos now insisted that judges, like military officers, put themselves under his personal direction and it was Marcos who had allowed the last big wave of land-grabbers to come in. For the Moros, as for other Filipinos, all possibility of future legal redress of their grievances had suddenly been taken away from them.

And then came the announcement from Malacañang, right after the martial law announcement, that all private arms were to be confiscated. The people were given a month to turn in any guns they owned or face arrest.

In the northern and central parts of the Philippines, and also the northern, Christian part of Mindanao, the decision to confiscate arms from civilians was at first welcomed. Few realized that in a few years there would be more guns around—in the hands of government-backed private guards, paramilitary units, and even some old-line Marcos opponents—than had been in circulation before martial law. But to the Moros, the confiscation of arms spelled an immediate crisis. It meant they would be defenseless against government soldiers and paramilitary groups such as the *Ilagas*—whom Marcos was soon to put in uniform as members in good standing of his new Civilian Home Defense Forces. Moreover, the Moros had a deep, religious-based warrior tradition dating back to the thirteenth century that had never been broken. To take a male Moro's weapon away meant that you were trampling on his faith.

So all at once, with the declaration of martial law, all families and factions of the Moslem Philippines came together. Politically, they demanded autonomy. Militarily, they joined in a guerrilla army called the Moro National Liberation Front—or more precisely, the Bangsa Moro Liberation Army, technically the armed force of the MNLF.

Up to now the Moro National Liberation Front had existed mainly on paper. Its principal advocate was an unprepossessing young political science professor, Nur Misuari. At the University of the Philippines, he had been at the heart of the anti-Marcos organizing that had been going on among the students and the intelligentsia. Although Misuari did not now advocate Communism, he had been a member of José Maria Sison's Kabataang Makabayan youth movement and had tried to keep well above the fray of Moroland's factional infighting.

By chance Misuari was visiting Mindanao at the time of the coup. He was hidden by his people and escaped the dragnet Marcos put out to round up opponents and make them political detainees. Now, under Misuari's leadership, the Moro Front, which had already had men trained in Malaysia, came into being as an actual fighting force. Just as all factions in Moroland drew together when Gen. Adna Chaffee invaded in 1901, so did they come together in 1972 right after the coup.

The first major engagement with government troops took place on October 20, 1972, just under a month after the coup and a few days before the deadline for turning in arms. Some said it was a planned Moro National Liberation Front action, others that it was spontaneous. Moro fighters, in the pattern they would follow all through the war, swarmed en masse into Marawi City and occupied the campus of Mindanao State University. A large contingent of government troops was sent in from the north. A head-on battle went on for days. Since there was no longer an independent press to report on events in the south, no one knew the number of deaths. Some said it was in the hundreds, others in the thousands.

Virtually every combat unit of the government military, except those units either guarding the Palace or carrying out search-and-destroy operations against the fledgling New People's Army in northeastern Luzon, was now sent to the far south. Soon there was massive fighting south of Marawi City in the much larger city of Cotabato. In Cotabato and elsewhere in the south entire companies of government troops found themselves encircled by Moro Front guerrillas.

Without a free press, few Filipinos ever knew how intense the fighting and devastation was while a given battle was in progress. Often the government-controlled media made no mention at all of large engagements, and when they were mentioned it was always after they were over. Such was the case in what became known as the Battle of Jolo, a battle that went unreported until it ended after a full month of fighting during which the government used blitzkrieg tactics.

The ancient city of Jolo, located on Sulu Island, the largest in the Sulu chain, is practically a holy city for the Moros. It was an early seat of Far Eastern Islamic culture. Therefore the Moros were particularly disturbed when, starting early in 1974, government forces began conducting brutal door-to-door searches for arms in Jolo. In response, on February 7, a contingent of Moro guerrillas, variously estimated at 1000 to 5000 strong, attacked to drive the government men out.

The government massed thousands of soldiers to win Jolo back. Tanks were driven into the city. With air force planes rocket-bombing and strafing the city and its environs, and three navy vessels bombarding it from the sea, virtually nothing was left standing after a month. When reporters from the controlled press were at last brought in, so that northerners could savor their reports of the government victory, they learned that there had been bodies of people of all ages everywhere, including on the grounds of mosques, churches and schools.

Some months before the Battle of Jolo, the American journalist Frank Gould, looking like a typical hippy with his long mustache and old clothes, had arrived in Manila. He had come from Japan, where he had worked on an anti–Vietnam War paper directed at American GIs. He visited the Visayan island of Negros and wrote an article about the squalid post-coup conditions there of sugar workers who before martial law had been among the most prosperous farm workers in the islands. Among the publications Gould wrote for was the venerable Hong Kong–based British *Far Eastern Economic Review.* After another stay back up in Manila, he headed much farther south and spent April and May traveling all through Moroland. Since he was a free-lancer, he was not bound to timetables like staff correspondents. He did what few other outsiders ever did in the Moro war. With his contacts set up in Manila before he left, he had a network of missionary priests and human rights lawyers to visit. Through these initial contacts he was able to meet up with Moro guerrillas. Also, before leaving Manila he had informed the government in broad outline of what he was doing, and he thus had contacts among the armed forces too. He even managed to travel with a Constabulary company on a military operation.

When he went back to Manila he began work on a book about the Moro war. One of his Manila friends recalled that he had 200 pages completed, which he took with him for further work when he returned to the south in July. He left another copy of the manuscript at the Manila office of the National Council of Churches, which gave him a grant to finish his work.

Fragments of the manuscript survive. In it he told how the people of Jolo had still believed that dying in battle would assure them a place in paradise. He quoted a Philippine Army officer who had fought at Jolo, echoing the comments of American soldiers in the Philippines sixty years before: "These people—you hit them with a .38 and it's nothing. You hit them twice, and they keep on coming. They have got that determination. They fight up to the last. As a matter of fact, there are no such things as 'surrenderees,' even on our side. If they overrun a detachment, we have to fight to the end. You can be sure that everybody is dead."

He also wrote of the attitudes of other Filipinos toward the Moslem minority, and again there were echoes of attitudes from the American past. "Christian Filipinos," he said, "tend to look on the Moros in the same way that many people look on American Indians. They regard the Moros as a quaint, picturesque people with curious customs, destined to gradually fade away but a good tourist attraction while they last."

He wrote of the fanaticism of the *Ilagas,* who by now were carrying Civilian Home Defense Forces arms: "Using a sort of supposedly magic oil and wearing magic amulets called *anting-anting,* the *Ilagas* believed they were impervious to bullets, provided that they followed an extremely complex set of rules, such as never taking a bath on Friday, not letting anybody walk behind them while eating, and not looking behind when fighting. Certain that they were protected by God, the *Ilagas* would not seek cover in battle. All casualties, of which there were many, were blamed on failure to observe all of the regulations."

To Gould such fanaticism was but one of the many old-fashioned aspects of the war, another being the guerrillas' preference for massed pitched battles over modern hit-and-run tactics by small units. He also noted their reliance on outsiders for money and arms, particularly the oil-rich Middle Eastern nations, to whom they were just one of many factors

in international politics. He found that there was little thought
being given to a postwar future, and that many Moro fighters,
although now united in the Moro National Liberation Front,
tended still to give their first loyalties to local clan leaders.
Although much of his own political background was as a self-
proclaimed anarchist, Gould borrowed a copy of Mao's writ-
ings on revolution to take south with him and share with the
guerrillas on his second trip from Manila to Moro territory.

At this point, he found, the Moro guerrillas were not blaming America for Marcos's excesses. "Certainly," he wrote, "the
rebels are not anti-American. Indeed, they had hoped to get
aid from the Central Intelligence Agency and wonder why
the United States continues to support Marcos. Pro-American
sentiment is indicated by the fact that in Cotabato there has
been a Commander Nixon [a *nom de guerre*], as well as several
Commander MacArthurs."

There may have been talk about help from America, but
the reality was that the Moros were getting considerable material as well as moral support from Moslem nations. In Gould's
time their major arms supplier was Libya. Moro leaders would
be welcomed in exile in such diverse nations as Pakistan and
Saudi Arabia. By 1984, the principal source of arms for the
Moro fighters was Iran, and Misuari was making his headquarters in Tehran.

From time to time conservative Moslem leaders in other
nations would urge the Moros to go slow since the government
they were attacking was allied to America. And Washington
did try to place restrictions on Marcos's use of American arms
in the south because of its concern for opinion in the oil-pro-
ducing Moslem countries. But among the actual combatants,
with so much fanaticism at work on both sides, there seemed
little room for moderation.

Gaston Ortigas, a government official who split with Marcos, made his way out of the Philippines by, as Filipinos say,
"the back door" in 1980 after he learned that a presidential

order for his arrest had been issued. The back door meant a lengthy voyage through Mindanao and then from small island to small island below it, eventually reaching sanctuary in Malaysia's state of Sabah on Borneo. Like most Christians, he had never before had contact with Moslems, whom he now credited with saving his life. Although the Moro war was in a lull by 1980 and the armed forces were concentrating on the New People's Army, Ortigas still saw constant fighting in the territory he passed through.

"The Moro fighting skills and tactics were very effective," he said later in America, where he had become executive director of the moderate opposition group called the Movement for a Free Philippines. "For instance, they got so they would let a military patrol move out from its base and instead of engaging it, the MNLF would slip in behind the patrol and quietly mine the trail of the road they had passed along. Then they would wait for the patrol to return to its camp and watch as the soldiers walked into the mine field least expecting it since they had passed through going the other way only a short time before."

Retaliation for such actions was severe, Ortigas said. "Members of a patrol heading back to a town, having been surprised by walking through a mine field, would come back and take out their frustrations on the civilians. By then, refugee camps of thousands of peasants and farmers had formed in the towns. Soldiers would come back to the town and in their anger shoot up the refugee camps. Many people died this way."

He also confirmed reports that the Moros still favored mass actions, meaning that "most of the casualties were on a larger scale." The Moros liked to hold territory, and thus it took massive operations to dislodge them, which was why the southwestern Mindanao coast, called the Cotabato Coast, was largely a ghostly no-man's-land. And the situation was even worse on the small islands off Mindanao.

As Ortigas described it: "The Moros found that the best

way to capture and hold territory was to seize small islands. But the [government soldiers] would always make a point to retake any territory in the hands of the Moros, so when the [soldiers] wanted to retake one of these captured islands, they would shell it with naval and aircraft bombs and gunfire indiscriminately. Civilians would die en masse." Several islands in the Sulu chain suffered that fate.

According to those who knew him in Manila, Frank Gould also wrote of massive civilian casualties from specific military operations, but that part of his manuscript was confiscated by the government and never returned. Since he was one of very few foreigners to travel with both the Moro Front guerrillas and the government troops, his own story sounded like the synopsis of a Costa-Gavras movie.

It is known that in July of 1974 Gould visited Tawi Tawi and other small islands where the fighting had been heavy. Then in a letter to his parents on August 11 from the southern Mindanao city of Zamboanga, he said there was a "colonel in charge of intelligence" who wanted him out of the country, but a friendly officer who was in charge of Moslem religious affairs in the area was supporting him. In a letter he mailed August 16, he told how he had tried to visit the wife of an attorney who had been jailed for subversion. He himself was taken into custody. A witness said later, "They manhandled him—they admit it—and took his papers," including his travel documents and presumably his manuscript. At about the same time, the National Council of Churches office in Manila was raided, and soldiers made off with the only other copy of the Gould manuscript.

After Zamboanga he traveled in northern Cotabato Province, where a Methodist missionary, Paul Van Buren, took his picture on September 27. It was the last proof that he was alive.

Five years later another journalist, Lawrence T. Johnson, writing for *Mother Jones* magazine, retraced Gould's route

and found he was well remembered. Johnson picked up the
network of priests Gould had used as contacts. "You couldn't
help but admire him," one of the priests said. "He had great
courage. . . . He had to document everything personally. I
can tell you, that kind of journalism isn't very popular with
the Philippine government." Another priest who saw Gould
just before he vanished said, "The military had already confiscated his travel papers and notes and had advised him to
return to Manila. But Frank wouldn't go. He knew more about
the MNLF and the Moro war than anyone else."

Eventually, through contacts he made in tracing Gould's
route, Johnson was led to a large secluded house on the out-
skirts of Cotabato City. There he met with a secretly anti-
Marcos officer of the paramilitary Integrated National Police.
Sitting facing each other across a table with glasses of Coca-
Cola and a tray of sliced mangoes, the officer told Johnson
that Gould had been killed along with two Moslem guides
and that their bodies had been dumped some miles north
of the city. They had been placed in a common grave, a reposi-
tory for victims of the disappearances that Filipinos called
salvaging. The murder, the officer said, had been carried out
by a special killer squad belonging to the intelligence branch
of the police.

An American embassy investigation came to nothing. After
months of holding back, embassy officials sent Gould's parents
eighteen pages of his manuscript that they had obtained from
the government. None of the details of massacres that Gould's
friends said were in the manuscript were in this fragment.

The Philippine government gave wildly contradictory versions of Gould's fate. At one point his parents were told that
he might have been eaten by crocodiles while going up a
river. They were also told he had left the Philippines and
arrived safely at the port of Sandakan in Sabah, though no
one there remembers a Caucasian, a rarity on this route, having turned up at the time.

Two years after the apparent salvaging of Gould it began to appear that the Moro war was winding down. The Marcos regime joined Moro leaders at the bargaining table in Tripoli, Libya. At one point when the discussions broke down, Imelda Marcos intervened: she flew to Tripoli and stayed up all night, she said, talking with her new "dear friend" Colonel Muammar al-Qaddafi. She ordered that a mansion be built for Qaddafi should he visit the Philippines; like the Coconut House built for the Pope, it was never used by its intended tenant since Qaddafi soon broke with the Marcoses. She also ordered work begun on a gigantic mosque, the first in the city, in downtown Manila. And eventually an agreement was signed that provided for Moroland's becoming an autonomous region.

But the Marcos government never honored the agreement. An election was held on a referendum for one version of autonomy that had been agreed to, but it was held in an area so wide that Moslems were in the minority, and hence it was defeated. Marcos announced he was giving the Moros autonomy anyway, but the terms meant abandoning the Tripoli agreement and letting Manila maintain so much centralized control over Moroland that there was little autonomy except in the imagination of the regime's propagandists.

The negotiations and the prospects for Moro self-government did, however, serve the purpose of bringing intra-community feuds to the surface in Moroland. Various other Moslem leaders challenged Misuari and began operating independent of him. Some Moros loyal to local leaders took up the government offer to surrender in exchange for cash payments—and guns. Some became professional surrenderees and turned themselves in for cash over and over again. With the situation this confused, the government was able to withdraw units from Moroland and deploy them against the New People's Army.

But the Moro war still did not come to an end. In the autumn of 1977, with the Tripoli cease-fire supposedly in effect, Sulu Island, the scene of the destruction of Jolo, became the scene of yet another conflagration.

On October 10, a meeting between the army's Brig. Gen. Teodulfo Bautista and a local Moro guerrilla commander, Usman Sali, was held at Danag, a marketplace in the municipality of Patikul, northeast of Jolo. General Bautista and the thirty-five soldiers with him watched as Usman Sali arrived for the meeting and extended his hand. The general responded, reaching out to shake hands, and just then 200 men standing behind Usman Sali opened fire. The general and all but one of his men, a man who faked death, were killed. It happened so quickly they were unable to return a shot.

Marcos allowed the news of the massacre to circulate, down to grisly details of how the Moros hacked up the bodies of the army men. What was not revealed was that in the time between the massacre and a previous meeting of Usman Sali and Bautista the rebel commander's son had been killed and his daughter raped by government soldiers.

Marcos protested that he was not going to let this massacre, or others like it, provoke his soldiers into retaliation against the Moros. Yet at the same time, following the usual contradictory patterns at Malacañang, he offered a reward for information leading to the capture, dead or alive, of Usman Sali.

The results were predictable. Moslem leaders told foreign correspondents that although Usman Sali remained at large, soldiers quickly took revenge for the Patikul massacre by shooting 400 civilians.

This constituted one of the still rare cases in which news of such activities got out, and the reason in this case was mainly that Marcos had wanted to publicize the affair. Another case of Marcos shedding light on the war for his own purposes came when the regime started talking in 1981 about a massacre of 119 soldiers on the tiny island of Pata in the Sulu chain. The controlled media gave the event heavy, sustained play. According to the government accounts, a military detachment had arrived at the island's main settlement "to pay a courtesy call on the Mayor," and Moro guerrillas had leapt from concealment and mowed down the soldiers with automatic weapons. Two months later Defense Minister Enrile announced that ninety guerrillas had been killed in the ensuing fighting on Pata.

Actually, as became evident later when witnesses gave their stories to foreigners, the courtesy call had been a ruse to put soldiers on Pata. The island had already been ringed by sixteen naval vessels. The plan was to carry out a surprise raid on a cache of weapons belonging not to the guerrillas but to well-organized Moro pirates who were practicing their traditional trade.

The leader of the pirates, one "Commander Unad," had previously been displayed by the government as a guerrilla who had "surrendered," publicized at Malacañang as a Moro Liberation Front leader who had changed sides. In fact he had continued to run guns, rob vessels, and stage kidnappings for ramsom.

Unad, one step ahead of military intelligence, led a band to meet the 124-man military landing party supposedly coming to visit the mayor. He put a gun to the head of the soldiers' commander and demanded that they put aside their weapons so that a peace conference could be held. As the soldiers were removing the shell clips from their M16s, Unad and his men started firing away and killed 119 of the troops. Some government soldiers were able to reload, and Unad and forty-six of his men were killed in the encounter.

Within twenty-four hours, according to two survivors who swam to a nearby island, the army had put reinforcements ashore. They disabled all the island's boats to prevent people escaping and then proceeded methodically to carry out revenge killings against civilians.

A naval bombardment of the island was followed by a thorough sweep, from one end of Pata to the other, by infantrymen. They burned down all the barrios and shot inhabitants.

The fighting spread to two more smaller islands. Again naval guns pounded the population centers, and soldiers went in afterward to shoot survivors and ransack and burn their villages and barrios.

One military regional commander admitted that there were more than 400 civilian deaths in the Pata operation. Another government source put the toll at 750. Nongovernment sources said this act of retaliation carried out on three islands, with further reprisals in its aftermath, brought the total of those killed to at least 2000.

It was but one of many such cases of mass killings still going on in the south. This one, like the Jolo and Patikul massacres, had been made public because the regime wanted to stir up public resentment against the Moros. But both government and Moro Front officials agreed that these publicized massacres represented only the tip of the iceberg in Moroland.

Other mass killings seldom came to light, but when they did they gave an idea of the recurring carnage. In November 1974, for instance, in the small, out-of-the-way town of Malisbong on the southwest Mindanao coast on the Celebes Sea, another 2000 Moslem villagers were reported to have been shot and killed. As related by a researcher for the American anti-Marcos organization Friends of the Filipino People, Severina Rivera-Drew, none of the dead were rebels. The real guerrillas, whose presence had attracted the soldiers, had left the town long before. The soldiers killed indiscriminately anyway, shooting some villagers inside their community mosque, taking others to sea and shooting them in boats. Rivera-Drew's account of the massacre, reconstructed from interviews with surviving witnesses, was entered in the *Congressional Record* by Congressman Tony P. Hall of Ohio in 1979. The heavy toll of civilian casualties from this one military operation was further verified by a secret military report sent to Marcos that leaked out. It discussed the burial by the army of "about

2000 women, civilians and children at Malisbong, province of Sultan Kudarat."

Shortly before he went home for the last time, Ninoy Aquino said he believed the Moro war could break out at any moment on a scale comparable to what it had been in the mid-1970s. Aquino, in touch with all the principal Moro leaders including Nur Misuari, had concluded that, with fresh material support from the Iranians, they were on the verge of uniting and staging the same sort of concerted uprising they had begun right after martial law.

While the killings continued in Moroland, the bulk of the army had been transferred elsewhere—all over Mindanao, up through the Visayas, in Bicol, in the provinces surrounding Manila and the provinces of northern Luzon—to do to the New People's Army and its supporters what government soldiers had learned to do to the Moros.

But the NPA, which had watched the Moro campaigns carefully and even at times joined with the Moro rebels in joint patrols, was determined to learn from the Moros' experience. National Democratic Front officials told us the New People's Army would never make itself dependent upon foreign arms, as the Moros had done; it would not risk becoming a pawn in other nations' politics, as had been the case when Libya and other Arab countries had cut off arms shipments. Moreover, for the time being the NPA would continue to move in small units, executing the perpetrators of atrocities, ambushing Army units, carrying out its Robin Hood–style version of "people's justice." Unlike the Moro fighters, its men and women would also continue to place as much emphasis on organizing and on bettering the conditions of the people among whom they moved as they did on actual military encounters in the field.

There would come a time, its leadership said, when the New People's Army would be able to stage massive operations;

but unlike the Moro guerrillas, the NPA would wait until it knew its supporters were too numerous and committed to be supressed even by Army tanks, Air Force planes and helicopters, and Navy gunboats. After the Aquino assassination, Communist leaders told us they thought the timetable for mass movements of guerrilla troops was being speeded up.

But even in the phase of small unit operations, the NPA guerrillas, not yet taking the risks the Moro rebels had taken, had proved they could tie up virtually the entire military, even after the dictatorship had increased its armed forces from 60,000 to 300,000.

Much in the manner that Gen. Arthur MacArthur had responded after he became convinced Aguinaldo's forces represented a nationwide and popular movement, the military of the dictatorship responded to the new show of support for the New People's Army not by compromising but by pushing ever harder. Not so many soldiers had been killed yet by the NPA's small units as by the Moros in their massive campaigns, but the NPA, never presenting the sort of target the Moros had presented, was causing the armed forces more frustration than the Moros had. And the government soldiers were now doing in every major area of the Christian Philippines what they had become accustomed to doing in the small and isolated part of the country where the Moros lived.

Marcos, brooding alone in his palace, was the symbol of the oppression. But there was not a man or woman in the Philippines who had not been touched, at least through their extended families, by actual, as opposed to symbolic, representatives of the dictatorship: government soldiers with American weapons.

11

THE POWER OF THE MILITARY

Government by Goon Squad

AS THE emphasis beyond Moroland switched from torture to outright murder following Reagan's inauguration in 1981, the regime's one last effective official institution, the enlarged military, was showing renewed vigor. The moderate and conservative, and also underground, opposition leaders, who had decried the soldiers' taking charge from civilians, now watched as the new military establishment tightened its grasp into a stranglehold through increased terror.

With America's human rights policy dead and the Marcoses back in favor with Washington, it seemed that most remaining restraints against marauding soldiers were being removed. More than ever people were being forced to choose between the Marcos-Ver enforcers, sent in from outside their provinces, and organizers and fighters of the underground National Democratic Front and New People's Army, who had appeared as their protectors and whom they knew and trusted, whatever their feelings about Communism.

Some of the military men had by this time grown rich and thus had a personal economic stake in maintaining the dictatorship. Many officers had also enjoyed real political power, sometimes de facto and often de jure, as governors and mayors, and of course as judges in the military tribunals. The presence of combat units, bloodied in the savage war with the Moros, in all parts of the country added to the people's feeling that their nation was being thoroughly militarized. And increasingly, as the rulers at Malacañang and in the ministries concentrated on internal intrigues and increasing their fortunes, the soldiers in the field were acting on their own.

In Manila itself the display of naked power by the military would increase to such an extent after the Aquino assassination that generals would start to regularly sit in on cabinet meetings, and also the caucus sessions of the regime's New Society Movement party, which handled all the business of the National Assembly. By the beginning of 1984 the people had begun to wonder if the military had not already staged something like a quiet coup of its own, with the generals already having replaced Marcos as the prime decision makers.

From 1981 on, as human rights workers found themselves totaling up more political murders than political arrests, civilians in all parts of the islands had to learn to live with military abuse as a fact of life. From the time Marcos found a friend in the White House and announced that with his New Republic a new era was beginning, the abuse increasingly went way beyond the persecution of specific individuals.

One horror story which shed light on how the military was operating began on a rainy September dawn in 1981, on the northeastern part of the resources-rich but battered island of Samar. Eighteen military men stormed into the bedraggled barrio of Sag-od, located on the edge of the huge San José Timber Corporation, a prime holding of the ruling elite.

Survivors later told human rights investigators how the soldiers went from stilt hut to stilt hut, ordering everyone to climb down the rickety ladders from their dwellings and form up in two lines in the road. One of the lines was composed of women and very young children, the other of the men and older boys. The women and small children were marched up the road at gunpoint, then off into the deep forest toward the nearby Sag-od River. When they were in the woods, they heard shots coming from the barrio.

Reynalda Durian, the twenty-five-year-old daughter-in-law of the leading Sag-od official, who had the traditional title of "barrio captain," told a nongovernment hearing, held two months later in Cebu City, that when she heard the gunfire she ran. A soldier ran after her and "threatened to kill me if I ran away again." Shortly afterward, while the group was being led across a forest stream by two soldiers, Reynalda Durian, with twelve other women and children, bolted again, this time managing to hide. Soon she heard more gunshots, now coming from the stream she had just left. Altogether the shootings at the barrio and at the stream took the lives of forty-five men, women and children.

An eight-year-old girl named Marela also testified at the Cebu hearings, which were held by a church group, the Ecumenical Movement for Justice and Peace in the Philippines. Marela and her little brother had been at their mother's side when the shooting started.

"When we were strafed, I fell flat on the ground, my mother lying sideward beside me," the girl said.

She was asked, "How about you, Marela, were you also hit when you were fired at by the soldiers?"

"I was grazed by a bullet on my hand," she replied. "I did not move again. When I fell flat on the ground, I was afraid the soldiers would hit me again."

Then, according to a transcript of the hearing, Marela went on to tell how her mother was shot "and my head got splattered by her brain." Her brother, too, was killed. When the soldiers left, Marela picked up an infant next to her, "then I placed him down again since he was dying already." She and the other children raced back to the barrio. Two kept running past the barrio into the forest, where they got lost and died of starvation and exposure.

"When we reached the barrio, we saw our dead menfolk piled on top of each other," Marela continued. Her father and the barrio captain were among the twenty men and older children who had been killed in the first round of gunfire.

She said that she still had nightmares about the soldiers. She and other survivors said they had recognized some of the men: they had seen them before, riding in the Jeeps of the San José Timber Corporation.

A Manila newspaper actually published a story mentioning that there had been a massacre, although it understated the number of victims and placed Sag-od in the wrong province. But it did report that local authorities identified the killers as security men from the logging concern. National Defense Minister Enrile, identified in leftist propaganda as the main owner of the concession, promptly announced that the armed forces would investigate. And the following month, the commander on Samar, Gen. Salvador Mison, told a provincial council that the killers were members of the New People's Army.

Some months later, however, the same general said he had no evidence leading to positive identification of the perpetrators. He said he had asked witnesses to come forward, "but you know how it is. . . . Nobody came." As had happened often before, and would happen again after the Aquino assassination, the regime was not even bothering to fashion a consistent cover-up story.

Other investigators, including those Amnesty International sent to the Philippines two months after the Sag-od affair, found it was not hard to unravel the true story. It centered on killers from a new sort of armed forces component that the regime encouraged but that neither Marcos nor his generals liked to mention.

Secret irregular units, similar to the *Ilagas* who fought the Moros, had come to form an integral part of the Marcos-Ver military establishment all through the islands. Many of these groups—such as Rock Christ, the Likos-Likos, the KKKKs, the Patiks and the Rizalistas—were, like the Dios-

Dios the Americans had encountered at the turn of the century, composed of wild Christian-animist fanatics. Some, such as the Rural Reformist Movement, whose specialty was beheadings, were tight right-wing political organizations controlled by Ver's intelligence apparatus. Some of the groups were so extreme they practiced ritual cannibalism as well as ritual mutilation of bodies—an odd development in what had once been the most modern of large Southeast Asian nations. Other groups were merely bandits, ready to hire themselves out as mercenaries, such as the bands of former Huks who served the regime in the vicinity of the American bases in central Luzon.

And by now it had become common for regular officers of the armed forces to have convicts released from prison into their custody and turn them into personal paramilitary bands—like the band Ver was reputed to have led thirty years earlier in the Huk campaigns. The soldiers, who had been recognized by the Sag-od survivors because they had served as private security guards for the timber firm, were members of the most famous convict band of all, the Lost Command. It was a unit of about 400 men, based in a mountainous area of northern Mindanao, led by a swarthy, silver-haired Constabulary lieutenant colonel named Charlie Lademora.

Lademora was a much-decorated government hero of the Moro war whose men—convicts, deserters, free-lance bandits—had been given their name by the government newspaper reporters, who compared their exploits to those seen in movies about the French Foreign Legion. After his service in Moroland Lademora had been given a seemingly soft berth far from the Moros as commander for a northeastern Mindanao province, Agusan del Sur, with his base camp in the town of San Francisco in the jungle-covered Diuata Mountains.

Numerous cases of extortion, robbery, rape and killing—committed in order to seize property—were attributed to Charlie Lademora's men. No witnesses dared come forth, but when he began attacking other government units he thought were poaching on his territory, provincial authorities complained to Manila. In 1979 he quit his post as provincial commander. But he stayed on. The New People's Army was active in his area now, and Lademora was still useful to the government.

The Lost Command fought the NPA but also expanded its other activities. It was extorting a share of all gold mined by small prospectors in the area. Its men were serving as security guards to a huge nearby British-owned palm oil plantation, set up by presidential decree by the Guthrie conglomerate with Philippine partners. In the service of the Guthrie interests, according to England's Catholic Institute for International Relations, the Lost Command drove out hundreds of farm families so that the plantation could be expanded. And the Lost Command was soon active on many other fronts.

A policeman in a neighboring province told how Lost Command men came in committing "killings, rape, robberies and senseless brutalities. . . ." The policeman described how Lademora's men kidnapped and killed a Constabulary sergeant on his own farm; how they kidnapped and raped twenty women all at once; how they had practiced extortion and had a stranglehold on all rackets, such as protection and gambling; and how fishermen and coffee bean growers, like the prospectors, were forced to give the Lost Command a share of their profits.

In San Francisco alone, the town that was still the site of Lademora's base camp, twenty-four murders went unsolved in 1981 because the police refused to investigate. But Lademora was welcoming foreign reporters, telling them he was still a Constabulary officer in good standing, posing for photographers in a camouflage jacket emblazoned on the back with a crushed skull, the title "Charlie's Angels," and the words "Courage, Guts, Death." One of his troopers was a sexy girl named Delilah who liked to pose with her AR-15 automatic, dark glasses cocked in her silky hair, and was said to go into battle in a sleeveless blouse and tight-fitting jeans. "I'm not a mad killer," Lademora told a free-lance journalist reporting for *Newsweek* magazine. "I'm a *reasonable* killer."

Over in Davao City, on the night before that 1981 Easter Sunday when grenades were thrown into the crowded San Pedro Cathedral, Lademora and some of his soldiers were seen in town. The authorities chose to explain the unsolved cathedral bombing—which had led to torture and killing of civilians—as the work, variously, of Moro rebels and the New People's Army. But if conclusive evidence was lacking regarding the Lost Command's implication in the Easter Davao cathedral bombing, the evidence was overwhelming that the Lost Command had been involved in the massacre at Sag-od later that year up on Samar.

Lademora had hired out some of his men to work as security guards for the big timber firm adjoining Sag-od. The NPA was putting particular emphasis on organizing there because of the firm's mistreatment of workers and its alleged ownership by high government officials. Defense Minister Enrile warned against "speculation" concerning Sag-od, but Amnesty International found good reason to believe Lademora himself had been present for the massacre.

Amnesty International heard that when word first reached his San Francisco camp from Manila that he was being implicated, Lademora took off for the capital, leaving instructions with his son to assassinate certain local Mindanao officials if he was not back in seven days. In Manila he checked into what was being said, purchased three wigs to use as disguises, and then he hurried to Samar. Soon he was back in San Francisco, bringing the bodies of security guards who had been killed, possibly by Lademora himself or possibly by NPA guerrillas. Amnesty International also learned that Lademora had rounded up a group of fake witnesses who were ready to say he had been with them on Mindanao at the time the Samar massacre took place.

Lademora was never asked by any government tribunal to explain if he or his men had done the killing at Sag-od. Witnesses confirmed that in addition to Lost Command members in the area there had also been regular army men, members of the Fourteenth Infantry Battalion. Survivors said these infantrymen had gathered up the bodies of the men and older children killed inside the barrio, put the bodies in the stilt huts, then set the huts on fire.

In total numbers, members of the Lost Command and other such irregular units apparently composed only a relatively small part of the total force of men under arms actively serving the dictatorship. But the fact that such units, which could not be touched by any system of military justice, were now routinely involved in government military actions all over the country was something new to the Philippines and added to the thickening atmosphere of terror. It was almost certain that thirty years earlier some irregular units, such as the one reputed to have been headed by Ver, were employed against the Huks. But they had been disowned by Magsaysay, whereas Marcos did nothing to distance his government from these quasi-independent terrorist outfits.

Before Marcos, civilians may have regarded the official military as a mercenary force, much the way the colonial forces of Spain and America had been regarded. But the military was also firmly under Filipino civilian control and had been set up as a professional organization, modeled almost precisely on America's own civilian-controlled military. Most of its top officers were trained in the Luzon hill city of Baguio at the Philippine Military Academy, which had been established as a scaled-down replica of West Point.

Using the Philippine Scouts and the Philippine Constabulary, which was originally intended as a national colonial police force, as its nucleus, the modern Armed Forces of the Philippines were put together during the Commonwealth period in the 1930s. This undertaking was headed by Douglas MacArthur, who went on leave from the U.S. Army to serve as a "field marshal" for the Commonwealth government.

After World War II, when the military was rebuilt for the new independent republic, it was again organized almost precisely along American lines. Much of the organization was carried out on the spot by American advisers, members of the American military assistance contingent that then, as in 1984, was connected to the U.S. embassy. At first the Constabulary was kept apart, reporting to the Department of the Interior. But since aiding local police fell outside treaty arrangements with America, and the Constabulary was anyway being used against the Huks as a regular combat force, it was integrated into Magsaysay's Department of National Defense, making it eligible, like the army, for American assistance in the field and also for officer training in the United States.

Aside from the fact that many people looked upon all soldiers as mercenaries, the Philippine military was kept apart from society because of the way it had been patterned on the American military. Officers, men and their families lived on self-contained bases. Civilian control was even stronger than in America since in the Philippines promotions to the higher ranks had to clear Congress. There had never, in the independent democratic republic, been a military man who sought high government office, as there had been in America. Also, there were no cases of military men putting together fortunes. Members of the armed forces were hardly ever seen at nonmilitary society events.

In organizational charts, the military of the dictatorship still looked much like what it had been in democratic days, even after its number of general officers had been increased tenfold and its overall strength fivefold. But the difference was that it was no longer part of a legal and constitutional system. There was no legally elected President above it, only a man who wanted to be dictator for life and insisted that his soldiers be a personal, rather than a national, force. There was no Congress, nor any other civilian institution, to which officers were held responsible. There was no legal constitution, only the successive martial law constitutions that the dictator himself ordered up.

In the new climate of martial law, it was in the armed forces' self-interest to see that the abuses set in motion by Marcos's policies were continued. The abuses ensured that fighting would continue, and thus that Washington was likely to see the armed Communist-led opponents of the regime as a threat to its own strategic interests in the region. The result, it was hoped, would be more money from America. As former Senator and Foreign Secretary Raul Manglapus said from exile after the Aquino assassination, "The most U.S.-oriented army in the world, the Armed Forces of the Philippines, continues to support that institutionalized violence because it sees mounting American aid to Marcos extorted in exchange for the military bases."

In the first five years of martial law, American military aid added up to more than $186 million, more than double that of the previous five years; at one point during martial law the Philippines became America's largest military aid recipient; and by the time of the Aquino killing, a total of $1 billion in U.S. support to the Philippine military had been pledged since the 1972 coup.

From the moment of his coup Marcos had begun to coddle his armed men in a way that never would have been permitted in democratic days. The state built fine homes for officers. Pay was raised—though often the foot soldiers never saw their paychecks and had to live off the land. Many armed government men received new benefits through large organizations Marcos created and expanded, such as the Philippine Veterans Bank. And the word quickly spread that no one would interfere with uniformed men taking advantage of their new positions to go into business, so long as their commercial activities did not interfere with those of Marcos, Imelda and their own tight little crowd of business cronies.

However it appeared on organizational charts, the military out in the provinces was no longer a professional organization but rather an organization to which no law applied. Its old standing was further undermined by Marcos's creation of the Civilian Home Defense Forces. The CHDF, which eventually had a strength of some 75,000, was as visible as the regular forces. Its only seeming purpose was to raise the level of the terror in order to keep the people under control. Its creation served to obscure the line between outlaw fanatics and regular troops since its members, some given uniforms and some not, came to include such groups as the *Ilagas* and the various old religious warrior sects.

In addition to the fanatics, the CHDF, which was always well armed and poorly trained, took in people by conscription. Military units sweeping through rural villages suspected of harboring New People's Army guerrillas would ask for Civilian Home Defense Forces "volunteers" and put out word that young men who failed to sign up would be subject to summary execution as subversives.

In the counterinsurgency battles, members of the CHDF often got the worst of it. At first they were assigned to their home areas, where they were considered traitors. Immobile but well armed, they became the easiest targets of the NPA. Later the policy was changed and they were sent as occupying forces to parts of the countryside where they were strangers.

Marcos also reached into the structure of the country's barrios to add to the forces at his command. He played heavily on superstition, propagating the reputation he had gained during his unprecedentedly long tenure, for possessing mystical, all-seeing powers. He reorganized the barrios, changing the word *barrio* to *barangay*, the precolonial name for hamlets.

There were now not just captains and councils but also armed barangay brigades and many other sorts of barangay officials and organizations. In places where government troops had their tightest control, these barangay groups were locked into his New Society Movement party.

One of these new barrio-level organizations was the *Barangay Kawal,* which means "Community Soldiers." Its members had to undergo a scary indoctrination in which the virtues of the dictatorship were supposed to be forever instilled.

Village priests came to learn of the rituals young people were being put through. In 1979 the Association of Major Religious Superiors issued a publication describing the bizarre rites:

> On the last night . . . the seminar takes on a new twist and [in an] atmosphere of mystery and suspense . . . the participants are blindfolded and led by circuitous and confusing routes . . . to another place of assembly. When their blindfolds are removed, they usually find themselves in a hall in which the only light comes from torches which flank full-length pictures of Marcos. This picture is invariably of heroic, more than life [size] proportions and is sometimes accompanied by a picture of Mrs. Marcos. . . . In the foreground there is a red-covered book of one of Mr. Marcos's writings. . . . A human skull often completes the setting. . . .
>
> After a brief exhortation touching on the greatness of . . . the New Society and its exalted leader . . . the participants are inducted into the *Barangay Kawal.* They are then told . . . that they will be sworn to defend with their lives and their total commitment the "Supremo" . . . of the New Society, Ferdinand E. Marcos. The participants are enjoined to strict secrecy regarding the dramatic events of the night.

These local forces were given assignments that included spying on residents, getting out the vote in rigged elections, breaking up local antigovernment meetings should anyone dare hold them, and forming up with military or police units when displays of force were necessary. Such groups were not just rural organizations; they were present even in the slums of Manila, where there are barrio, or barangay, boundaries between hovels.

All members of the various barangay organizations—including youth groups responsible to a national youth organization headed by Marcos's pretty Princeton-educated daughter Imee, as well as the local militias—were encouraged to inform on suspected opponents of the dictatorship. The complex of intelligence organizations, starting on the barrio level and working up to General Ver's all-encompassing intelligence apparatus, may have become the most elaborate in any nation that did not have external enemies.

Intelligence services of the Philippine military proliferated to the point where the average Filipino could not keep track of them. Although their operations were supposed to be kept secret, the government wanted it believed that everywhere you went someone was watching and listening.

No one trusted the telephones or the mail. If you talked politics, you did it in whispers. Early in the martial law period, before he went public with his dislike of Marcos, former Senator Doy Laurel used to ask people to merely nod and smile to each other in silent, secret communication that they disagreed with something Marcos was doing.

NISA, Ver's National Intelligence and Security Agency, was supposedly ubiquitous and was far more spooky to Filipinos than the CIA and FBI were to Americans. Filipinos believed that NISA had agents not just in every government office but in every foreign embassy and consulate in the Philippines and in every Philippine embassy, consulate and tourist office abroad. NISA, which like the CIA had control officers and agents of its own and was also charged with coordinating the other intelligence agencies, did more than listen and watch for antiregime plots or evidence of the catchall crime of "subversion" committed by the many enemies the rulers made. Under National Security Code provisions, made public only in 1983, three years after Marcos decreed them, government criticism of almost any kind could be construed as a crime punishable by death. The regime did not go in for formal executions, but there had been so much salvaging, and also open murder, that if the regime said something was a capital crime the regime was taken at its word.

"Rumormongering" became such a capital crime, policed by NISA officers and their agents and informants. It was another added duty to the standard NISA tasks of interrogating and torturing political prisoners. Amnesty International found, as we did, that civilian and military officials openly conceded that when NISA was involved no rules of prisoner safety ever applied.

NISA was linked with Ver's 15,000-man Presidential Security Command. It had authority over CISA, the Civil Intelligence and Security Agency set up for civilian spying jobs. The regular military forces retained their own intelligence branches that had been created, following the American pattern, when they were first set up—and added more. General Headquarters had its J-2 intelligence branch with an alphabet soup of initialed offshoots including the ISAFP, for Intelligence Services of the Armed Forces of the Philippines, and field units called MIGs, for Military Intelligence Groups. The Constabulary had its C-2, spinning off into CSUs, for Constabulary Security Units, plus the CIS, for Criminal Investigation Services, which was Ver's old outfit; it also had SOGs, for Special Operations Groups; CANU, for Constabulary Anti-Narcotics Unit; COSAC, for Constabulary Off-Shore Anti-Crime Unit, and more.

AVSECOM, the Aviation Security Command, the SWAT-team unit that was supposedly ordered to guard Aquino, came under the Constabulary, as did its parent group, METRO-COM, the country's centralized urban police command, which was also represented on the tarmac when Aquino was shot—and both AVSECOM and METROCOM had intelligence functions. Then each of the other branches of the armed forces had its own intelligence units—G-2 for the Army, N-2 for the Navy and A-2 for the Air Force—with further offshoots.

No outsider—maybe no insider—knew the exact total of undercover intelligence operatives working for the dictatorship. But it was possible, using government figures and the estimates of analysts with international organizations, to get a fairly clear picture of the size of the uniformed forces under the dictatorship's control. The analysts usually left out the *Barangay Kawals*, which a former military intelligence colonel told us had a strength of 400,000 by the time of the Aquino assassination, and whose strength Marcos was to claim in 1984 was 1.4 million. By then authority in the provinces was breaking down to the point where no one could be certain that any local members would fight people of their own areas for the rulers. But even without the local militias, the dictatorship's troop strength was impressive, especially when it was understood that the Philippine military had no role other than to control the Philippine people.

In 1971, the last full year of civilian supremacy in the Philippines, the total armed forces count came to less than 58,000 troops including all members of regular units and a small home guard militia of around 400. At the time of the Aquino killing the dictatorship had a regular Army of 60,000, and there were 42,000 men in the Constabulary, most of them formed into regular combat units. The Air Force had 16,000 members, the Navy 28,000, and the estimated full-time strength of the Civilian Home Defense Forces was 75,000. In addition, Marcos had long since brought all local police forces under the command of the Constabulary's General Ramos, making their members part of a new organization called the Integrated National Police, adding an estimated 65,000 men to the armed forces' total manpower. It was by this count—apart from the thousands of progovernment mercenaries and cultists not taken into the CHDF and the unknown numbers in the barangay units—that the dictatorship had nearly 300,000 uniformed armed men to deploy.

And Marcos did deploy them. Although he spent far greater sums on civic action programs and in bribes to try to get New People's Army members to surrender than Magsaysay had had at his disposal during the Huk insurrection, the NPA at no point showed a drop in its numbers. It was probably true, as Marcos claimed, that he restrained some of his generals who wanted to solve the NPA problem by starting a blitz all through the 1200-mile-long island chain, but nonetheless he all but abandoned attempts to peacefully bring the NPA into the fold and instead fell back on brute force, both to kill NPA members and to terrorize civilians who might support NPA soldiers and organizers.

The Sag-od massacre was no isolated incident on Samar, where the regime had lucrative private business interests to protect from the 1.25 million people who lived on this third-largest of the Philippine islands. In addition to logging, Samar has many mineral deposits to exploit, and Marcos had guaranteed foreign investors that they would be free of trouble if they took advantage of the opportunities he offered them, including a strike-free labor force whose wages were the lowest in Southeast Asia. Americans and Japanese, for example, were partners in a big copper mine at Bagacay on the western side of the island. To the east, Germans were mining chromite around Girporlos. And while in Mindanao the Japanese had been given control of fish processing, here on Samar the local fishing industry had been nearly destroyed after the dictatorship allowed Japanese trawlers to violate regulations that would have kept them 7 kilometers from shore.

Before torture had given way to murder in most of the rest of the country, military killings had become routine affairs on Samar. One vicious round occurred in 1979 when the Sixtieth Constabulary Battalion, which had just been protecting the logging interests of Marcos cronies and Japanese investors in Luzon's Cordillera and the Ilocos provinces, was transferred to northeastern Samar.

The Sixtieth took up positions in eleven municipalities in the vicinity of the city of Palapag. Soon after they arrived, soldiers dumped a human head at the door of Palapag's town hall. At the fishing harbor of Laoang, two priests and a cemetery attendant reported that soldiers buried three more heads late one night. Outside Palapag, soldiers cornered a woman named Nida Ortiz, suspected of being an NPA member, and shot her and two male companions. A foreign correspondent described how her long hair dragged along the ground as her body was displayed "trussed like a pig" for the town to see. Nida Ortiz had been Palapag's beauty queen.

The list of such incidents seemed unending. But there was much more going on. General Ramos told us that there had been only "two or three cases of hamleting" in the Philippines, that those cases had been at the request of barrio captains who feared for their people's safety, and that the practice had been ended, but Samareños knew better.

Three different times people in Samar were driven away in large numbers from their fishing villages on the coast and their farmer barrios in the mountainous interior. Declaring sections of mountain ranges and strips of the coast "free-fire zones"—the equivalent of the old American "dead lines"— the military authorities ordered everyone living there to leave. And, despite what Ramos claimed, few went back.

In 1978 a presidential order came down to evacuate a stretch of the southern part of Samar's western coast. According to church researchers, about 600 families, meaning many thousands of people, were chased out of their houses and herded into three refugee centers inside towns. Their rice fields were burned. In the refugee centers, children's diseases spread and epidemics of cholera and dysentery broke out.

The next year, 1979, refugees were in flight in greater numbers, this time in the northern part of the island. Some

50,000 Filipinos were uprooted by soldiers between early June and mid-August. Displaced persons now lived three and four large families to one shack, taking turns sleeping on the bare floors. Some families had no structured shelter at all, sleeping on slats of wood to which their pigs and chickens were tethered. In 1981, another 6000 people, this time from the western part of the island, were uprooted. Military commanders told them to move fast because search-and-destroy missions were to begin instantly and if they remained in their homes they would be shot.

At the same time, military murders outside the hamleted areas and free-fire zones were increasing. Amnesty International described an incident on July 23, 1981, when a dozen soldiers from the Twentieth Mechanized Infantry Battalion burst through Juanito Salas's farmhouse door in barrio Osmeña in the southwestern Samar town of Maraput. They dragged Salas and his sixteen-year-old brother-in-law, Antonio Abon, outside. These two and another prisoner were taken to a remote spot, tied to banana trees and beaten. The soldiers then rounded up six more villagers. All nine were now taken to a Constabulary camp and handed over to drunken interrogators.

They were forced to sing while the soldiers banged their heads as if they were drums, using two-inch-thick pieces of lumber, until they bled. They were made to dance. They were made to strip, masturbate, kiss each other and then punch each other. Then they were taken outdoors behind the barracks. Three, including the teenager Antonio Abon, were shot to death.

The other six were carted to the division headquarters of the original arresting soldiers, where they underwent a week of beatings. Next they were taken to Camp Lukban, headquarters of the Armed Forces' Eastern Command, the center for security throughout the eastern Visayas. They were hung from above while soldiers used them as punching bags.

Finally, a month after Juanito Salas's arrest, he and the others still alive were released, told never to return to their mountain farmlands again. Amnesty International learned that the Twentieth Mechanized Infantry Battalion had been brought in for the purpose of scaring people in order to put down labor unrest at a British-Philippine logging company, German B. Aranes, Inc.

With the year 1981 proving a watershed for increased military brutality, reports of atrocities came to church groups from all other parts of the Philippines. Shortly after Reagan came into office and Marcos proclaimed that martial law would be lifted, some 5000 peasants gathered just east of Manila, in the town of Guinyangan in Quezon Province, to protest military abuses and the low coconut prices the government was setting. Members of the Constabulary's 232nd Company fired their weapons directly into the crowd. Two peasants were killed and twenty-one were wounded. It was not a high toll of victims, but this kind of methodical brutality by soldiers was something new to this part of the countryside.

The forthcoming June 1981 voting, in which Marcos would have himself re-elected—the election Vice-President Bush praised because "we love your adherence to democracy"— was the occasion for a new round of killing. The countrywide boycott, set in motion by the left and joined by the moderate opposition, resulted first in strong words from the palace. Marcos told his people on television that it would be a mortal sin not to vote. Cardinal Sin said the dictator had his theology wrong. Then Marcos turned to terror again. He ordered his military to get the people to the polls even if they had to do so at gunpoint. In all parts of the country there were incidents of military-instigated terrorism to break the boycott. Former Senator José Diokno, who knew military brutality well from his two years as a political detainee and his years since as a human rights leader, spoke of scores at a time being killed as soldiers fired into civilian crowds.

Some 40 percent of the voters either stayed away or cast blank ballots, which were numbered and hence traceable, in spite of the terror. A typical example of this use of terror occurred at Camarines Norte Province in Bicol on southern Luzon shortly before the balloting. At the time, the NPA was pressing hard in Bicol and the infamous Sixtieth Battalion had been brought up from Samar to join other Constabulary troopers there. Some 3000 small farmers and farm workers were marching toward the town of Daet to join a boycott rally when a company of Constabulary men fired into the marchers, killing four and wounding fifty. The nuns who had been collecting cases of human rights abuses counted up five such mass daylight encounters with the military. But human rights lawyers again pointed out that this hardly told the whole story, since there were so many encounters with the military for which they could not produce witnesses, and so many suspected salvagings going on around the country, as well as those incidents of people being murdered at night, their bodies found by would-be boycotters as warnings in the morning.

It got worse in 1982, the year Mr. and Mrs. Marcos went to Washington. For example, in Nueva Ecija Province north of Manila, five men last seen quietly playing a local board game disappeared; they were later spotted in military custody; still later three were found stabbed to death, and the other two were never seen again. West of Manila on the Bataan peninsula, scene of the last battle before the Japanese occupied the Philippines in World War II, five young suspected leftist activists surrendered to Marines who surrounded the house they were in. Instead of taking them prisoners, the Marines ordered them back inside, witnesses reported, and riddled the house with automatic weapons fire until all five were dead. In northwest Mindanao a band of *Ilagas,* turning their attention from the Moros to the New People's Army, raided a house and slashed twelve suspected Communists to death.

On the south end of the Visayan island of Leyte, Constabulary soldiers, peppering a hut with their automatics, killed nine peasants, seven of them between the ages of three and eighteen. In Bulacan Province north of Manila, a Constabulary patrol arrested five people they said were "peasant organizers." The next day their hacked up bodies were found by a roadside in another town. Down in Bicol, five civilians who had built a barracks for a regular infantry unit were shot to death upon completion of the job.

In Mindanao, at the isolated village of Dimalinao in the forests of the Zamboanga peninsula, two Air Force helicopters appeared over a group of huts in a clearing. Minutes later fighter planes rocketed the settlement with bombs. Then troops waiting in the jungle burst into the clearing. What they found was a mother weeping over the remains of her infant daughter; a man dead in a field with a wounded child clutched in his arms; another dead villager and half a dozen others wounded.

Church investigators discovered that the soldiers had been ordered to attack a New People's Army unit and had been specifically told the NPA soldiers were located far from the Dimalinao settlement.

The Task Force nuns, the activist above-ground human rights lawyers, the open oppositionists and also those underground tracking abuses on behalf of the National Democratic Front, all continued to emphasize that the stories they told gave only a partial picture of what was happening in the islands. And as the military violence got still worse in 1983—the year Reagan was supposed to visit the Philippines—we continually found, as we moved about Manila and the provinces, that everyone had fresh stories, usually not yet reported in any publications, of more military abuses. When we decided to take an overall view of the islands during a period of a few weeks that year to get a picture of what the NPA was doing, we found that nearly every NPA action we uncovered had been carried out in direct response to the intensive wave of murders by military men.

And increasingly the violence, we found, was becoming almost capricious. One night in northern Mindanao one of us sat at a round dining table in the darkened home of a banana plantation manager near Davao City, which before martial law had been by far the most economically sound and socially progressive city on that big southern island. The talk now, however, was of how everything was out of control. Government militia killers were pretending to be bandits; kidnap gangs were pretending to be part of the armed forces. In broad daylight on city streets and in barrio compounds people were dropping dead from the bullets of unseen assailants, and no one was bothering anymore to approach government officials or officers for redress or protection.

As the plantation manager's private security force patrolled the walled-in house that night, his chief of security sketched out the violent lay of the land. Charlie Lademora was still in charge at the Guthrie plantation to the north. "On balance," the security chief said, "the Lost Command kills civilians." Lademora's men hardly bothered with the NPA now since there was "no money in it."

Increasingly the big agribusiness and mining employers of Mindanao were coerced by the government to employ as security guards trigger-happy soldiers the government military itself could no longer control—those who had been hauled out of military stockades early in the Moro wars and pushed into battle in the south. Although such guards were commonly identified as Lost Command members, the security chief said that there were similar units all over now. Of the half-dozen military undesirables this particular plantation had been forced to take on, two disappeared after the first day, and one of the two killed a town judge. Two more had also left, presumably to pursue their careers as bandits or racketeers. The two still on the payroll were the main reason that all 138 of the plantation's security guards were made to turn in their weapons each day to the company armory.

In the period right after the 1972 coup, martial law had

had a good effect on Mindanao, according to the security chief, who was no liberal and bore an eerie physical resemblance to G. Gordon Liddy. He said he had not been antigovernment, in fact at first he was resentful that Communist propaganda had "made a Satan of our President." But the period of peace and order after the imposition of martial law had been very brief. Soon bandits were roaming the region in greater numbers than before, and the soldiers proved worse than the desperados they had supposedly come to eliminate.

In the security chief's view, military corruption and abuses exceeded any lawless acts that had gone on before the coup. Civilians now were slaughtered in their huts on the faintest suspicion of NPA sympathies. Roadblocks were set up, and Constabulary troopers let people pass only if they had money for small bribes and could produce travel papers—something that was unknown in democratic times, when you could travel the Philippines as easily as you could travel America, with no identification required.

Soldiers, poorly paid when paid at all in the provinces, were now doing anything for money, the security chief said. "Military uniforms are sold, any military issue is for sale. Armalites [American designed M16 automatic rifles, by now made under license inside the Philippines] are for sale, and bullets down here have become a medium of exchange." It was no secret how the NPA was getting its hands on American weapons to add to those it stole, and how it was getting the uniforms it sometimes used to disguise its men.

Several recent Davao City area robberies, including one at the Bureau of Fisheries and one at a lumber company, had been committed by men from the Air Force, the Constabulary and the Civilian Home Defense Forces. There was no doubt who the criminals were because they had been caught in the act and word got around town, just as there was no doubt about many killings by military men that the controlled press blamed on the NPA.

A Davao City–based human rights lawyer, Billy Aportadera, who worked with José Diokno's Free Legal Assistance Group, told us that the city "verged on anarchy" because citizens "do not trust authority anymore." He said that people wanting to report crimes "would find roadblocks in their way to the [Constabulary] headquarters and at night the road is barricaded, they cannot get through at all." A city court judge, Enrique Inting, had just fled with his family after receiving threats on his life for sentencing criminals, including paramilitary troops, brought before him. Hardly a day went by without at least one brazen daylight killing in Davao City. In March two women church workers, Hilda Narcisco and Annamarie Morales, were picked up by military men; according to an eyewitness account, thirty-six hours of sexual abuse ensued "from the very start, inside the car." They had been arrested on a Presidential Commitment Order that charged them with "subversion." Such officially reported, Malacañang-ordered political arrests totaled more than 800 in 1982. In 1983 the rate doubled.

Human rights groups had gruesome photos to show of victims of military murder sprawled on the floors of huts with their intestines ripped out, lying facedown in pigsties, stretched out headless and otherwise mutilated. More bodies were photographed where they had been thrown in front of town halls and in village squares. But the disruption in life that the political arrests and murders caused was nothing compared to the massive dislocations caused by setting up free-fire zones, chasing civilians from their homes and herding them into strategic hamlets.

Reports that surfaced well after the fact indicated that some 20,000 people had been hamleted in Isabela Province in northeastern Luzon when Marcos staged his first massive attack on the NPA there right after he imposed martial law. Hamleting had been a standard practice ever since, usually hidden from the public but occasionally coming to light, as it did on Samar.

On Mindanao, in the crucial year 1981, the year Manila

was given the green light by Washington, massive hamleting took place in a 300-square-mile hilly farming area in barrios that were part of the municipality of Laac, later renamed San Vicente, in the northern part of the island.

Laac was one of the many rural regions of the country where the NPA had gained great influence with small farmers. The military had struck back, adding Constabulary troops from a special mobile strike force battalion to the troops of the regional command.

The citizens of Laac had gone too far with their defiance in the June 1981 presidential elections. When the voting was over it turned out that in more than half of the twenty-nine barrios that made up the Laac district, no one at all had showed up to vote. Father Eligio Bianchi, an Italian who was serving then as a priest for Laac and who later would be expelled by the military, told a visitor at the time of the boycott, "It was only then that we discovered how extensive the NPA influence was in this municipality."

In the months after the election still more troops were sent in, this time composite battalion-size groups including regular Army, the Marines, elite paratroop units and the commando Scout Rangers. Then in September, with 2500 soldiers stationed in Laac, the NPA staged an ambush in which five soldiers, two members of the CHDF, and two civilians were killed. In October, the hamleting of the region began.

Between 25,000 and 30,000 of Laac's 39,000 people were told to move. They were ordered to tear down their houses and take the material and rebuild in clusters far from their fields, along roadsides and around the edges of barrios, where they could be watched. While they were building, the order came to pick up and move again, now to the centers of barrios where they would be packed even more tightly together.

They were ordered to leave a side of every hovel open, with no wall, so passing patrols could see who was inside. A list of authorized occupants was tacked up inside each new makeshift dwelling. No one was allowed out of the immediate barrio area during a curfew that was in effect each night from 5 P.M. to 5 A.M.

Farmers now had to walk miles to the fields where they raised livestock, corn, coffee and cocoa beans. The fields suffered from lack of attention. Monkeys and other wild animals were able to raid the crops. Livestock went untended and died off.

Conditions in the cramped open-sided huts became desperate. Malaria and diphtheria accompanied malnutrition. The water supplies became contaminated with human waste. In the first months of this round of hamleting on Mindanao, church workers said, 200 people died as a direct result of dislocation and congestion. Visitors to the area found the people tightly locked in, their clusters of huts surrounded by bamboo stake fences. Mothers were seen, covering the heads of sick children with threadbare blankets, dashing through the tropical rains to the nearest sizable town to visit a doctor and get back before the curfew began.

Farmers told visitors that many individual men in uniform only behaved as ordered, but their orders were extreme. Farmers refusing to tear down their houses and abandon their farms were burned out and shot. Human rights lawyers and church workers were accused of pro-Communist sympathies and expelled. Farmers and members of their families suspected of having helped the NPA before the hamleting were tortured. A church organization counted forty-eight civilians killed while in military custody in Laac between October 1981 and the following February.

In November 1981 the order came down that some of the hamleted victims of Laac were to be uprooted yet again and bunched closer together. Seven thousand of them were marched into the Laac town center. While helicopter gunships hovered overhead, they were made to swear their loyalty to the Marcos government. The Manila press reported the event as a gathering of NPA guerrillas who were switching to the government side. Gen. Alfredo S. Olano, the regional commander, was philosophical about what was happening. "You can't have heaven all the time," he said. It was "a choice between security and production. I think if I had to choose, I'd say security was more important." Besides, "families should learn to live together, with other families."

By the end of the year, hamleting had spread to six provinces on Mindanao, the Ecumenical Movement for Justice and Peace reported. Meanwhile tens of thousands more were ordered into guarded centers in the high mountains of northern Luzon. And the practice spread to areas in central Luzon and also to the Bicol peninsula.

The guerrillas, as it turned out, were denied little by hamleting, since they had long since set up their units as highly mobile groups operating in wide fronts, units that could scatter across provincial lines if confronted with the government's superior forces. The worst setback they admitted to was on Samar, where, according to an internal Communist analysis, it took the NPA just six months to get re-established after the most extreme wave of hamleting there. On the bigger islands of Mindanao and Luzon it was much easier to quickly move far from hamleted areas.

In the spring of 1982, as commanders in the field were explaining why hamleting was necessary and Malacañang was claiming it did not exist, Defense Minister Enrile announced that everyone would be allowed to return to their homes and said that hamleting had never been condoned by the Marcos government in the first place. But in the following year, 1983, human rights lawyers fanned out across Mindanao and found that almost nothing had changed. Even in Laac, where the government had admitted to hamleting and said it would be stopped and reversed right away, only 10 percent of the farmers had tried to return to rebuild their homes. The irregulars of the Civilian Home Defense Forces and also regular forces in Laac were still running wild, the lawyers found. They were extorting cash from hamleted ex-farmers, coercing them into supplying recruits to the CHDF, and torturing on the flimsiest of excuses, in one case for the crime of carrying an outdated tax certificate.

Away from Laac there was not even the pretense through 1983 and into 1984 that hamleting was over, despite what Enrile kept saying. A contingent of lawyers from the Integrated Bar of the Philippines traveled to five different areas of military occupation around the country and found tens of thousands of people still locked up. The local military authorities told the lawyers they had received no order from Enrile countermanding hamleting.

In the latter half of 1983, José Diokno described in some detail hamleting going on in northern Luzon. He said that lawyers who worked with him had seen it at first hand in six provinces. In the north, he said, "farmers are still being ousted from their villages. Homes and granaries are still being burned. Little objects for us, but highly important for the people in the barrios, like chickens and pigs are being taken away and [people] are being told, 'No, you can't stay, these are pro-NPA villages, you must get out.' That's happening up north. Exactly the same thing is still happening throughout several provinces of Mindanao."

Earlier, Amnesty International had decided to check up on claims coming out of Malacañang that military men who abused civilians were punished. In one of the books published in Manila under his name, Marcos had admitted to a mere seventy-nine cases of such abuse. He had said that these cases were either resolved and the culprits punished or were under investigation and headed for a "swift" resolution. Three years after the book came out, Amnesty International found that only twenty-seven of the seventy-nine cases had even been investigated. Of these twenty-seven, "punishment" had been ordered in only six. Of the sixty military men involved in these six cases, two went to jail, one was dismissed from the service, and the rest were let off with light reprimands. The regime would continue to announce that military men were about to be punished, and Amnesty International or local human rights groups would continue to find that the soldiers judged guilty had gone free in the end.

When one of us was traveling in Bicol in 1983 he encountered one Monsignor Domingo Nebris, who had once served as military chaplain at Malacañang Palace and was in town now with a spoiled acting group of Filipina beauties. "We came to entertain the troops, like Bob Hope," the hearty monsignor announced. But he said he knew the soldiers' reputation and so, after the entertainment, "I asked them, would you sell your beloved wives? Of course not. Then why would you sell your honor, I asked them. That is just as important. This corruption, these abuses, you should have no part in them. They do not become you. They do not become our country. This I told them." Back in Manila, Monsignor Nebris and his message to the troops came up in conversation with a nun who now worked in the slums but had known him years before. "Nebris said that?" she asked. "Too late. He should have said it when he was at the Palace."

Nebris had been at the Palace in the heady early days of martial law when to the people around the Marcoses it seemed that the President could make no mistakes. By chance the prices for the major Philippine commodities—timber, copper, sugar, and copra, the dried meat of coconuts from which coconut oil is made—were at an all-time high, and Marcos was taking the credit. Also, many people were hailing their President as having instantly solved all law and order problems. Imelda was at work with her plans to "beautify" Manila. Entrepreneurs were getting rich overnight as partners with the foreign investors who were suddenly allowed to come into the country. And the military, in the past despised by many of the people and considered by all of them to be outside the mainstream of society, suddenly found itself caught up in all the new activity, its members emerging from the hall of mirrors as key players in the New Society.

This was the time—the first time ever in the Philippines—that military men were routinely taking over functions of government. They had also been chosen to police the streets and countryside, simultaneously hunting out "subversives" and criminals. A flurry of General Orders, Letters of Instruction and Presidential Decrees were coming out of the President-turned-dictator's office, and the armed forces were charged with carrying them out.

Filipinos for the first time were seeing soldiers knock on the doors of their social superiors—opposition politicians, college professors and artists—and hauling them away in military vehicles; the soldiers were patrolling city streets during the nightly curfew; they were confiscating firearms, breaking up peaceful public gatherings, and standing guard at the nation's padlocked newspaper, radio and TV station offices.

All important criminal cases, including those for nonpolitical crimes such as drug offenses, now went before military tribunals or one-officer provost courts instead of civilian courts. Even after 1981, after Marcos said civilian rule would return, the cases that were dragging along in the military courts remained in military hands. And since Marcos held the written resignation of all judges, civilian judges proceeded with such caution that it was clear the military was still supreme.

In 1983 one of us went to a civilian courtroom in Quezon City, one of the municipalities made part of Manila, to observe a series of subversion hearings in a civilian courtroom. Other prisoners, such as Sison and Buscayno, were still on trial in military courts, but those in this court had been arrested after Marcos had supposedly ended martial law and hence theoretically were under civilian jurisdiction.

We were particularly interested in the country's second most prominent prisoner after Sison, Boy Morales, the handsome young former high-level government planner who had become an underground leader of the National Democratic Front, and in the well-known antigovernment priest, Father Edicio de la Torre, another high NDF figure. And in addition we were interested in a human rights lawyer, Efran Moncupa, who had already been convicted on lesser subversion charges than those hanging over Morales and de la Torre, and had by now been held for more than nine months even though his charge carried a maximum six-month sentence. All were to come before a judge named Eduardo Tutaan that day.

Judge Tutaan's courtroom was dominated by a large portrait of Marcos. Before the day's hearings began, the prisoner Moncupa told of how "detainees only go free when Marcos approves." Morales gave his permission for an interview before the court was gaveled to order. But then a military guard in civilian clothes, carrying a walkie-talkie, snapped, "You are not allowed to interview the prisoner. Permission must come from my commanding officer." Morales shrugged his apologies and took his seat for the hearing. His lawyer, Fulgencio S. Factoran, Jr., said he would speak with Judge Tutaan.

When the proceedings began, Factoran stood up and asked Judge Tutaan to allow, as was customary practice, the "foreign visitor to have a few words with one of the defendants," and explained that a prisoner guard had just forbidden it here in the judge's own courtroom. The judge listened, then said softly, "I am only conducting a hearing."

"Yes, I know, your honor," the lawyer said, "but there is a military guard interfering with your custom in your courtroom to allow conversations between visitors and defendants."

The judge leaned toward the lawyer and spoke even more softly. "My powers are limited." Then in almost a whisper he asked, "Why are you trying to embarrass me?"

Factoran and some other outspoken urban human rights lawyers connected with Diokno were known as the "Mabini group" after the intellectual Apolinario Mabini, who had advised General Aguinaldo in the late nineteenth century. The night before they had explained to us how the civilian judiciary was a farce. They had cited complex cases in which the courts had proven powerless before the overriding dictates of Marcos. They had described how the once independent Supreme Court, which since the Marcos coup had never overruled a presidential decree, had never backed up lower-level judges who had tried to make decisions based on law, not on the wishes of the Palace.

Judges, like Tutaan in the Morales hearing, were not the only authorities who found their roles undermined by the military. After the 1972 coup, members of the armed forces had been given jobs of great authority throughout what had once been a civilian bureaucracy. Soldiers became bill collectors, employed to get payments from farmers or order foreclosures under Marcos's mortgage-style system of what he called land reform. The majority of martial law Presidential Regional Officers for Development—authoritative men called "PRODS" who had the clout to cut through red tape for pet building projects of the regime—were military officers. One general had taken over an antismuggling agency run by the Ministry of Finance. Other generals were running postal services, prisons, civil aviation, the railway system, public housing, the maritime authority, rural electrification—a long list of agencies that were supposedly civilian. They also headed various new government economic planning and research organizations. They had their own Philippine Veterans Development Corporation, established in 1973 to "provide investment opportunities" for retired military personnel, complementing the functions of the veterans bank. There were top officers running government insurance companies, shipping lines and various joint ventures between the government and the Marcoses' private business friends.

The most ambitious barrio development organization of the 1980s, the KKK—standing for *Kilusang Kabuhayan sa*

Kaunlaran, "Movement for Livelihood and Progress"—was largely in the hands of the military. It gave uniformed men the go-ahead to get into further government-guaranteed entrepreneurial ventures. These new small businesses provided soldiers with independent sources of wealth. Boy Morales had conceived the KKK, then concluded that, particularly since it was in Imelda Marcos's jurisdiction, it would never amount to more than a means for rewarding government supporters and buying off potential government enemies. Its prime purpose was as the machinery the government hoped to use to buy off—rather than to intimidate—voters in the scheduled May 1984 National Assembly elections.

Previously, the anterooms of the offices of civilian government authorities had often been filled with petitioners seeking government assistance. Now these petitioners were seen waiting outside the offices of generals and colonels, and also those of lower-ranking officers.

In some cases civilian holdings were seized by the government and turned over to the military almost as booty. Early in martial law, the huge Fernando Jacinto conglomerate of fourteen companies—steel, transport, insurance, real estate and others—was taken because of "outstanding obligations with the government." Marcos put Defense Minister Enrile in charge and named his then armed forces chief, Gen. Romeo C. Espiño, as the new board chairman. Espiño later retired from active service in favor of Ver, but he remained a Jacinto director and stayed on the boards of other commercial companies as well, including the Manila Hilton Hotel.

Occasionally there was talk that various officers, now that Marcos had introduced the coup d'état to the Philippines, were planning to take over. One such coup conspiracy, hatched by junior officers, was uncovered in 1978, Marcos said. In 1980 he vetoed the demands of another group of junior officers, who thought that he should distance himself from the Americans in renegotiating base rights.

Meanwhile military men in the countryside went on stealing rice and chickens. The graft and theft began with soldiers in the field and extended up the ranks to their commanders at regional headquarters. On Samar, soldiers were making peasants buy food and beer for them, dig their foxholes and supply them with women. As elsewhere they got a cut of gambling and prostitution proceeds. But their commanders were getting bigger pieces of the action.

On April 4, 1982, the mayor of the city of Calbayog on Samar's west coast was murdered on a tennis court. The authorities blamed the killing on the New People's Army. But it turned out that the mayor, pushing an antinarcotics drive, had happened upon a huge marijuana plantation. Four other people who found the marijuana farm had been murdered earlier. Local civilian officials told foreign journalists on the sly that it was run by an intelligence colonel from General Ver's National Intelligence and Security Agency, NISA.

In the far south, southern Mindanao and the Sulu chain, military officers were known to have taken control in the legal barter trade that Marcos allowed between the Philippines and Borneo in order to curb smuggling by the Moros. Moslem boatmen carried lumber and rice and other foodstuffs to Borneo, to be shipped to Japan, and picked up American cigarettes and Japanese consumer goods in exchange. Military men from the north now used Moslem front men in this trade even as they fought Moslem guerrillas.

Everywhere the military was taking charge of gambling. It had long been extensive in the islands, since there are many Filipinos who, like Englishmen, will bet on anything. Routinely the military commanders became the gambling overlords. A young American consular officer whose territory included the central and southern islands reported, in a dispatch obtained by us and other writers, on the corruption he found all around him. He told how he had picked up reports that Gen. Alfredo S. Olano, the Constabulary commander for eastern Mindanao, personally pocketed $500 a week by letting a local gambling syndicate operate.

In Davao City in early 1983, a high-ranking regular army officer had complained to a businessman friend that the $1450 he had had to pay to General Ver on the side for his last promotion meant a financial hardship for him, and the monthly payments that Ver demanded were a further drain. The officer, though, had been allowed to take care of his problem, the businessman explained. He had gotten control of enough extortion, betting and prostitution income to resolve his cash flow situation.

But in the confusion following the Aquino assassination, it was not the fact that they were involved with both legal and illicit businesses that made the local commanders the center of attention. It was the fact that they were the only government authority visible in the provinces at a time when the central government seemed to be falling apart.

We knew a man in one part of the country, prominent in his city, who had gone to the regional Constabulary general and told him he should ease up on the demonstrators who were protesting the Aquino assassination. The general himself was not unpopular in the area, the businessman told him, emphasizing that when Marcos went and a military government took charge in Manila, the general would, if he behaved well now, be accepted as the region's military governor.

The general replied that he had been thinking along similar lines. The trouble was, he said, there were colonels under him who were reporting directly to Ver, and so he had to be careful. Could the protestors, he asked, be persuaded to choose as their targets in the demonstrations "those above and below me?"

This attempt by an independent businessman and a general to strike a deal in the provinces summed up an important aspect of the climate that prevailed after Aquino was killed. After eleven years of martial law the economy had fallen apart.

The government had had no contingency plan when, in the mid-1970s, the world price of Philippine-produced commodities had dropped. Its response had been to use palace favorites to further squeeze the producers of the commodities. And the dictatorship could come up with no other response to the world recession of the early 1980s than to use government funds to bail out those same men who had been squeezing the people on its behalf. After the assassination the first concerns of most people were not so much for political as for economic survival.

Many of the supporters of the regime now seemed to be running for cover. It was not just in Manila that government bureaucrats now appeared in the ranks of the regime's opponents. In America some consular officials were seeking out members of the exile opposition to say that they had become secret sympathizers.

But although some were trying to cover themselves with the opposition, anyone who planned to stay in the Philippines knew he or she could not function unless in the good graces of the military. Marcos had enlarged the military for his own purposes and now it was a monster. As his health got worse, as generals came out in the open as prime participants in government decisions, it became clear to many people where their future in the Philippines lay.

In the past, patronage by the Marcoses had been enough. Now, with Marcos faltering, all he seemed to be leaving behind was the new institution of a politicized military in what had become a largely militarized country.

At the same time, with the economy turning sharply downward yet again, the corruption on all levels continued. No one believed that the military, now that it was out of the barracks, would suddenly lose its new interest in politics. And no one believed that the officers and men who had made money out of the dictatorship would calmly let reformers attack the overall corruption that prevailed.

12

THE LOOTING OF THE ISLANDS

The Palace and the Cronies

FOR the people of the barrios, the members of the military may have been the most visible thieves and grafters as well as the most visible oppressors. But just as Marcos had rotated military postings to prevent any one regional commander from setting up a serious power base in the provinces, so had he created and maintained firm centralized control over the doling out of the largest shares of what his regime stole.

It was true that, in the new martial law atmosphere of state-sanctioned corruption, members of the armed forces were among the big winners. But individual military men were restrained from gaining economic power on such a scale that it could loosen the economic stranglehold that Malacañang maintained. In this one area—the splitting up of the spoils—Marcos had upheld the country's tradition of civilian supremacy over its armed forces.

To do so, he did not hesitate to toy with the people's welfare. It was no secret why in the Philippines, unlike neighboring countries, wages kept going down and social services actually contracted, long before the Aquino assassination brought the Philippines' economic shambles to world attention. It was no secret what lay behind the conclusion of a World Bank study that in the Marcos era purchasing power had gone down "in both urban and rural areas, in all regions, and practically all occupations," resulting in a gap between the rich and the poor that had become "worse in the Philippines than elsewhere in the region . . . exceeded only in Latin America."

This situation was the result of methodically applied practices of favoritism that had transferred most of the nation's wealth—like its positions of military power—to actual relations, or members of the extended family, of the Marcoses. The extended family in the Philippines means friends so close that the ties between them have the strength of blood ties. The concept is mixed up with the concept of *utang na loob,* the socially binding "debt of gratitude" that can supersede any state laws.

Following up on his belief that he could deny power to others by denying them money, Marcos had used his favorites, men totally bound to the Palace, to take charge of the nation's natural and human resources and its big economic ventures. In the process of creating a new elite—in effect a new superclass of very rich individuals who for the most part had been outsiders to wealth and power before martial law—the country's economic structure was changed.

The Marcoses and their friends, always spoken of disrespectfully simply as "the cronies," grabbed what it was worthwhile to grab; where direct ownership was not in their interests, the cronies put into effect national skimming operations. The superclass insinuated itself into newly created middleman positions between the people who produced and the customers who bought Philippine goods. And the cronies had a safety net. If they ran into trouble, they knew they would be bailed out with treasury funds—just as they knew that, if they wanted to increase their wealth, they would have the backing of the dictatorship.

The name "Octopus" that Filipinos used when talking about the state-backed private conglomerates and monopoly mechanisms came from the title of an anonymous study put out by a Manila business firm whose officers were outside the Palace circle. Although the Octopus paper was widely circulated by the militant opposition, it was originally intended not as a political document but as a guide for honest businessmen. It listed hundreds of holdings—in such areas as agribusiness, industry, tourism, transportation, construction, minerals and timber—that had been taken over by the Marcoses and the cronies; its purpose was to warn businessmen about what fields to avoid in order to remain safe from the dangers they might face if they competed head-on with Marcos and crony companies.

To the people who suffered most under the dictatorship, however, the Octopus could never be avoided. It was omnipresent, changing the nature of the workplace. With the cronies in charge, the people were not getting anything approaching fair compensation for their labor. Too much was siphoned off. The workers in the new industrial export zones were denied even the low minimum wages that had brought American, Japanese and other foreign capital to these zones after the 1972 coup, as were the men and women who worked on plantations. Nearly all people working in agriculture and industry discovered that they were putting in more time for the benefit of the Marcoses and the cronies than for themselves or for their old bosses and landlords.

The new monopolies, backed by the government but set up as private national cartels under the cronies, were designed to control domestic industrial production and to handle every aspect of the nation's prime commodities, from financing to production to shipping. With legal restraints removed, with the voices calling for fairness and moderation silenced, the cronies quite naturally became ever more audacious in their wheeling and dealing.

Their acts were often so outrageous that they would have been hard to believe if portrayed in fiction—but this was the case with so much that went on in the martial law Philippines, such as the creation of Imelda's new royal capital. Like Imelda's edifices and her slum-hiding facades, the acts of the cronies were the new reality in the islands. And this new reality, although it always caused suffering, was also the backdrop to rollicking tales.

One of the choicest bits of low comedy concerning the cronies and their Octopus operations had to do with an undertaking concerning coconuts, the Philippines' leading export crop. In this particular crony caper, an attempt was made to corner the world market in coconuts. The scheme was so far-reaching that for a time it looked as if action would be taken even in America to bring it to a halt—though, not surprisingly, the Reagan administration quickly called this action off.

In early 1981, lawsuits were floating around federal and state courtrooms in California. Reports in Los Angeles and San Francisco newspapers described a Justice Department criminal complaint against three American companies dealing in coconut products—primarily copra, the dried coconut meat used for coconut oil, and the refined oil itself. The complaint cited violations of U.S. antitrust laws prohibiting artificial price regulation. There were also civil lawsuits brought by private parties, riding on the Justice Department action, claiming damage to commercial enterprises as a result of the price fixing.

Through presidential decrees Marcos had, early in the martial law period, taken hold of the coconut industry by setting up a special privately held bank, a private producers' federation, and a private milling and marketing company. Since the milling and marketing agency, the United Coconut Mills, Inc., controlled 93 percent of oil-making capacity and 80 percent of the country's coconut products exports, and since the Philippines was the world's largest coconut producer, it looked as if cornering the market and thereby manipulating world prices was well within the cronies' grasp.

When the price of coconut oil in the United States, the

biggest market, went down from 53 cents a pound to 40 cents in July and August of 1979, word went out, according to federal witnesses before a grand jury in Los Angeles, to keep Philippine copra and coconut oil off the market. This meant shipping no more copra or oil, and not releasing stored oil, until the shortage drove the price up.

The immediate targets of the Justice Department, according to reports coming out of the grand jury, were the three firms doing business in America: Pan Pacific Commodities Corporation, Cranex U.S.A. Corporation and Crown Oil Corporation. All three were subsidiaries of Philippine companies under the control of the government-backed, private coconut control bureaucracy. Federal prosecutors said they were confident of winning criminal indictments. One company had held more than 34,000 long tons of oil off the U.S. market. This was an amount equivalent then to a month's U.S. consumption. An officer of the company, who had formerly worked in the big crony milling and marketing firm in the Philippines, told the prosecutors he had imported oil but stored it on orders from his bosses in Manila.

Quite aside from U.S. action to break the coconut conspiracy, the idea of cornering the coconut market had already turned out to be another of those martial law events that were at root merely silly. The manipulators in Manila soon discovered they had no leverage at all since it is so easy to use other vegetable oils as substitutes for coconut oil. The cronies had cornered the market and in the process decreased the worth of their product. In the best of times for the coconut industry, coconut oil furnished only 8 percent of the vegetable oil used in America. And now there was yet another factor that the manipulators had overlooked: the Carter administration's grain embargo against the Soviet Union. The American market was awash with domestically produced soybean oil; the artificial shortage in coconut oil was hardly noticed.

The three American firms whose officers were called before

the grand jury had already found themselves forced to unload their hoarded supplies. They had announced that they would not sell until the price went up to at least 42 cents, but the price they had actually gotten was 25 cents a pound. Pan Pacific alone took a $10 million loss right away, and there were greater losses ahead. Civil suits brought in state courts in San Francisco by private companies, under California's own antitrust statutes, were settled to the satisfaction of the plaintiffs for many millions of dollars more. And by now part of the market was lost forever. During the fake shortage, some American customers of Philippine coconut oil had invested in refining and processing equipment for substitute oils; they had changed the contents lists on their bottles, and never did go back to oil made from copra.

The American subsidiaries of the Philippine companies involved in price fixing did get a boost from Washington, however. Philippine representations to the Reagan administration's State Department were successful. The Justice Department quietly dropped its pursuit of criminal charges.

But inside the Philippines the greedy if absurd move to corner the coconut market had done its harm, and the cronies were not the ones who suffered. It was, rather, the people who owned coconut farms or worked on them—the coconut industry being the single largest source of income to Filipinos. Since the start of martial law these people had been squeezed by Malacañang, via the cronies, so that the rulers could be cut in on the profits. Now the cronies made up their new losses by again lowering the prices to the millers, and the millers responded by again lowering prices to farmers and hence worker wages.

The squeeze on the coconut industry was never a matter of straightforward taxation; rather it was a matter of private individuals, with the state behind them, taking a personal share, an operation that many said amounted to nothing more than state-sanctioned, mob-style extortion. By the start of

1984, the cronies had very slightly loosened their grip on the coconut industry in the face of national unrest. But even now, according to commodities traders, Philippine farmers, who in line with world market prices should have been receiving about 20 cents a pound for copra, were actually getting less than 13 cents.

At other times before and after the cornering of the coconut market, the gap between external world prices and internal Philippine prices had been even greater. Much of the reason for this gap had to do with Marcos's maneuvering to get a close friend and palace habitué, Eduardo M. Cojuangco, Jr., into position as the chief operating officer of all the components of the complex private coconut control bureaucracy Malacañang had set up.

The burly Cojuangco, still in his thirties when martial law began, was godfather to Marcos's son and grandson. Marcos in turn was godfather to Cojuangco's eldest son, whose first name was Marcos. And there was something else that linked the two men: Cojuangco was from Tarlac Province, where before martial law he had been known primarily for being the archenemy of Ninoy Aquino.

Up in Tarlac there were two feuding branches of the Cojuangcos, a distinguished family that was second in the province only to the Aquinos and had produced powerful congressmen. One branch was extremely wealthy, with interests in banking as well as sugar; from this branch came Corazon Cojuangco, who became Ninoy's wife. The other, less successful branch was headed by Eduardo Cojuangco, whose principal activity before martial law seemed to be sending out his bodyguards to do battle with the bodyguards of Ninoy. After Ninoy was thrown in jail and Eduardo sided with Marcos, the split between the two branches of the Cojuangco family became deeper. All this was fine with Eduardo, since Malacañang proceeded to turn him into a dollar billionaire, the second richest man in the country after Marcos himself.

To underscore Marcos's support of the various firms that interlocked to form the coconut monopoly, the Ministry of National Defense became a direct participant. The firms were all run by Eduardo Cojuangco, but the chairman, sometimes called honorary chairman, of these firms was Defense Minister Juan Ponce Enrile.

In the most blatant grab for profits from coconuts, Marcos decreed in the mid-1970s that a "levy" be imposed on all coconut producers. In order to pay the levy, the coconut millers reduced the price they paid to the farmers. The funds collected were placed in Cojuangco and Enrile's United Coconut Planters Bank, housed in a lavish new structure that has become a Manila landmark. The bank refused to account for a penny of the estimated $1 billion in levy funds that were on deposit. To assure secrecy, Marcos ordered that there could be no government audit. The bank and its funds, he announced, were private.

A bank spokesman did say that some of the levy money had gone to develop the coconut industry. But the only industry development operation—a firm that sold new hybrid coconut trees—was owned by Eduardo's side of the Cojuangco family. The levy was lifted in 1981, but the national coconut cartel and all its components kept on with the squeeze. It had been bad luck for the regime that world prices for coconut products had fallen; but it was by design that the farmers and millers could not even get the world prices.

After martial law brought Cojuangco to the kind of prominence he had only dreamed of when Ninoy was still able to operate in Tarlac, he was suddenly popping up everywhere in the business community, taking control of all sorts of companies. He also, as a member of the dictator's extended family, achieved celebrity in many other areas.

For example, Cojuangco had a fan's love of basketball, and so Marcos appointed him to a new position which made him the czar of the sport in the Philippines. He was officially charged with promoting basketball for the glory of the New Society and New Republic.

Basketball is a sport much loved in the Philippines, even though few Filipinos approach six feet in height and thus Filipino teams are restricted largely to competition with each other and with teams from other Asian nations, such as Japan, where most people are relatively short. But now there were professional Philippine basketball teams manned by tall Americans. Cojuangco owned one such team. He spread the word that secret presidential decrees had turned his Americans into Filipinos, eligible to represent the Philippines in international competition. In December 1983 a Philippine team was turned away from a tournament in Hong Kong on the grounds that most of its players, though they carried Philippine passports, were Americans, not Filipinos.

Cojuangco was also the number one booster of the team of his alma mater, an expensive Manila college called La Salle. Shortly before we went back to the Philippines in 1983, Cojuangco, watching a game in which La Salle was losing, started a riot by ordering his bodyguards to push through the crowd of spectators and start beating up kids from the opposing team's college.

That such a man should be elevated said a great deal about the atmosphere of Malacañang after the death of democracy. Marcos apparently did not care if his appointees appeared to be bullies and clowns so long as they remained loyal. It may have seemed to outsiders that it was absurd that such men should control the economy, but from the dictatorship's standpoint it made perfect sense. Men like Cojuangco would never have been able to advance as they had if it had not been for Marcos; without him, his wife and his generals, they had no place to go.

When Filipinos talked conspiracy theories concerning the Aquino assassination, Cojuangco's name came up as frequently as did the names of Marcos, Imelda and General Ver. Being the wealthiest crony, he had the most to lose from an Aquino comeback. If Aquino had not been killed, Cojuangco would have instantly lost his position as number one in Tarlac. Also, it was hard to see how any future leader not a part of the Marcos-Ver system would have let him keep the vast holdings he had accumulated in the Marcos years.

Like Enrile, Cojuangco was in on much more than the coconut monopoly. Enrile was big: in addition to coconuts, farm lands in Isabela and the legal business of crony firms, he had been part of the timber land grabs, and he also had multimillion-dollar property holdings in such places as San Francisco and Dallas. But Cojuangco was bigger. He controlled at least nine large industrial and agribusiness firms and banks apart from coconuts. He owned tobacco fields on Luzon and rice lands on the remote island of Palawan west of the Visayas and Mindanao in the Sulu Sea. Aside from his Luzon estate in Tarlac, where he functioned like a feudal lord, he also reigned over his own private island in the Visayas off Negros. And among much else, Marcos, after making Cojuangco the czar of basketball, had put him in charge of horse racing. When, in early 1984, Marcos decided that he had better show his face in public, he turned up at Manila's race track.

Cojuangco was the biggest, but there were others who were nearly as big and whose Malacañang-supported ventures were equally all-encompassing and outlandish. The reason, for example, why sugar growing areas had become so depressed during martial law had a lot to do with the activities of an old friend and fraternity brother of Marcos's, Roberto S. Benedicto.

In 1983, according to reporters who spoke with him, Benedicto did not seem the least bit worried when the Philippine Central Bank ordered penalties against his own Republic Planters Bank for having failed to meet its reserve requirements. Then on June 6, Malacañang issued Presidential Letter of Instruction 1330, which voided the penalties. "It's favoritism. It's demoralizing. And it isn't the way to run a central bank," one high government official, who asked that his name not be used, told a foreign reporter at the end of the year. But it was clearly the way business went on in the dictatorship.

Benedicto, one of the few cronies who had been rich before martial law, by this time controlled not only his own vast sugar estates on Negros but everyone else's too. Benedicto was head of a martial law government commission—another skimming operation—that was the sole buyer of Philippine sugar, the second biggest export after coconuts. For a time he headed the government-owned Philippine National Bank, through which the large sugar transactions were financed. Later he controlled two private banks, one set up specifically for the sugar industry.

Benedicto's official powers included the authority to seize sugar mills he found were not meeting contractual obligations, or which his commission merely deemed to be "inefficient." He also still owned outright his own sugar mills, competing with those he was meant to police on behalf of Malacañang. He owned one of Manila's government-controlled newspapers, the *Daily Express,* and five television and thirty-six radio stations that Marcos had seized right after he staged his coup. In addition, Benedicto had his own shipping line, whose vessels traveled mostly to Japan. At one point he was sent to Tokyo as the Philippine ambassador, and he was considered one of the key figures in the opening up to Japanese investment that Marcos had ordered. He was a man you had to see, if you were doing business with the Japanese. And through his own firms in a variety of spheres he personally exercised direct control over hundreds of millions of dollars in the Japan-Philippines trade.

But primarily Benedicto was known as the man most responsible for worsening the conditions of the sugar workers, just as Cojuangco was blamed for the sad fate of the coconut workers. In the mid-1970s, as Marcos's luck changed and world prices for Philippine goods began their decline, the price of sugar dropped sharply. By this time agreements under which America had subsidized sugar had run out, and workers in the cane fields would have been hurt even without martial law cronyism. But when the price dropped, sugar farmers were not getting even the world market price. Because of the monopoly cartel system headed up by Benedicto, Philippine producers were receiving a fixed price of 12 cents a pound even as world prices reached 46 cents. The sugar producers, like the coconut oil producers, tried to make up for lower prices by cutting worker salaries still further. On the sugar-growing island of Negros, malnutrition and disease spread as a result of crony skimming just as they had spread on other islands because of military hamleting.

And yet crony operations continued to produce laughter as well as tears, for the graft knew no bounds. One of the closest of the cronies, Rodolfo Cuenca, a college dropout ten years younger than Marcos, went overnight from being a small-time contractor to running by far the biggest construction company in the Philippines, one of the biggest in all of Asia.

Like the other cronies, Cuenca accumulated a variety of enterprises after the coup. A typical venture was his Galleon Shipping Company, set up with $100 million in government-guaranteed loans. When the ships Cuenca purchased from Japan proved uncompetitive, Marcos issued a presidential decree making Galleon the only Philippine flag carrier permitted to operate container vessels from America's west coast to the Philippines. But there was nothing comparable to Cuenca's cornerstone operation, the Construction and Development Corporation of the Philippines, which won nearly every big contract inside the Philippines, including contracts to fill in land in Manila Bay for Imelda's royal edifices. He had the contract to build the splashy new Manila International Airport. He built Marcos's gift to Imelda, the Leyte-Samar San Juanico

Bridge, after which the military's torture tactic of suspending a victim like a bridge was named. Cuenca also, with government guarantees, got more than $1 billion in construction contracts abroad.

Much of the non-crony business community had turned against Marcos before the Aquino assassination because he had used government funds to bail out Cuenca's construction company when it went bankrupt in the 1980s. But Cuenca was best known for an ongoing operation he controlled. He had been given the contracts to build two fine new highways, one running north from Manila and the other south. They were forever being hailed by the regime as proof that it had revitalized the nation's infrastructure. These were not really government roads, however. Rudy Cuenca had been given, along with the contracts to build them, the franchises to operate the highways as private toll roads for forty years; he was still personally pocketing the tolls.

There were a handful of others whom the Marcoses similarly made big-time magnates, and in each case there were aspects to their empires that prevented anyone from considering them legitimate businessmen. One of the scandals of the regime was the squalid conditions of workers in new industrial projects set up to entice American and Japanese investors with the lowest-paid, most thoroughly subjugated labor force in the region. One who benefited most from this labor situation was Ricardo C. Silverio, also ten years Marcos's junior, who went from being a dealer in textile remnants to head of an industrial empire that made him what the *Far Eastern Economic Review* called the "star of crony capitalism."

Like Benedicto, Silverio had strong Japanese connections. It was considered by the regime a key sign of progress when Silverio's Delta Company began turning out Toyotas. Actually it was only the crudest kind of assembly of imported components, but to hear Malacañang Information Ministry people talk you would have thought the Philippines had become a major automobile producer.

Almost all of Silverio's companies had to fall back on government bailouts. In March 1983 the controlled press said Marcos wanted to investigate why a Toyota assembled by Silverio sold for more than a Toyota imported directly from Japan, but the investigation was never carried out. Businessmen knew they had to buy from Delta if they wanted to stay on the good side of the authorities.

And then there was Herminio Disini, only forty-seven in 1984, the man who, with his Japanese partners in his exploitation of public lands, had been largely responsible for turning large areas of Luzon's Cordillera and even parts of the Marcoses' Ilocos provinces into a war zone. Before martial law his only business had been a small cigarette filter company, the Philippine Tobacco Filters Corporation, which he had operated out of a modest one-room office. Then he had married Inday Escolin, who was a first cousin of Imelda's, and soon he was seen frequently on the links in business golf foursomes that included Marcos himself. Marcos issued instructions that henceforth Disini would pay only a 10-percent duty on raw material imported for filters, while all his competitors would have to pay a duty of 100 percent. Suddenly Disini had all the filter business to himself.

He quickly put together his Herdis Group, a $1 billion conglomerate of fifty companies that ranged from tobacco, timber and mining to computers, real estate and vending machines. Perhaps his most dazzling venture was to serve as the middleman between the government and Westinghouse for a contract to build a nuclear power plant near Manila.

According to rumors in the business community, his commissions on the Westinghouse deal may have totalled $4 million, the figure from various sources, or may have been $35 million. Years later he was, businessmen said, still receiving commissions on materials imported for the venture though it remained far from completion. Whatever the precise truth about the alleged commissions, the rumors added to Disini's stature.

As part of the regime's national sports program, Marcos put Disini in charge of golf, just as he had put Cojuangco in charge of basketball and horse racing. Although he had not been a social figure before martial law, Disini was elected president of the most exclusive club in the country, Manila's Wack Wack Golf and Country Club. Another millionaire golfer told us that at first the Wack Wack members were surprised; but they decided that, given the climate of the times, it was fitting that Disini be the regime's representative in the golf world. He was not a popular partner, the millionaire said: "He cheated. He even hired caddies to help him cheat."

In 1981 Disini's empire seemed to fall apart. But Marcos, as was his fashion, came to the rescue. By the start of 1984 Disini, with continued government help, was still wheeling and dealing, dividing his time now between Manila and Switzerland.

Disini may have been keeping a discreet distance from Malacañang, but most of the cronies were very much in evidence. Antonio O. Floirendo, for example, who was about Marcos's age and was believed to be the crony closest to the Marcos family, remained a fixture at the palace. Before the martial law era he had been a Ford dealer in Mindanao's Davao City. After the 1972 coup he became the country's banana king.

Many people had been driven from their homes to make way for Floirendo's new plantations. The largest part of what he produced was destined for Japan, but he also became the grower for the largest American banana exporter in the Philippines, United Brands. People had also been driven from their homes to add acreage to the pineapple plantations of the American firms Dole and Del Monte, which after martial law made the Philippines, rather than Hawaii, their central growing area to take advantage of the martial law labor situation.

The fact that the crony Floirendo was associated with an American firm, like the fact that the American pineapple growers were expanding in the Philippines, was not lost on

New People's Army organizers. But there was also another purely internal factor that caused outrage about Floirendo's rise: he was given a jump on competitors because he was allowed to use lands owned by a huge Mindanao prison colony. He was even allowed to use the inmates as his workers.

When one of us was traveling in the south he kept hearing Floirendo referred to as "the most hated man on Mindanao" because of the way his security forces terrorized his workers and the small farmers whose land he wanted. But by now Floirendo seemed nearly untouchable. A frequent member of Imelda's traveling entourage, he was also engaged on his own in high living abroad—entertaining Philippine government figures, for example, at a $1 million mansion he maintained in the rich Makiki Heights district of Honolulu. Because he was a crony, not an independent businessman, the New People's Army knew that hatred for Floirendo could easily be transformed into hatred for his benefactors.

No one thought Floirendo and the other cronies were operating by themselves. For a crony to own something was the same as for Malacañang to own it. And anyway the rulers often did not even bother to use front men. Actual Marcos family members, as opposed to cronies fronting for the family, sometimes did not bother to conceal their holdings. Imelda herself admitted to chairing some twenty-three private enterprises, many of them businesses run for profit, for which there was direct government assistance.

The dictator's younger brother, a physician, Dr. Pacifico Marcos, had been made chairman of the Medicare Commission—another American mirror-image undertaking—which deducted money from workers' paychecks. All nongovernment labor leaders complained of how it failed to pay claims. Pacifico also openly owned mines, coconut estates, insurance firms, hotels and a bank. Pacifico's son, Mariano Marcos II, had in turn put together an empire that included entertainment ventures.

One of the dictator's uncles, Judge Pio Marcos, had yet another conglomerate. It included a sugar mill, shipping firms, mines and a group of cemeteries. One of Marcos's sisters, Fortuna Marcos Barba, also had an oceangoing shipping line and, with other varied ventures, was in real estate and travel. And there were many other Marcoses who had big businesses of their own and sat on the boards of others. Even the dictator's spry old mother, Josefa Edralin Marcos, had become a major entrepreneur, involved with interisland shipping, food processing and tobacco.

A Palace defector, Primitivo Mijares, who had been Malacañang's chief censor at the start of martial law and was later to disappear under suspicious circumstances, told how Marcos's mother also got into the Rice and Corn Administration, an organization set up to keep control of the staples in the Filipino diet. He said she, like other family members and cronies, used her influence to obtain for her friends lucrative retailing licenses for handling the basic foods on which the people depended. Even the staples were part of the Octopus.

Altogether, close blood relatives openly owned forty-eight large private commercial companies; estimates of major firms they controlled behind front men were never less than in the high hundreds. Not all of these people were Marcoses; some bore the name Romualdez, Imelda's maiden name. Imelda put Malacañang off limits to many Romualdezes— those who were wealthy before martial law was imposed and had, she felt, snubbed her. But she was extravagant in the favors she bestowed on fellow poor-relation members of the Romualdez clan.

Her youngest brother, Alfredo "Bejo" Romualdez, was a Navy officer who was given control over organized casino gambling. Early martial law decrees had banned casinos, which had functioned openly for years. But soon the Marcoses themselves were inaugurating casinos opening up all over the country, all under the stewardship of Bejo Romualdez, with Imelda, quite naturally, considered to be the real owner. It had turned out that the Marcoses did not object to gambling; they objected to anyone except themselves controlling the take.

The first of the legal New Society gambling establishments was a floating casino on a ship in Manila Bay. Urban guerrillas set it afire and sank it in 1979. The Manila casino was then transferred to one of the plush new hotels, the Philippine Village out by the airport. The lobby of this once elegant hotel quickly filled up with pimps and prostitutes. When we were there in 1983, we found that even in the gambling areas there were pictures from the Marcoses' trip to Washington. In fact, there were pictures of the Marcoses looking down from the walls of the official pawnshop that had been set up in the hotel's shopping arcade.

Bejo had the gambling, but it was Imelda's favorite brother, Benjamin "Kokoy" Romualdez, who was in on the biggest action, behaving always with an arrogance that confirmed all rumors concerning his being the designated bag man for the First Family. He served as governor of the island of Leyte, a job Imelda had given him after ousting a Romualdez cousin she disliked. Concurrently he was ambassador to the United States, where he was first sent, succeeding an uncle, to pave the way for the Marcoses' 1982 trip. Included in his share of the martial law spoils were key holdings of the Lopezes, the family of Marcos's old legal Vice President, taken over by Marcos in order to destroy their political power base. He had what under the Lopezes had been one of the country's most prestigious newspapers, the *Manila Chronicle,* and he had the Lopezes' Manila Electric Company, the nation's largest utility. But it was not just Lopez ventures that concerned Kokoy; foreign businessmen knew that nothing could beat having Kokoy Romualdez on your side if you wanted to make money in the Philippines.

As for Ferdinand and Imelda Marcos's personal fortune, no one could give an exact estimate. We spoke with one defector who had been in a position that put him as close to Marcos as anyone except Imelda during the legal phase of the presidency. In 1972 this man and another top official, who had left the Philippines but had not broken openly with the regime, got together in New York to try to figure out what the Marcoses owned. They calculated the fortune at that point, just before the enactment of martial law, at $300 million in tangible assets, a sum unprecedented for an elected Philippine president with no inherited fortune to have accumulated.

After martial law was declared, according to this source, all the standard corrupt practices of the regime had given way to a new system whereby the dictator took a flat 10 percent of all big Philippine business transactions, giving much of the money to his wife to spend and salting the rest of it away, mostly abroad.

The two men met again in New York in 1980 after eight years of martial law. Calculating as closely as they could, they estimated that by now the Marcos fortune had risen to $3 billion in tangible assets. By 1984 the common figure bandied about Manila was $5 billion, though people making this and higher estimates, including government officials speaking on the sly, always added that by now the Marcoses owned so much that they themselves probably did not know their total worth.

Whatever the real sum, it did not matter, for Marcos had accomplished his purpose. If money was indeed power, he had almost all the power. The Philippines, with its 53 million people, was a one-man business, with relatives and cronies responsible for day-to-day operations and the military responsible for seeing that competing interests did not interfere.

Not everyone who talked about the Marcos wealth talked about Marcos himself disparagingly. Those who looked up to him had never thought he was against graft and bribery; he had never pretended to a reputation for honesty. He was admired, instead, for his once brilliant mind, his show of learning, his shrewdness, his ability to get what he wanted through cajolery, bribery and intimidation.

Marcos tended to confirm that his wealth was unlimited, always coming up with whatever money was needed for any political purpose. After declaring martial law he talked about how he kept his holdings, through what he called "a blind trust," in the Marcos Foundation, an institution far more secret than the Shah of Iran's old vehicle for family enrichment, the Pahlevi Foundation.

What was known for sure was that early in his adult life, right after World War II, Marcos had set out to raise himself above his moderately well-off family. Before the war his father had served as an appointed governor on Mindanao. After the war, in which the father had died in circumstances never explained, young Marcos had put in extravagant war reparations claims for thousands of head of cattle he said had been slaughtered on Mindanao as part of the war effort. He was turned down. No evidence was found that the Marcoses had owned more than a few cows. But then he went to Congress, and afterward the money never stopped flowing.

In his early days in Congress he pushed through a bill that had the effect of allowing congressmen to sell import licenses. This was during the presidency of Elpidio Quirino, whose administration's corruption was considered a prime motivating factor for the Huk rebellion. What came out about Quirino, after Magsaysay made him a one-termer in a landslide election, indicated that his government was the most crony-ridden in Philippine history—until Marcos.

At first no one paid much attention to what the young congressman from Ilocos Norte was doing; so many people were doing the same thing in Quirino's time. But Marcos took it all a step farther. Working with the Chinese, he set up the Virginia tobacco business in the Ilocos provinces as his own moneymaking machine. Ninoy Aquino told us Marcos even had fake cigarette package revenue stamps printed for his front men so they could evade taxes. Since he worked so closely with the Chinese, the rumor began to spread that he was the illegitimate son of a Chinese merchant. There was no verification of the rumor, but he had always had powerful Chinese allies around him; it was widely believed that there were Chinese in the background even in the 1980s who were as rich and powerful as the cronies.

"It's simple," Ninoy Aquino said. "The Chinese do not talk. The Filipino talks. . . . When the Chinese makes money he is happy. When the Filipino makes money he wants political power. . . . That's the reason the Chinese went all the way for Marcos. He was dependable. Marcos cultivated them because they were a source of money."

Imelda Marcos herself spoke of the stacks of currency from many countries that her husband showed her in a wall safe just after the marriage. Presy Lopez Psinakis—daughter of the entrepreneur Eugenio Lopez whom Marcos destroyed and wife of the anti-Marcos exile leader Steve Psinakis—told more, speaking from the perspective of one who had once been closer than anyone else to Imelda. Presy had introduced Imelda to high society for the first time. She told of "suitcases full of cash" delivered to the Marcos home by Chinese businessmen as Marcos campaigned, on a ticket with her uncle Fernando Lopez as Vice President, for the presidency in 1965. A former senator, Jovito Salonga, told of seeing, shortly after that election, a deposit slip for a Marcos account in the Chase Manhattan Bank that a man in the New York Philippine consulate sent to him secretly. "It wasn't too big an amount, around $250,000 or $275,000. Since it was just after the campaign and in Philippine pesos it was a lot of money, I wanted to expose that, but on second thought I said to myself, give the guy a chance."

But soon Salonga, like Aquino, was exposing misdeeds. The first had to do with Marcos's illegally lifting restrictions on Japanese investment before a treaty with Japan had been signed. Another time Salonga led a Senate investigation into a stock manipulation scheme undertaken by Marcos business pals in which, he said, "millions were made." At the Plaza Miranda rally bombing in 1971, in which Salonga and the other opposition Senate candidates were severely wounded by grenades, the principal speakers had been about to talk on the subject of Marcos's personal finances.

All of this became an academic subject after the 1972 coup, which allowed the Marcoses to stop pretending they were not dipping into the treasury. By 1983 Marcos played down concern with defending his family against charges of corruption. What bothered him now were those World War II medals he still kept on display even though most of them had long since been proven fake.

No matter that everything else seemed in danger. Despite the growing threat to his regime from increasingly outspoken above-ground politicians and clergymen, combined with the actions of a well-organized urban underground and a nation-wide rural guerrilla army, the most publicized political arrests now were of people who questioned his wartime achievements.

Most of the medals he possessed had been awarded him nearly two decades after the war by his predecessor, President Diosdado Macapagal. According to Macapagal's defense secretary, Macario Peralta, the medals were part of an agreement that Marcos would honor his promise—which he broke—not to block Macapagal's bid for a second term. Since then military historians inside the Philippines and also in America had combed through all the dispatches, Philippine and American, concerning the engagements Marcos claimed to have led. The dispatches did not back the claims. That he had spent at least a small part of the war as a guerrilla had been verified. And pictures of him in uniform right after the war did show him sporting three campaign medals. However, his claims that he had been a major guerrilla leader, and legitimately "the Philippines' most decorated war hero," were claims made only in his own accounts or those he helped others write.

With the medals Macapagal gave him in hand, Marcos teamed up with an American to write an account of his claimed wartime adventures, *For Every Tear a Victory,* which he used as his 1965 campaign biography. That same year a movie about his supposed wartime exploits was made and released by the filmmaking in-laws of the man who was his campaign manager and would become his executive secretary—and later an exiled former senator—Ernesto Maceda. The book and movie were said to have won him the election. The war stories had, thus, once served him well. As his world fell apart, he seemed to be thinking he could become the man he once was if he got people to believe those stories again.

In Ferdinand Marcos's part of Malacañang Palace it was the wars of fiction, not the real war his regime was fighting with the New People's Army, that predominated. And in Imelda's part of the Palace the fantasy was even more bizarre.

By mid-1983 the economy was in worse shape than it had ever been. The country had just been rescued from defaulting on its foreign debt by an emergency International Monetary Fund and World Bank loan—an $843 million bailout. Marcos had just ordered "stricter belt-tightening" measures, such as cabinet-level pay cuts, to deal with the growing balance of payments deficit, approaching $2 billion for 1983. But Imelda had decided that what her people really wanted was to see the sort of pageantry that appeals to the British.

Having failed some years back in her attempts to get Prince Charles interested in one of her daughters, she decided that the wedding of her other daughter, in the seedy Marcos-Ver hometown in the north, would be the precise equivalent of what she had called the "fairy tale" British royal wedding. The event, held about two months before the Aquino assassination, was to be the most extravagant Imelda function yet.

She was still dreaming of outdoing the old elite who had looked down on her. And her husband was no closer to reality as he pored over the drafts of his ghost writers still charged with making up and elaborating his World War II exploits.

When the economic crisis had hit in the 1980s, the Malacañang solution was to throw money at the cronies. Now, just before the Aquino assassination, as the crisis became as much political as economic, Malacañang was consumed with pure fiction—on the one hand heroic war stories, on the other fairy tales.

13

THE CHICKENS ROOST IN AMERICA

Hunting Down Enemies Abroad

WHEN observed from a distance, the activities of the dictatorship often appeared merely frivolous. Before the Aquino killing, Americans, literally half a world away, sometimes saw the comic aspects while failing to grasp how sinister was the tyranny in the most Americanized part of Asia, the most Americanized country in the world. But when the long arm of Malacañang reached out 10,000 miles into America itself, some Americans found to their peril that the tyranny was not being played out in isolation. And when it developed that U.S. agents were cooperating with, not trying to combat, the agents of the Philippine dictatorship, there was immediate cause for alarm.

Sometimes the secrecy in which General Ver's overseas operatives worked was penetrated by opponents of the dictatorship. And specific incidents came to light in America's own dark spy and counterspy world that proved cases of collusion. Moreover, whatever the full extent of American-Philippine cooperation in intimidating the dictatorship's exile opponents, one thing was certain: U.S. agencies were aware from near the start that Ver's men were going after opponents inside America, including opponents who held American passports.

"Top secret sensitive" reports of the U.S. Senate Committee on Government Operations that we obtained showed that the collusion had not begun with Reagan. Though it became much more blatant from 1981 onwards, it had started in the early days of martial law while Nixon was still President.

Just before pulling his coup Marcos had had a long private conference with the then U.S. Ambassador to Manila, Henry Byroade; just afterwards, the first organization to publicly congratulate Marcos and offer support had been Manila's American Chamber of Commerce. No one produced any documents proving conclusively that any Americans knew about martial law in advance, though many years later Byroade admitted that he and Marcos had discussed the possibility. In any event, few Filipinos believed Marcos would have gone ahead with the coup if he had not, at least tacitly, been given a green light by Washington. Furthermore, as the U.S. Senate committee found, one thing Washington did certainly know early in the martial law period was that Marcos was prepared to pursue his enemies inside the United States.

"The CIA became aware in October 1973 that the Philippine government had become increasingly concerned that President Marcos's enemies in the U.S. might be developing, or had already, an influence that would adversely affect the Philippine government," the Operations Committee's counsel, Mike Glennon, wrote in a classified 1979 report. The report said that since 1973 Ver had been sending military intelligence officers to the United States "for the purpose of infiltrating, monitoring and possibly counteracting the threat of anti-Marcos groups. . . ."

There were three Marcos foes mentioned by Glennon as leaders of groups representing what the Philippine regime then considered "the threat"—former Senator Raul Manglapus, once the leading independent advocate of peaceful reform and now head of the big, mainstream, and rather conservative U.S.–based Movement for a Free Philippines; former

Manila Mayor Antonio Villegas, a middle-of-the-roader who wound up, instead of pursuing the cause, retiring to a ranch in Nevada; and the old deposed business tycoon and brother of Marcos's former Vice President, Eugenio Lopez. "Knowledgeable CIA officials were not aware of what means might be used to 'counteract' those groups," Glennon said, "but it did not rule out the possibility of violence."

The committee investigator went on to disclose that in the spring of 1973 Ver's elite Presidential Security Command had sent spies to the New York area. Their cover was that they were to serve as bodyguards for Marcos's daughter Imee, a student at Princeton, but "the real mission of the several officers was to infiltrate and report on the activities of the anti-Marcos groups. The CIA listed 19 Filipino intelligence officers assigned to the U.S. on this occasion."

Glennon's report said that sometimes in this early period American officials tried to discourage Ver's spies out of concern over "the possible intimidation of Filipinos in the U.S.," but on other occasions they let them operate freely. A Philippine agent who contacted an American federal agent offering assistance in handling "problems among the Filipino immigrants" in San Francisco was waved away. But "on at least one occasion . . . fear of reciprocal action [in Manila against] the CIA prompted it to attempt to prevent the investigation of certain foreign agents present in the United States whose activities were unknown but suspect."

Glennon related that on December 12, 1973, the "CIA chief of station in Manila asked Ambassador William Sullivan that the embassy assist in preventing the investigation of Philippine diplomats in the U.S. Specifically, the chief of station asked that the embassy make clear to the State Department that the embassy's 'position is that there should be no active investigation of official Philippine government representatives in the U.S. without advance consultation with the embassy and CIA headquarters, the reason being that such investigation would result in reciprocal [action] against American intelligence personnel in the Philippines.' The FBI thereupon terminated its investigation of certain Philippine diplomatic personnel believed to be on intelligence assignment."

In the ten years that followed, as we found through our contacts with the opposition during Reagan's first three years in office, many exile opponents had been hounded by Ver's operatives. In 1983, just before the Aquino assassination, we got hold of a secret internal U.S. Defense Intelligence Agency publication, later also leaked to the Democratic congressman Don Edwards of California, that gave fresh evidence that Washington was not unaware of what Ver's overseas operatives were doing.

The report from the DIA, the Pentagon's intelligence branch, took note of a new breed of unusually high-level military attachés who had recently arrived at the Philippine embassy in Washington, all handpicked by Imelda's brother, Ambassador Kokoy Romualdez. The new officers could be counted upon to aggressively pursue contacts at the Pentagon, the DIA report said. They were led by Brig. Gen. Angel Kanapi, who had last attracted attention as superintendent of the Philippine Military Academy when a cadet died in a hazing incident. Around General Kanapi was assembled a team of subordinates that included a Constabulary officer, Lt. Col. Roman Maddela, a man well known as an undercover operative because he had been the escort for the Philippine-American Victor Burns Lovely, who had accidentally injured himself with a bomb in Manila, then been taken by Maddela to the United States specifically to testify against opposition leaders in exile.

The DIA document, noting that these and other high-level officers were now in place in Washington, observed that among their duties would be the monitoring of "dissident activity in the United States." The report said, without comment, that "the attachés will undoubtedly report on, and possibly operate against, anti-Marcos Philippine activists in the U.S."

Such news would have come as no surprise to members

of America's intelligence community who had been concerned with the Philippines and with the activities of exile Filipinos. And it certainly would not have surprised the opposition leaders themselves. Because they had grown up believing that America was the land of free expression, and because they identified culturally with their former colonizers, they had come to the United States when they had known they were threatened at home. But the United States had not proved to be the completely safe refuge they expected.

Most Filipinos in America, whether antiregime activists or not, believed, with some good evidence, that they were always being watched. They believed that if they spoke out against the dictatorship possibly their own lives, and more likely the lives of family members back home, would be in danger.

It did not matter where they stood in the political spectrum. At least two exile members of the far left had been killed; many had been harassed. But so too had moderates and conservatives. From the time in 1981 that Reagan sent Haig to Manila and the Justice Department began attempting to make a case against the moderates before a federal grand jury, those who wanted a peaceful return to democracy were convinced of what they had suspected. They were certain from this point on that Washington would place its concern for the Clark and Subic bases, and the Reagan-Marcos relationship, above its concern not just for the human rights of people living in the Philippines but also for the human rights of Filipinos and Filipino-Americans living in the United States.

On the left, a turning-point case of intimidation inside America occurred with the murders of two twenty-nine-year-old Filipino labor leaders in Seattle in June of 1981, the same month that Haig delivered Reagan's message about going after exile opposition figures, and also the same month that Bush confirmed in public in Manila Reagan's secret promise to Imelda of unqualified support for the Marcos dictatorship.

Gene Viernes fell dead when several bullets hit him while he was at work as dispatcher at the Seattle local of the Alaska Cannery Worker's Union, an affiliate of the big West Coast International Longshoremen's and Warehousemen's Union. Silme Domingo, the local's secretary-treasurer, took four gunshots to his body but staggered out into the street, called for help, and spoke the names of his assailants before collapsing. He died the next day.

Both men had been part of a reform slate that had recently won key positions in the local. Two members of a known criminal gang, who admitted they were connected with an old-guard faction of the union, were tried and convicted of the killings, as was the admitted gang leader who had given the hit men their assignment. But the old-guard faction leader himself, the Filipino president of the local who was being squeezed out by the young reformers, was not indicted even though it came out in court that he was the owner of the murder weapon, a .45 automatic pistol.

This man, Tony Baruso—who would be convicted of embezzlement at the end of 1983—was an ardent and vocal supporter of the Marcos regime. Shortly before the Viernes and Domingo murders, he had actually been honored as a guest at Malacañang Palace. Viernes and Domingo were on the opposite side. Viernes had also been in Manila recently, for the purpose of conferring with members of the outlawed Communist-supported May 1 Labor Movement, the most widely backed antiregime worker organization in the Philippines. Then back in America Viernes and Domingo had been instrumental in the passage of a Longshoremen's Union convention resolution to look into labor repression in the Philippines.

Baruso was arrested but immediately released. He refused to cooperate in the proceedings against the accused killers. When called to the stand, he took the Fifth Amendment 136 times.

In September 1982, supporters of Viernes and Domingo,

both of whom had been long associated with the Philippine underground National Democratic Front, filed a federal court lawsuit in Seattle putting into legal context the suspicions that the murders were not cases of union gangsterism but were political murders ordered by the Marcos regime. Calling Baruso an agent for Marcos, the suit said the real reason he was never charged was that he was being protected by certain agents of the CIA, the FBI and U.S. military intelligence, who were listed as defendants in the lawsuit. Other defendants were George Shultz, Alexander Haig and FBI Director William Webster. The mere filing of a lawsuit may have proved nothing, but the *New York Times* columnist Tom Wicker took a close look at the suit and concluded that "these charges seem serious enough for Congress to look into."

Actually, Reagan administration criticism of, and opposition to, exile members of the far left, in keeping with the way the administration colluded with Malacañang, had never been so vocal and open as had its harassment of the exile moderates. But, as we had seen inside the Philippines, the left, especially after Reagan's inauguration, seemed to be emerging as a more potent antiregime force than was the center. And although most efforts of the Reagan administration—like those of the Marcos government—against Filipino dissidents would continue to focus on the old-line democratic politicians who had been Marcos's rivals before he imposed martial law, it was clear by now even in the exile opposition ranks, still dominated by moderates, that the left was moving to the forefront. And so the left was increasingly a factor that had to be considered by the leaders of both the Philippine and the American governments when formulating their plans to suppress opposition to the Philippine dictatorship.

Among the most important of the exile leftists was a genial, personable and highly persuasive Ph.D. from Cornell, Joel Rocamora. Like Ninoy Aquino, he had been a political detainee right after the 1972 coup. Before that he had been a close associate, at the University of the Philippines, of the man who would become chairman of the Philippine Communist Party, José Maria Sison. Rocamora now was based across the Bay from San Francisco at Berkeley, where he headed the Southeast Asia Resource Center. It was there that some of the best documentation of what was happening in the Philippines was carried out, just as this organization's predecessor, the Indochina Resource Center, had done work in support of opposition to the Vietnam War. Rocamora's close associate, the respected economic and military expert Walden Bello, who had a doctorate from Princeton, meanwhile ran an office in Washington that, although both men leaned leftward, served all opposition factions as a hard-pressing lobbying group to get U.S. congressional support for a change of policy toward the Philippine dictatorship.

There had been a period when few exile moderates spoke to exile leftists such as Rocamora and Bello. But by the time of the Aquino assassination the leftists in America, as in the Philippines, were working closely not just with various Philippine Marxist groups and splinter groups but also with most prominent middle-of-the-road exile proponents of a return to democracy.

One reason the moderates cooperated with the leftists in America was that, although they had thought of themselves as proponents of the American way, they had found they were the ones who had most to fear from Reagan's America. Even so, the moderates still worked night and day, as had their leader Aquino, to try to solve the problems of their devastated islands without a major bloodletting.

But although basically men and women of peace, these exile moderates had not always acted within the law. Many of their allies were convinced that the moderates had had something to do with sending urban bombers, and possibly even the actual explosives, to Manila in 1980. Such urban actions were not yet a part of the plans of the Communists, who were successfully acting to deny control of the country-side to the dictatorship and saw the encirclement and capture of urban areas as something that would come in a later phase of the struggle. Moderates and conservatives had meanwhile trained urban guerrillas of their own, some of them told us, at camps in Malaysia and also in America, probably in Arizona. This had put them in technical violation of federal statutes forbidding the use of U.S. territory as a launching point for political action abroad. But since America had not prosecuted other anti-Communists who trained within its borders to infil-trate their homelands, the Philippine exile moderates and con-servatives were surprised when they found themselves treated like criminals by their host country.

By the late 1970s and early 1980s moderate Filipinos had become so disillusioned with the Marcos regime, and so de-spairing of a peaceful return to democratic ways, that some extremely unlikely individuals had become revolutionaries. A case in point was that of Doris Baffrey. On first meeting she appeared a classic Filipina beauty with her long hair, fine dark skin and high cheekbones. By chance, one of us had had lunch with her back in the summer of 1980. The name Baffrey was that of a Peace Corps volunteer she had met and married. In 1980, by now divorced, she was living in New York, working for the Philippine government, and using her maiden name, Nuval.

Her job was at the showy Fifth Avenue consulate Imelda had ordered erected, where she served as part of a team han-dling the New York operations of the vast Ministry of Tourism that Marcos had created after his coup. Doris Baffrey had been recommended by one of New York's leading travel edi-tors as the only person in the consulate who knew her subject. The business of the luncheon, in the luxuriant Maharlika Phil-ippine restaurant that Imelda had ordered built into the consu-late basement, had had to do with travel, not politics. Small talk centered around such matters as Baffrey's discovery of such nontropical activities as ski weekends. She must have considered her luncheon companion an utter fool for feigning the belief, as she did herself, that Manila was a perfectly plausible tourist destination.

That autumn she was in one of Marcos's political prisons. She had gone to Manila and set off a bomb in the Philippine International Convention Center. Her action had all but destroyed the regime's much-vaunted tourism program, leaving the country with little in the way of foreign tourists except men coming for clear-cut sexual reasons.

The bombing, during ceremonies at the American Society of Travel Agents world convention, had been the last of a series of about fifty explosions set off that autumn for which an organization called the April 6 Liberation Movement claimed credit. It was a movement led by moderate political figures, named for an all-night "noise barrage" protest—mainly conducted by housewives beating on pots and pans and motorists honking their horns—as a demonstration against the rigged National Assembly elections in April of 1978.

The 1980 bombings had been designed to create a climate of unrest in order to, movement leaders said, "destabilize" the regime. The bombings were a follow-up to the previous year's Light-a-Fire Movement, another radical campaign conducted by moderates, in which a series of buildings, and the Manila Floating Casino, all of which belonged to the Marcoses or their cronies, were burned down. The bombs set off by the April 6 urban guerrillas were relatively small ones. As with the Light-a-Fire actions, attempts were made to avoid casualties. Warnings were issued beforehand to people at the places that would be bombed—all symbolic targets, principally banks, government office buildings, department stores and hotels owned by the new elite.

Altogether some sixty-five people received minor injuries in the 1980 bombings. Two or three were seriously injured and one woman, an American, was killed in an explosion at the Rustan Department Store, a once basic department store that had become more like Bloomingdale's after Imelda took it over. When Doris Baffrey set off her bomb in the Convention Center a dozen people were cut by flying debris or dazed by the blast. But the real damage was to the prestige of the regime.

Marcos himself was in the hall, and the whole point of the convention had been to assure world tourists that he had made his country safe. The convention instantly disbanded. All delegates rushed to their hotels, packed, checked out and dashed to the airport. Hundreds spent the night there after all seats on that evening's outbound flights had been taken.

Doris Baffrey was one of the government's best catches that season. The authorities had a confession from her; better yet, she had come from the United States, where many of the plotters who worried Marcos most, once-popular mainstream democratic politicians, were living.

But she was no pushover. She would tell her Constabulary interrogators nothing about any confederates she may have had. On December 8 she was invited to have lunch with the commander of the unit that had arrested her and others in the April 6 Liberation Movement, Col. Ramon Montano, head of a Constabulary "Special Operations Group."

She was first taken to Montano's office. Together they went to one of the Camp Crame dining rooms. To her surprise, they were joined there by three Americans. Two of the men were introduced as FBI agents attached to the American embassy and the third as a member of the embassy's legal affairs section. In a letter smuggled out of prison Baffrey said she naturally assumed the embassy man was from the CIA. After lunch they returned to Montano's office. He left her alone there with the three Americans, who proceeded with their own interrogation. They wanted the same information the Filipinos had wanted.

"Questions ranged from my personal life, life in New York

and finally the bombings," she wrote. "They were, to say the least, unsatisfied with my vague answers—to the point that they resorted to name-calling." She said they told her, "You've got crap coming out of your ears, and it's coming out of your mouth."

For four and a half hours the Americans played good cop and bad cop, at one moment pumping her for information, at the next making offers. They promised that she could see her four-year-old son, Dagul, then living with her sister in Houston, if she would be an informer. She turned down this and all of the other offers. One agent asked, "What kind of mother are you?" When she cried, they made fun of her. "Look, guys," one said, "she's crying." Then another got back to the child: "Isn't there something you want? Little arms? Little feet?"

It all might have ended there with her staunch refusal to talk. She had already been tried, convicted and sentenced. She might have served out her six-month term and returned home to America to live with her child. Such almost certainly would have been the case if Reagan had not just been elected President. As it turned out, she was looked upon as the chief, and the last, hope to achieve the objective agreed upon by Malacañang and the Reaganites to prosecute the moderate anti-Marcos exile politicians.

When we went back to the Philippines in 1983 we were wondering whatever had become of Doris Baffrey. One of us made inquiries through mutual friends at the Ministry of Tourism and drew a blank. But the other—not the one who had had lunch with her in 1980—discovered through underground sources that she was still at Camp Crame, twenty-eight months after having received her six-month sentence. Along with a Filipino he went to Crame to try to visit her.

At the entrance to the barren building where she was being held four guards looked up from their rummy game. Foreigners needed special permission, one of them said, to see what he called "special detainees." But the Filipino was led to her cell—and it turned out Doris Baffrey had quite a lot more to say.

The FBI had continued periodic visits. The last had occurred in the summer of 1982, about seven months earlier. The agent who had been assigned to follow through on her case and continue the interrogation was John Grant, who was well known to moderate exiles. Grant, working out of the legal attaché's office at the U.S. embassy, had made a name for himself by getting another captured Filipino-American bomber to talk—Victor Burns Lovely, the man who had accidentally blown himself up in his room at the Manila YMCA. Grant had seen to it that Lovely, a Los Angeles food importer and grocer, was taken back to America by the Constabulary's Colonel Maddela, after a painful, staged, nationwide television appearance in which Lovely had implicated everyone up to Aquino. Now Special Agent Grant was continuing to make the same sort of offers to Baffrey that he had made to Lovely. If she would become his informer and go before a federal grand jury in San Francisco that had been called into session by the Reagan Justice Department, he would put her in the Federal Witness Protection Program.

Baffrey, twenty-seven years old now, this time was not making social talk; but although she had become extremely thin she was much the same self-confident-appearing young lady she had seemed two and a half years earlier at Imelda's New York restaurant. In New York she had worn jeans, in sharp contrast to the other government-connected ladies dining at the consulate restaurant, who were dressed to the teeth at midday. In Crame now she wore a plain red blouse and white exercise shorts. She spoke with scorn of how Special Agent Grant had said the Americans would "set me up" in the United States, "give me a new identity and make me look like Gina Lollobrigida. . . .

"I said, 'No thank you. I like my face and body.' "

"There was a time when [Grant] put a yellow legal pad in front of me and told me, 'Name your price,' " she said. "I told him, 'What are the combined budgets of the FBI and CIA?' He said to me, 'You dumb shit!' "

On his last visit, Grant had applied the pressure as never before, she said. On that final occasion he was accompanied by a Filipino military officer. They told her she could get a pass from jail so that she could go off and think over Grant's offer and reach "the right decision." She said she was given the clear idea that this would be her last opportunity to walk out of Camp Crame so long as the dictatorship survived.

She was sure she knew what Grant and her Filipino captors had decided upon as their strategy. If she did go out on a pass, the temptation to make an agreement to stay out would be great. "I dreamed of America and my son for several nights in a row. I wanted so much to go back." But in the end she turned them down. "I called after a week, on a Monday, and told [the Filipino officer] I would rather be a prisoner behind bars for a few years" than have to live with what they wanted her to do "for the rest of my life."

We were still checking with Manila early in 1984 and as far as anyone knew Doris Baffrey was still in Camp Crame. Lovely, a maimed and broken man at thirty-eight, trusted by neither side since he had changed his story so often, was in Los Angeles. When his mother suffered a heart attack and died he became convinced she had been murdered by Marcos's agents. We had been part of the effort to persuade him not to get even by, as he threatened, dousing himself with gasoline and setting himself on fire in front of the White House.

Also in 1984, well after Aquino's murder, lawyers for moderate exile leaders were telling us that U.S. federal investigations were still going on into their clients' political activities. Despite the lack of evidence, federal prosecutors were leaving the cases open, still hopeful of obtaining indictments.

On another front, Reagan's Justice Department, after taking a head count, was still holding back on submission to the Senate of the Philippine-American extradition treaty, already signed by the Marcos and Reagan governments. This was the treaty that would have given the State Department, not the courts, the authority on politically sensitive extradition decisions concerning Filipinos. In lieu of such a law, the Reagan government was still withholding political asylum from most Marcos foes.

Political asylum for Filipinos had virtually ended even before Reagan's Justice Department ordered coordinated FBI visits without warrants to moderate opposition leaders across the nation. Word coming out of the San Francisco grand jury which had begun investigating the Philippine opposition in 1981 was that at first Ninoy Aquino had been the most wanted man—just as he had been in Lovely's televised confession in Manila. A Justice Department official, however, told a reporter that there had been second thoughts about Aquino, not because he was considered less involved in the attempts to destabilize the Marcos regime but rather because of who he was. "It had been commented," the official said, " 'Jeez, this guy may be the next President of the Philippines.' "

Well into 1984 the man who continued to come under the heaviest pressure, as had been the case even before the pressure intensified with Reagan, was the suave, fifty-two-year-old, bearded Greek-born American Steve Psinakis, who had possibly worked as hard as anyone alive, inside or outside the Philippines, to overturn the dictatorship. Until the mid-1970s, Psinakis had never been involved in politics. In 1959 he had left his job with an engineering consulting firm in Reading, Pennsylvania, to take what seemed a better job in Manila. There he had become associated with the dynastic Lopez family, which included the pre–martial law Vice President, Fernando Lopez, and the country's leading pre–martial law entrepreneur, Eugenio Lopez. Steve had married Eugenio Lopez's daughter, Presentacion "Presy" Lopez, who in 1984 was still among the most celebrated of all Filipina beauties. Even now, in reduced circumstances, this woman, whose exquisite figure and features belied her resolve, looked more like an international style setter than the totally committed political activist she had become.

In many ways Steve and Presy were as unlikely revolutionaries as young Doris Baffrey. It was his career as a mechanical engineer, nothing else, that had first taken Psinakis to the Philippines. He had gone to work for the Manila Electric Company—before its American owners sold it to Eugenio Lopez—as production manager. After the utility was purchased by Lopez he had risen to the position of operations manager and assistant to the president. He and Presy had fallen in love. They were married abroad in 1970. The fact that they had both been previously divorced—divorce is not recognized in the Catholic Philippines—had been too much for Presy's devout father. At the time martial law was declared Steve and Presy had become exiles already, though only for this purely personal family reason, and were living in Greece.

It was the treatment received by the Lopezes at the hands of Marcos, and by Psinakis himself at the hands of both Philippine and American agents, that had turned Steve into a political being. That he was effective was attested to by the fact that he wound up at the top of Marcos's enemy list, as indicated by Marcos's own statements and repeated attempts to silence him. Steve also was at the top of the lists of those American officials who had become obsessed with the preservation of the Philippine dictatorship. One can only guess at the vast amounts that have been spent already on investigations and interrogators at home and abroad, on informers and free-lance spooks, on auditors and eavesdroppers, on FBI raids and on federal grand juries, in the effort to get the goods on Steve Psinakis and undermine his efforts as a lobbyist.

His run-ins with Marcos agents had begun just before his brother-in-law, Eugenio "Geny" Lopez, Jr., was arrested without charge and thrown into a cell at Fort Bonifacio as a personal prisoner of Marcos's. For Geny to even be taken to visit a dentist required an order with Marcos's own signature. It was, naturally, the Marcos agents that first worried Steve most. Speaking as an American citizen of long standing, Steve tried to alert his government to the nature of the Marcos dictatorship, little realizing that eventually an American right-wing radical would reach the White House and the Philippine opposition would be referring to the people in Malacañang increasingly as the "U.S.–Marcos dictatorship."

Steve's long journey into politics originally had to do with how the once high-living Lopezes had been the people Imelda looked up to and envied most in the years before martial law. Even after the post coup regime set out to destroy the family, Imelda kept on sending couriers to San Francisco to tell the Psinakises that the First Lady just could not understand why her "dear friend," the aristocratic Presy, now refused to meet with her on any terms. She could not understand why Presy would not answer the messages she sent even though, using Presy's brother as a hostage, the Marcoses were practicing extortion against the Lopezes. The way Geny's life could be saved, emissaries told her father, was if he transferred the bulk of what he owned to the First Family. One by one Eugenio Lopez, Sr. was signing over to the Marcoses and their representatives all of his biggest holdings, including his power company; his once influential daily, the *Manila Chronicle,* of which Geny had been publisher; his many radio and TV stations, and various other properties he owned.

Marcos himself, like Imelda, was bent on revenge. Before the coup, after Vice President Fernando Lopez had turned against him, the *Chronicle* had become one of the loudest voices exposing not just the corruption but the ineffectiveness of Marcos's legal regime. Also, the Lopez family, Malacañang decided, had to be destroyed as an economic force in keeping with Marcos's belief that he could make his potential rivals impotent by cutting off their funds.

In late 1974, Geny and a fellow detainee who was also a personal hostage of the President, Sergio Osmeña III, grandson of a past President and son of the man who had run for President against Marcos in 1969, began a hunger strike. In the course of the hunger strike Marcos finally announced formal charges against them; they had, he said, been plotting his assassination.

It was at this point that Steve decided to devote all his considerable energies to the anti-Marcos cause in response to Geny's personal appeal. Geny wanted Steve and Presy to make use of the hunger strike to draw attention to the tyranny. "It was a direct appeal from a member of the family for a good cause," Steve told us much later. "I agreed to respond and have devoted all my energies ever since to fighting Marcos and for the restoration of democracy in the Philippines."

It was at that point—with Steve now living, like his father-in-law, in San Francisco—that the threats began. Right after receiving Geny's message, Steve flew to the East Coast to try to arouse interest in the news media and in Congress. A few days after he checked into the Waldorf in New York, the phone in his room rang.

"You better pack up and go home," said the caller in heavily accented Filipino English. "Forget about this or you'll be dead." A few hours later, Steve recalled, "there was another call, from someone else, an American. The message was the same.

"Those calls scared me the most because they were the first and I was very new at all this then. I called the police. Politely, they made me feel foolish, for there was nothing they could do and I had no evidence any calls were even made."

During the next couple of years back in San Francisco, after he was working full-time for the cause, "cars went past me with men pointing guns," he said. And the calls and the direct threats never let up. "In 1979, I was walking through [San Francisco's] Union Square on a nice summer day and a guy came out of the crowd of shoppers. He walked along with me just long enough to tell me, 'If you don't quit your campaign we'll kill you,' then just melted into the crowd. He was big for a Filipino, heavy-set, with a crewcut. He was well dressed and presentable, blending right in."

That year Steve and Presy, their funds dwindling were operating a fast-food restaurant, Pick-a-Pita. Steve was heading to work before dawn one morning when a car pulled up beside him while he was stopped for a red light at Market and Third streets in downtown San Francisco.

"There were two guys in the front seat. The driver was a black fellow, maybe thirty years old, and the one sitting next to him was a white man with a graying beard. The guy on the passenger side, the one nearest me, smiled and motioned to me to roll down my window. I did, and said to him, 'Yes?'

"Suddenly he pulled a gun, reached across and actually touched it to my temple. He said to me: 'You son of a bitch. You don't seem to believe we mean business. This is your last warning; if you don't wise up, next time we'll let you have it.'

"I thought, this time I've had it. All in the split second he held the gun to my head I thought, the setting is perfect. No witnesses. And worst of all, I saw a silencer. Why would they go to the trouble of putting on a silencer if they weren't going to shoot?

"I just froze. I didn't do anything. I felt neither afraid nor brave. I just sat there, waiting for the gun to go off. It didn't.

"Their car, a late-model dark blue Cadillac, pulled out ahead of me and I mechanically followed. Then suddenly the driver slammed on his brakes in front of me. I nearly hit him from behind. Then he did it again, two or three times, all in the space of about a block. Then he turned left on Sacramento Street and I kept going to the restaurant.

"I don't know why he did that, but obviously he wasn't trying to hide his plates. I scribbled the number down—433 DGH—and thought, why bother? It's probably a stolen car or stolen plates.

"I told the [San Francisco Police] and wrote to the FBI, only because Mike Glennon [the Senate Government Operations Committee counsel] told me I should when things like this happened, even with no evidence for it."

We asked Psinakis about the response from Washington, since we knew it was a major complaint of his that U.S. officials were indifferent to law violations by General Ver's men.

"Not even a fucking acknowledgment."

On another occasion when men with guns in cars threatened Psinakis in the middle of the day, "They made me laugh. It must have been a *tuta* [a disparaging Tagalog word meaning "lap dog"] of Marcos, because they had covered the license plates. I couldn't take that one seriously. What was I supposed to think, that they'd shoot me on a city street and drive away in a car with covered plates? That would have attracted more attention than plates that weren't covered.

"I'm not saying I wasn't scared. I was scared, every time there was an approach. But I never gave them the satisfaction of showing my fear. By laughing at them, I discouraged them."

At his home in the quiet Balboa Terrace section of San Francisco, Psinakis kept a memento of another attempt to silence him, a painted wooden board that was pitched into his backyard. On it was written, "Good luck. Hope you survive, fucker."

The phone threats were still being made to Psinakis after the Aquino killing. They were being made to most members of the opposition. We were being threatened too. Just as earlier in the year in Manila a late-night caller, claiming to speak for General Ver, had gotten through to one of us, such calls were coming now in California. While Vanzi stayed in Manila for the Aquino funeral, men kept pushing the downstairs buzzer to his apartment and disappearing before the building's guard could catch up with them. One phone caller with a Filipino accent told his wife, "He's reporting lies about our country. He won't live a day after he gets back to San Francisco."

Steve had warned us, correctly, at the outset of our project that such threats would come, just as he had warned us that our phones would be tapped, our homes possibly bugged and our tax returns probably audited. But compared to Steve we were mere spectators on the sidelines, and nothing yet had happened to us that was comparable to a disturbing call Steve had received from Manila at 3:20 on the morning of February 3, 1976.

The call was from his brother-in-law Geny Lopez, who was still a hostage although he had stopped his hunger strike on Marcos's personal, soon broken, promise to meet the hunger strikers' demands that political detainees be released. The dictator, Geny said, was repeating a charge he had made before that Psinakis was plotting the assassination of Marcos and Imelda and the kidnapping of their daughter Imee at Princeton. Defense Minister Juan Ponce Enrile had personally gone to Geny and asked him to tell Psinakis that "two can play the game as well as one." Enrile, on instructions from Marcos, had taken Geny from jail to his home to make the overseas call to Steve.

Psinakis recalled telling Geny, for the benefit of others listening in, that what he and Presy were bringing to light about the dictatorship constituted weapons enough in their war with the regime. "By then I'd been ignoring their threats. I guess they thought it was time to try something new."

Although friends and family were often desperately worried about him, Steve had come to revel in the threats that he and everyone else opposing the dictatorship were getting. It proved, as he wrote in an editorial page article for the *San Francisco Examiner,* that he and Presy were causing consternation by being "relatively successful in documenting and presenting to the U.S. Congress and the international press several cases of Marcos' criminal activities, not only in the Philippines, but also in the United States."

It had been Psinakis who had gotten the word out about the "extortion and terrorism" Marcos used to take over his tycoon father-in-law's holdings. When Marcos first made his accusations that the Psinakises were planning to kidnap and kill his daughter Imee, in the summer of 1975, Psinakis had replied with a publicity-generating federal court libel suit against the dictator.

It was mainly Psinakis and an exile newspaper publisher, Alex A. Eslamado, who had publicized the case of a desperate Filipino, Napoleon Lechoco, who in 1974 had pulled a gun on the Philippine ambassador to Washington, Imelda's uncle, Eduardo Romualdez (Kokoy's predecessor), and held him for hours trying to get the release from Manila of Lechoco's sixteen-year-old son. Lechoco was a lawyer who had worked with an antigraft organization in the Philippines to expose Marcos crony corruption. After he surrendered to authorities in Washington he was tried, convicted and sentenced to ten years in prison; but then he was acquitted in a second trial. Psinakis not only made sure that the most eloquent witnesses were obtained for the second trial to testify to the horrors of the dictatorship; he also came up with evidence, and spread it all over the country, that the Kissinger State Department and the Marcos government had brought influence to bear in the first trial that prevented testimony by anti-Marcos exiles ready to tell the jury what kind of regime it was that had driven Lechoco to his act.

Psinakis was a regular columnist for Alex Esclamado's weekly *Philippine News*, the leading Philippine-American newspaper, which had been virulently anti-Marcos since before the start of martial law. Like the Psinakises, and starting before them, Alex and his wife, Lourdes, were full-time, self-

described "freedom fighters," working constantly and effectively to get the Philippine story out.

After writing an exposé of one grand-scale Marcos regime
scam for the newspaper, Steve uncovered an apparent assassination plot against himself. He had gotten hold of the tape
recording of a telephone conversation in which it sounded
clear that at one point General Ver had sent two of his subordi-
nate generals to the United States to set up the execution
of Psinakis and another American involved in that exposé.

Whether the plot was real or not was not the main point,
Psinakis maintained. He was more bothered by the fact that
the FBI, having been given a copy of the recorded conversation, failed to do so much as interview the American who
had made the tape. "What excited them more than anything
was the taping of the conversation. 'So,' they told me, 'you
have been taping conversations on the telephone secretly.
That's illegal.' And it was not, of course, I who did the taping."

While Kissinger was still conducting American foreign policy, Psinakis had been told directly while visiting the Justice
Department in Washington that it was not in America's interest to protect him against General Ver's agents. It was a sign
of what would come with the much more right-wing government of Reagan, when the Justice Department would actually
try to get Psinakis indicted on criminal charges for pressing
his anti-Marcos campaign. But whether confronting indifference or the threat of prosecution, he, like Alex and many
others in the exile opposition, never bowed to either American
or Philippine intimidation. On a wide range of fronts he pursued the fight. For example, when thieves stole documents
at a Los Angeles convention of the moderate opposition Movement for a Free Philippines, Steve went to work. He turned
up eventually with meticulously detailed evidence that the
thieves were hired by Philippine agents.

The most sensational of the exposés in which he played
a part concerned the case of Primitivo Mijares, the former

chief censor of the Philippines' controlled press, who fled to Washington and testified at length in 1975 before the House Committee on International Relations. Mijares gave, in the kind of detail known then only to Palace insiders, a shocking picture of the human rights atrocities being perpetrated by the regime.

Before Mijares disappeared—last heard from in a letter to a journalist dated January 7, 1977, and mailed during a stopover as he was flying back to Manila—he had not only exposed the dictatorship in general. Mijares had helped Psinakis and the *Philippine News*'s Alex Esclamado, through taped phone conversations with Manila and actual records from a bank where $50,000 had been deposited in his name, to show how the regime had clumsily attempted, in America, to bribe him not to talk.

Steve's most dramatic triumph took place at the start of October 1977. He masterminded and financed the escape from the maximum-security military prison at Fort Bonifacio of Geny Lopez and Sergio Osmeña III, who, after Ninoy, were then the best-known political detainees. Steve spent months in the planning. Finally, on the appointed day the two men got out through bars that had been loosened on their cells. They crawled through the prison compound and met up with Geny's two sons, who were waiting outside with a car. After switching vehicles and clothes they made their way in the early-morning hours of October 1 to a remote private airstrip on the South China Sea coast.

A blue and white six-seater Cessna 320 soon appeared overhead, dipped down and landed. With the plane still turning on the landing field, Lopez and Osmeña, along with Geny's sons and a lawyer friend, jumped aboard. The plane took off and headed to Hong Kong.

There to meet it was Steve Psinakis, who had bought the Cessna, hired an Israeli-American fighter pilot, and orchestrated all other elements of the escape. While the men fleeing the Philippines waited in the Hong Kong transit lounge, he picked up their boarding passes using the passports of his children and went aboard a Japan Airlines plane bound for Los Angeles with the escapees. At Los Angeles International Airport, he escorted them through immigration, getting on the phone to Washington. Carter State Department officials let the escapees remain in the country pending asylum, which was soon granted.

When Steve first became active, some opposition leaders were dubious about his motives. Since he had previously been apolitical, and since it seemed that an early end to martial law might restore Presy's inheritance, they wondered if he were not operating on his own with selfish motives. But as martial law drew on, it became plain that the families Marcos had destroyed no longer even dreamed the Philippines would ever be what it once was. Psinakis became a close friend of, and even adviser to, Aquino after Ninoy came to America in 1980. He also was a key figure in bringing the moderates together with the leftists, who had no sympathy for any oligarchs, whether the name was Marcos or Lopez.

Some anti-Marcos Filipinos—including some members of the Lopez clan back in Manila—made their peace with the regime; they would not be as rich as the cronies, but at least they would be allowed to keep on doing business in the Philippines. It was a matter, after all, of family responsibility, they said. They said that anyway they were business people, not revolutionaries. But to Steve and Presy, these people had become compromised figures. In the course of their fight against Marcos they cut themselves off from, often became bitterly at odds with, many of their old associates, including some of Presy's closest childhood friends and even members of her immediate family.

Steve was, quite simply, a driven man. And Presy was a driven woman. They had demonstrated that they would sacrifice material wealth, and all chance of a return to the high

life they had known, for the sake of restoring Philippine democracy. Steve by now was at home with the most radical
of Marcos opponents. It was Steve who had first introduced
us in Berkeley to Joel Rocamora of the Southeast Asia Resource
Center, which led to our own close work with the left. Steve,
taking a more direct course than that of some moderate opposition figures, would not even speak to Marcos supporters,
not even for tactical purposes.

That he and Presy would become such directed and self-
sacrificing members of the cause had seemed unlikely back
in September 1972 when the coup occurred.

At the time martial law began, Steve and Presy were living
very well indeed. In the summer of 1972 they had had a
reconciliation with Eugenio Lopez, Sr., when he came to see
them in Greece on one of his regular world tours and gave
them his blessing. They first heard the news about the September coup while they were in Greece in a phone call from
the elder Lopez, who was then in San Francisco, where he
received a telephone call from his brother, Vice President
Fernando Lopez, informing him what Marcos had done and
warning him it was no longer safe to go home.

Then began a period in which Steve and Presy practically
commuted between Greece and San Francisco, where Lopez
maintained a mansion in the wealthy Sea Cliff district. On
October 29, 1972, Steve, Presy and her father were sitting
at a baccarat table at Caesar's Palace in Las Vegas when they
saw someone familiar.

It was Kokoy Romualdez, Imelda's formerly ne'er-do-well
favorite brother. Kokoy, not yet a diplomat, had apparently
come to America specifically to see them. As Steve recalled
it, the senior Lopez "was civil with Kokoy but basically ignored
him." Kokoy was saying, "Can I have a word with you? I
have something to say," and the old man was concentrating
on his cards.

But Steve and Presy did agree to speak with the brother

of the woman to whom Presy had once been extremely close. They went to a cocktail lounge inside Caesar's and listened as Kokoy made his pitch. "The First Lady," he said, always referring to his sister by that title, never by name, "still considers Presy her best friend." As Steve and Presy recalled it, he said, "The First Lady would dearly love to have you return to the Philippines." Moreover, he said, "the President mentioned that Steve was a very respected executive and power engineering expert. Steve, he would like you to come back as 'consultant to energy development' in the Philippines."

Over and over Kokoy repeated his offer. The Psinakises, he said, could be very helpful to the "First Family" in building the New Society Ferdinand Marcos was heralding. Steve and Presy avoided direct replies. They had no intention of becoming part of the dictatorship. On the other hand they knew, now that there was no law operating except the will of the Marcoses, that their family was in a vulnerable position. They parted, telling Kokoy they would think about what he had said.

Two weeks passed, and then suddenly came word that Geny had been thrown in jail. And Steve was convinced that, this time at least, there was nothing sincere in Imelda's overtures to Presy. "What Kokoy was really up to," Steve said much later, "was that they were looking for a hostage to use so they could keep the very powerful father quiet and expropriate the Lopez holdings. Presy, Eugenio Lopez's only daughter, would have been the ideal hostage. When they realized they weren't going to get her, they took Geny instead."

Steve and Presy had continued to move between Greece and San Francisco, still thinking that the dark days of the dictatorship would somehow come to an end, Presy's father would get his holdings back, and Geny would become a Manila newspaper publisher again. But by late 1974—with Geny's hunger strike and plea for help, and Marcos's continuation of political detention, torture and killing—they realized that their thinking was wishful dreaming. By the time the old man died, on July 1, 1975, their world travels had ceased and they were totally immersed in their new lives as antigovernment political activists.

"Our phone bills alone some months were running $5000 to $6000," Steve said. In the months before his death his father-in-law had continued to help pay their expenses. But then the subsidies stopped, while the cost of the lobbying and dissemination of information continued. Psinakis had established such wide connections that he was getting "Dear Steve" letters from the biggest names in the Senate and House, but all this cultivating was expensive.

"Once, during Geny's hunger strike, we sent a two-page telegram to every member of the U.S. Congress and important people in the media and the administration, and for that one cable alone the cost was $5000," Steve related much later. "I didn't realize then, when Presy and I first started, that there's a service where you can send the same message to all members of Congress for around $400.

"We went through hundreds of thousands, and now it's almost all gone. All our investments, Presy's jewels of $100,000, her real estate, our savings, it's all gone.

"Since the start of our commitment in late 1974, we have devoted full time and have had no regular income. My earnings would have been several hundred thousand. I was at the prime of my career. There were savings and properties worth several hundred thousands more. It was all spent on the cause and to survive. It's dwindled down to practically nothing today. Through a period, we did save and earn a little from odds and ends—a restaurant, some real estate, some counsulting work I was able to do. Now even that has gone."

After the year Reagan came into office, what little time Steve had left was spent working on his own grand jury case. But Psinakis, though not a Filipino himself, had achieved his goal of becoming the main thorn in Marcos's side, at least before and after Ninoy's three years of exile freedom. Steve was always singled out by name, and his name was constantly repeated, in the vituperative speeches Marcos was making about exile "terrorists." And just as he drew Philippine agents, so did he draw American agents after March of 1981 when the new attorney general, William French Smith, issued Reagan-approved guidelines increasing the FBI's latitude to infiltrate and investigate. The first coordinated visits to all the Philippine opposition leaders, Psinakis included, occurred that same month.

But this was nothing compared to what would happen later in the year. On December 17, 1981, at 11:30 at night, the doorbell rang at the Psinakis home. Steve opened the door and saw agents all over—four right in front of him, others in the yard, and more pouring out of vehicles lined up at the curb. The first four entered, showing identification. They produced a warrant when Psinakis refused permission for them to start a search.

Immediately one of the agents, for reasons Steve never understood, charged, shouting and swearing, up to the top of a staircase where Presy and a houseguest, an activist named Charlie Avila, were standing. The agent grabbed Avila, wrenching his arm behind his back, and slammed him against the wall.

Psinakis, holding back his two large dogs—Prince, a German short-haired pointer, and Princess, a springer spaniel— let out a shout. "Hold it! I will not permit any violence in our home—and, especially, foul language in front of a lady." "Take it easy up there," said another agent, whom Psinakis remembered as being one Al Cruz, whom he knew slightly from a previous visit.

A third agent, Frank Doyle, who had whipped out the search warrant, now ordered Psinakis to take the excited dogs into the backyard. The moment he did, a gunshot boomed in the darkness and Doyle was screaming, "Don't shoot! Don't shoot! This is the FBI!"

Psinakis resisted an urge to cut and run. If he had, he

thought later, "there is no doubt the trigger-happy agent would have kept on firing until the 'escaping terrorist' dropped dead."

It turned out there were what Psinakis estimated to be twenty to thirty lawmen—local police and sheriff's deputies as well as the FBI—who remained both inside and outside the house during the three-and-a-half-hour search that was conducted. The FBI men looked through everything, even opening wrapped Christmas presents beneath the family tree. Steve, Presy and Charlie Avila were ordered to the kitchen and kept under guard, not permitted to watch the search. Avila asked to leave and was told to "stay put." Agents went through his briefcase and shoulder bag, even though the search warrant did not mention Avila. They found and took an unloaded pistol, confidential papers, and pictures of activists inside the Philippines that were in the bags Avila was carrying.

More agents had entered the house by now. They spread out through all the rooms, even slipping into the bedrooms of the three Psinakis children, Yuri, fourteen years old, Michael, ten, and Geni, five, and looking under their beds for evidence.

The warrant that Steve examined authorized a search "for certain destructive devices" and mentioned that the devices were described on "attached affidavits." There were no attached affidavits.

Psinakis got his lawyer, a noted criminal attorney named George T. Davis, on the kitchen phone.

Steve recalled later how Davis had exploded. "They're playing with us! The search is illegal. Have you told them? Have they stopped?"

"I told them, George, but I don't know if they've stopped. There must be at least twenty agents all over the house and I don't know what they're doing. We're locked up in the kitchen."

To Psinakis, the reasons for the search became clearer later. The agents were ostensibly looking for bomb-making components similar to those which they said an "informant"—whom Steve was convinced was a Marcos agent—had reported finding in the Psinakis garbage. A delivery man had already told Steve that he had seen a Filipino stealing his garbage bags early that morning.

The agents found no bomb parts. But there was more to the search. They methodically went through the files and correspondence that Psinakis kept in his upstairs study. "Their primary objective was to gather intelligence information," he said. "They hoped and expected to find correspondence and documents which would identify my contacts with the underground forces in the Philippines and/or other sensitive information which would help Marcos to not only suppress his opposition in the United States but, in fact, to round up all those in the Philippines who were connected with me and any other opponents of Marcos.

"Three weeks after the raid I learned from my own intelligence sources in the Philippines that copies of the documents seized or photographed by the FBI from my files were on the desk of General Fabian Ver in Manila.

"A week later I learned that more than twenty people had been arrested in Manila for 'interrogation.' Most of them were tortured and two disappeared and were presumed salvaged."

Psinakis would not elaborate further on the men and women captured by Ver's men in the Philippines through his papers taken by the FBI. He said to do so "would jeopardize other friends in the Philippines and my defense if I were indicted and brought to trial" on the Neutrality Act violations the U.S. attorney's office was trying to pin on him.

There was corroboration for what he had learned. Some of it we heard later from secret sources in Manila. Meanwhile, two months after the raid the *San Francisco Chronicle* ran an exclusive front page story about information gathered for the grand jury "being funneled to authorities in the Philippines." The story said Justice Department officials had passed on to Ver in Manila "photocopies of documents seized during an FBI search last December of the Balboa Terrace home of Steve Psinakis." The story went on to say that the federal prosecutions of Marcos foes that Reagan had promised Marcos were by now centered almost solely on Psinakis. A year later a federal investigator told a UPI reporter, Spencer Sherman, doing a free-lance article for *Mother Jones* magazine, that "investigative reports" compiled during government probes into the anti-Marcos movement in America were still being sent to the Philippines for General Ver to examine.

It was sufficient evidence so that the California press never dismissed Psinakis's charges of Reagan administration collusion with Marcos and Ver as paranoia. The California media covered Philippine events much more thoroughly than the media elsewhere in the nation because Filipinos, partly due to the exodus during the martial law years, had come to form the state's largest ethnic Asian group, outnumbering even the Chinese.

All Filipinos in America with whom we spoke were convinced that if they acted against Marcos their actions would be noted at home. One of us had the sad experience, after we began work on our book, of losing cautious longtime Filipino friends who now feared to associate with us. The apparent killing of Mijares in 1977 because of his activities in America had made Filipinos everywhere feel more vulnerable than ever, in much the same way that the first killings under torture of political detainees had brought home the true nature of the threat Filipinos faced.

Those who had seen the Mijares disappearance as a warning to themselves found their fears reinforced five months later when his fifteen-year-old son in Manila also disappeared. After two weeks, the boy's body turned up at a funeral parlor near Manila, where it was identified by family members. The body bore the marks of severe beatings and multiple stab wounds.

An object lesson was also made with the family of one of the most active anti-Marcos exiles, Heherson "Sonny" Alvarez, who lived in New York but traveled widely as secretary-general of the Movement for a Free Philippines. He served as unofficial second-in-command first to ex-Senator Raul Manglapus and later, after Ninoy's release to Aquino. When Doy Laurel and other oppositionists from Manila came to America they were usually escorted during their visits by Alvarez.

Before the imposition of martial law Alvarez had been a delegate to the Constitutional Convention that was in the process of reforming the system—despite massive bribes distributed to many delegates by Marcos, who wanted to see that the system was changed in a way that would permit him to stay on after his legal term. The Constitutional Convention, like every other legal body dealing with the political life of the nation, became irrelevant after the coup.

Sonny Alvarez had both establishment anti-Marcos political ties and ties to the left, including ties from a time he had visited China against the wishes of the legal Marcos government. He had escaped from the Philippines right after the coup, and shortly after that his young wife, Cecile Guidote Alvarez, one of the nation's most celebrated theatrical directors, had also escaped to join him.

In 1974 Alvarez received a letter from a priest in his family's home province, Isabela, in northeastern Luzon. It said, "Your brother Marsman is dead. The people know who killed him, but they are terrified to talk openly about it." The priest described how the "killers had completely beaten up his face and his jaw was broken. They cut his nose and clawed out one of his eyeballs. They pulled out all of his teeth except two, and they cut his tongue. His skull was broken at the back."

The family was in shock, the priest said. Then six weeks later, Sonny and Marsman's father died of heart failure and the priest wrote again, this time asking Sonny to get word to the rest of the family that he was well and safe.

"But be prudent," he advised Sonny. "The people I have talked to agree that your brother, who was a harmless and pleasant young man, was killed because you have refused to cooperate with the dictatorship. The province [where Enrile was the biggest landowner and the NPA had established its first big front] is in a state of terror. Anyone who meets the displeasure of the powers that be pays very dearly for it."

The priest went on to explain why there was no doubt who the killers of Sonny's brother were. Marsman had last been seen alive in the custody of a special U-2 police intelligence unit consisting of a lieutenant and a squad of soldiers. They were escorting Marsman out of a small town he had been visiting. The body was found the next morning.

Much later Sonny told us, "The region was so terrified by the killing that my father could not find a coroner or a doctor to perform an autopsy." And that, Sonny said, was just the sort of situation the regime wanted.

"I see it as a method of cowing the opposition" both in the Philippines and in America, he said. "By killing in a very diabolical way and making big propaganda out of it, you're able to silence a few more. The techniques are the same as in Brazil—torture beyond the need for killing."

Sonny said he did not hold up his brother's case when trying to rally support against the dictatorship, for that would be playing into Malacañang's hands—spreading the fear. "I never mention it in my speeches. It propagates their work."

Sonny had long since learned to live with the periodic anonymous threats made on his life. So had all the other leaders, including the prominent Washington-based reformer Raul Manglapus, though he told us of one threat that had been too big to ignore.

In 1977 and 1978, the former senator and foreign secretary said, "information was given to me that General Ver wanted me assassinated." Manglapus described how a certain Filipino living in Chicago had contacted a friend of his, former Ambassador Eduardo Quintero, now an exile politician, who in the early 1970s had exposed the way Marcos had tried to compromise delegates to the Constitutional Convention by actually passing out envelopes containing cash. The man in Chicago had told Quintero that Ver had offered to drop criminal charges against him in the Philippines if he would kill Manglapus.

Quintero reported all this to Manglapus; then they went to Chicago together to question the man further. The man insisted again that he had been approached directly by Ver. He said that Ver, who made several trips to America, had gone personally to Chicago to put the proposition to him. Again, as with Alvarez, the main point seemed to be how people would react to such stories. Manglapus said that what he learned in Chicago "might have been real or it might have been their goal only to intimidate."

Out in San Francisco Alex Esclamado, the crusading anti-Marcos publisher of the *Philippine News*, by now considered the threats an integral part of the life he had chosen. He described how always "the threats come after the paper has made, or I have made, a particularly strong attack on the government." As with everyone else on the antigovernment side, the anonymous threats were stepped up in the period after the Aquino killing. Usually, he said, they came over the phone and were veiled—more like the threats one of us had received in his hotel room in Manila than the direct threats received by the wife of the other while he was reporting on the Aquino assassination. Alex said a typical call would go, "Well, I've just come from Manila and heard what you've been doing. What's so bad about the President? I would like to see you some day."

There had also been occasions when he had been followed while driving his car. "They made it obvious. They would stay behind me, then swerve and race past me and a man in the car, usually a Filipino, pointed his finger at me, the Filipino's way of threatening there will be a shooting."

At the same time some agents were threatening him, others were trying to buy him out. There had already been four such attempts to silence him this way—reminiscent of the time agents had been sent to bookstores and libraries to get all copies of a privately published book damning the regime, *The Conjugal Dictatorship*, that the one-time press censor, Mijares, had written. It was also reminiscent of a time we had been told by a man close to Marcos that there would be "more money than you guys have ever seen before" should we agree not to write our own book.

In 1975, Alex said, he had been offered $750,000 to $1 million for his newspaper, "as a starting point for negotiations." In the years that followed the offers were increased finally to "$9 million for me and $3 million for my staff, and I was to stay on at the paper as a front man." At the same time, advertisers had canceled out, saying they had been threatened by Marcos agents. Esclamado said that the paper, although it was the largest and most widely read publication in the generally prosperous Filipino exile community, usually operated in the red.

Back in Washington, Dante Simbulan, a one-time Philippine Army officer who left and was now head of the Church Coalition for Human Rights in the Philippines, told of intimidation similar to that of the old-line moderates. Echoing what we had heard from the author and lobbyist Walden Bello and other Filipinos in America associated with the left-leaning groups, Simbulan spoke to us, from his office at the National Council of Churches building, of what had happened shortly before the Marcoses' visit to the Reagans.

Simbulan had been criticizing the regime for flying movie

stars and starlets to the United States to try to stir up pro-government sentiment among apolitical exiles. One day, he said, "I got a visitor, a big muscled Caucasian who looked like a wrestler. He said he was a tourist from New Jersey and had found one of our leaflets." He hung around the office for a while, looking over the literature Simbulan's group put out to help with its efforts in lobbying Congress and alerting Filipinos and Americans to the nature of the dictatorship. He went away carrying pamphlets with him.

"Then when the movie stars came," Simbulan said, "we went to watch the people's reaction and there he was again. He was with the security people from the Philippine embassy. He was helping to try and intimidate anti-Marcos people. We confronted him and said, 'We thought you were a tourist.' No, he said, he worked for the embassy, had been all the time."

Only someone who knows what it is like to be a foreigner in the United States and feel at the mercy of the Immigration and Naturalization Service can fully appreciate the fear that an American, any American, can instill in the average immigrant, whether or not he or she is an illegal alien. The fact that most Filipino immigrants are primarily concerned with advancement through education and careers means that only a relative handful of the estimated 1.5 million Filipinos in America would dare fly in the face of what seemed to be authority.

We had often noted how Marcos had resorted to overkill to intimidate his people inside the Philippines. That Filipinos knew Ver's agents were allowed to operate in America, and that Filipinos here did not believe their relatives were safe at home, should have been enough for either Marcos or the Reagan administration's purposes. So too should have been the fact that no one was interfering with the Ver agents' use of American goons across the country. That the FBI should be brought in on the prodictatorship side, and moves made to either tamper with the American justice system, as in the Reagan extradition treaty, or turn it against Filipinos who believed in democracy, as in the grand jury proceedings, was surely much more than was needed to back up the dictatorship.

In lack of restraint, as in so much else, there continued to be elements of the dark side of official America that were being used to assist the rulers so far away in Malacañang Palace.

14

DON'T CRY FOR ME, FILIPINOS!

The First Lady and the "Little People"

WHEN it came to the royal style of Imelda and the new superclass, America was still too egalitarian to always serve as a guide. Reflections from the United States may have sufficed for organizing a military complex, building images through flackery, even turning espionage systems against your own people. But in other areas something beyond the example set by the old colonizers was required.

From Latin America came the idea of exalting a caudillo's wife, just as it was Latin America that had provided relevant modern models for political detention and torture, arranged disappearances, and death squad murders. Filipinos were quick to compare their glamorous First Lady to Argentina's late Eva Peron.

They did so without affection. Imelda never did receive the massive outpouring of adulation that Evita had inspired. Some put her closer to the former Shahbanu of Iran, a woman who claimed that her husband, the son of a plebeian usurper, was the embodiment of 2500 years of royalty. Imelda had been so anxious to impress her friendly rival the Shahbanu that during Iran's opulent 2500th anniversary celebration of its supposedly unbroken royal line she had taken to Persepolis,

uninvited, her entire retinue of cronies and crony wives, European royal pretenders, international beautiful people, celebri-
ties and Hollywood admirers.

Her luck had not held in England, where she had been
refused an invitation to the 1981 royal wedding that she had
once dreamed would feature her daughter Imee instead of
Lady Diana Spencer. But in June of 1983, at the very time
the regime was plotting how it would handle Ninoy's impend-
ing return, Imelda got what must have seemed her revenge.
In a *déluge-après-moi* atmosphere of abandon in the midst
of national economic collapse, she made the wedding of her
younger daughter, Irene, a full-blown state occasion. And for
this occasion she transformed the backwater birthplace of Ferdinand Marcos—and Fabian Ver—in such a way that no one,
whether those she called "my little people" or members of
the old elite she had envied, could fail to see what truly good
living meant.

It was not just the new international airport and the $10
million deluxe hotel, done in Spanish colonial style, that had
been rapidly constructed on her orders in this part of the
barren Ilocos provinces. It was not just that General Ver's
old home, like the homes of other relatives, had been torn
apart and then reconstructed to give the impression that the
chief of staff and various Marcos cousins had come from landed
gentry. The entire Marcos birthplace of Sarrat had almost
instantly been replaced with a town that could only have had
its origins in Imelda's imagination. She had made Sarrat, she
said, into a precise replica of a seventeenth-century Spanish
colonial town.

It was pure make-believe, since no historians recall any
such show of splendor in this part of Spain's old empire. No
historians hint that there were even towns here characterized
by comparable charm. But facts had never before gotten in
Imelda's way, and this time she topped herself.

The wedding guests found that Sarrat had all of a sudden

become a town made up of houses—some of them livable dwellings and some of them facades—that all fit Imelda's chosen motif. In addition to these European houses and facades that had pushed aside native huts, there was now elaborate landscaping all through Sarrat and especially along the mile-long route the imperial horse-drawn carriages of the bridal procession would take. Before the wedding day, workmen had stayed up all night to put papier-mâché blossoms on freshly planted flowering trees that had failed to bloom on schedule.

The center of town now was dominated by a great brick hall whose only designated function was for one-time use for the wedding reception. Because the new hotel and the newly created ancestral homes were overflowing with cronies and other members of the entourage, yet further accommodations had been provided. The members of the National Assembly had all been ordered to attend, and for them an ocean liner, with 500 luxury cabins, was anchored offshore.

The lowest estimates of the cost of the wedding were in the tens of millions of dollars. Information Minister Greg Cendaña, seeming more harried than usual, refused to reveal the true cost of what Imelda had done but admitted that the Philippine government had "contributed." He would not talk at all, however, about the recent international bailout loans or Marcos's recent cry for an austerity program.

Daughter Irene, a shy, pretty twenty-two-year-old whose main interest was music, was of course given away by her father the dictator. They went together to the old Santa Monica Church, built centuries ago by Spanish friars, in a silver carriage from Austria drawn by a team of seven white horses that had been flown in from Morocco.

Like all momentous events in the New Republic, everything that went on in Sarrat that day was directed with care to be shown live, and then repeated over and over, on national television. The groom, Gregorio "Greggy" Araneta III, twelve years Irene's senior and scion of the sort of old-money Manila family that used to snub the Marcoses, came first to the church and was shown there on TV, waiting for Irene's entrance with her father.

The old church is not large, but wide-angle lenses were used by the government television crews, who got their cameras to the highest rafters. We saw the version of the wedding that was shown on Philippine television. The elaborately decked-out flower girls and train bearers, the sponsors and ushers, the dazzling guests from so many different worlds, were all made to seem part of a panorama comparable to what had been seen two years earlier in London. Clever camera work gave the modest friars' church the illusion that it had been built on the proportions of St. Paul's Cathedral.

Later in 1983, after the turmoil touched off by Aquino's murder, Imelda announced that she was, for the moment at least, giving up such ostentation. She was, she said, canceling the Third Manila International Film Festival, scheduled for January 1984.

The question of the film festival had inspired a Filipino in-joke in the daily protest marches that Imelda's suddenly emboldened subjects were conducting. It seemed as if everyone was wearing Aquino T-shirts, the most common one featuring a picture of Aquino above his pet name "NINOY" and the Tagalog words for "You are not Alone." Now some of the braver marchers had taken to wearing a T-shirt that on the front had the words "MARCOS, You are not Alone," and on the back a picture of George Hamilton.

"Dear George," as she called him, Imelda's favorite dancing partner and the inspiration of her film festivals, had long been the center of gossip that would probably have been unprintable even in the old days when the Manila press was free and free-wheeling. During the 1983 festival, she told an interviewer that Marcos had drawn her attention to a newspaper that had "a full page picture with George Hamilton and I dancing away."

"In fact," she said, "last night it was a disaster" because

they had been dancing in her Malacañang disco "right in front of the President. Poor George, I pulled him to the dance floor because, first of all, we dance so beautifully together. I like dancing with people who are perfect dancers, and he's neither too tall, nor too short, too fat or too thin. You know I am tall. It was so much fun. I really don't mind the newspapers because in the end, it's one's conscience. My conscience is clear and God can take me any time."

She went on to say that some years back she had discussed all this with Pope Paul VI just before he died, telling him that "God is love, and I know I have loved, [therefore] I'll go to heaven." The Pope had been moved, she said, and replied, "Oh, how childlike, how wonderful."

But whatever the state of Imelda's conscience, and whatever the real nature of her relationships with foreign men and women with whom gossip linked her, it was her spending in the face of poverty that had made her the regime's most unpopular member. She had kept 8000 shift workers busy twenty-four hours a day to get the Parthenon replica on Manila Bay ready for her First Manila International Film Festival, set for early 1982. In the haste, thirty-five workmen were killed when a wall collapsed on them, but the rest hardly missed a beat in the frenzy to finish on time. An urban guerrilla group, protesting the expense at a time when Manila's slum poverty was worse than ever, had threatened to blow the marble structure up, with the result that many guests, including Charlton Heston and Ali McGraw, begged off. A group of French stars, including Jeanne Moreau, sent back their invitations, then advertised in a French magazine to say how misplaced such spectacles were in a land where the poor were getting poorer.

Hollywood producer Michael Viner, who was at the 1983 festival, told us how prostitutes were thrust upon him in hotel lobbies where festival people stayed. He also told how production equipment had disappeared as it passed through customs when he had made a movie in the Philippines. H. Gray Fred-rickson, Jr., the co-producer of *Apocalypse Now*, told us of the "million dollars that went down the drain in bribes" a few years earlier when that movie was being made in the country. A well-known Hollywood columnist described the lavish attention heaped on her at Imelda's order during the 1983 festival, and said that when she left and read the non-Philippine newspapers on the plane, her reaction was, "My God, we were reading about a murder here, an execution there, and tomorrow it's a hundred people more in prison."

In the midst of the 1982 festival, a family crisis took place that grew into a state crisis. It was revealed that in December 1981 Imelda's older daughter, Imee, whom many had consid-ered the heir apparent to the dynasty the Marcoses thought they were founding, had secretly married a thirty-two-year-old Manila playboy and amateur sportsman, Tommy Manotoc, in Arlington, Virginia. The trouble with Manotoc was that he had just been divorced in America—divorce still not being recognized in the Philippines—from a celebrated beauty queen who had also, it was rumored, been a friend of the President's. The couple came back to Manila. Just before the festival, Manotoc disappeared.

Manilans thought they had seen the last of him, but forty-two days later came the announcement he had been rescued from "Communist terrorists." At a press conference, flanked by Ver and Enrile, Manotoc gave a sketchy, coached account of how he had been held in the mountains until his captors, surprised by government soldiers, fled after a gunfight and left him behind. He refused to say more.

This real-life melodrama of sex, power and violence was the high point of their stay for the Hollywood visitors. Pro-ducer Viner said the consensus was that Marcos had ordered Manotoc kidnapped in order to keep Imelda from murdering him.

Among the many versions of what had happened to Manotoc, the one nobody believed was that he had been kidnapped by the New People's Army. The NPA had never used such tactics, in fact had stated often it was against them since kidnappings of innocent people always brought discredit on the kidnappers.

Whatever had really happened, the Manotoc affair was a blow to Marcos and Imelda. They only had three children. Irene had always foresworn public life, concentrating on her musical studies. The son, Ferdinand "Bong Bong" Marcos, Jr., had been put in charge of the Marcoses' Ilocos Norte Province, but he was mainly an absentee governor; he had never undertaken any major government project, had dropped out of school, and seemed to have no aspirations to power. Only Imee, who had headed the New Society's youth movement and constantly appeared in public inaugurating First Lady uplift projects, had seemed to have the ability and the will to carry on the dynasty the Marcoses wanted to create—and now, as one who knew her said, "she had given it all up for love."

The most commonly accepted version of the affair was the one the Hollywood crowd spread—that Marcos himself had had the kidnapping staged in order to protect the young sportsman until Imelda cooled off. Imelda's rage when she could not get her way was something with which Filipinos had long been familiar.

They were put in mind of how she had acted that time before martial law was in effect, after the famous Dovie Beams tape was played at rallies and on the campus radio station. The tape—which carried the love groans and gasps, Dovie said, of herself and Marcos—had been made for the purpose of self-protection. Events proved she had not been overly cautious. After she had made her self-publicized exit from the country, both the caretaker of the house Marcos had set her up in and a man who had acted as a go-between for them turned up murdered. Much later several people we talked with in Manila told us how Imelda had angrily showed them nude photos she had found of Dovie Beams.

Such high jinks in the First Family were a constant source of amusement to Filipinos, but they also contributed to the mounting hatred for the regime. Sexual escapades at the top were not unusual in the islands, but they became something else in view of the new sex scene that had developed at the bottom after the dictatorship took everyone's legal protections away.

A reporter who talked with children working the area told how Imelda had responded to a piece in a European magazine about a child prostitute in the downtown Ermita district. The little girl had actually been taken to the palace in 1982, the children said. She had been berated by Imelda herself, who kept saying, "You are dishonoring our country." Then the girl was set free. She turned up at her old stand. But after several police beatings she had disappeared from Ermita, the other children said, and no one knew whether or where she was now practicing her trade.

What was going on in Ermita could be seen by anyone. Such activities, of course, had gone on in secret before, as they do in any very large city. But this open child prostitution scene, which had burst forth in Ermita in 1981, the year the regime had begun to dispense with cosmetics in many areas, could not have existed without a wide range of officials, from local police up to the all-seeing Metropolitan Command of the Constabulary and the Ver intelligence apparatus, knowing about it. Still, what most upset government officials was not that it existed but that it was brought to light by the foreign press.

One of the most conservative and moral members of the administration, the technocrat Placido L. Mapa, Jr., minister of economic planning, a member of the conservative international Opus Dei Catholic society, told one of us in a long and friendly session that child prostitution worried him. It was a sign of moral decay. But when he was reminded that almost all of the customers present in Ermita were foreigners—which seemed to say something about the nature of the dictatorship's tourism program—he began speculating that maybe we had been mistaken and had actually seen Filipinos. What the child prostitution problem came down to, Mapa then concluded, was "that there seems to be a press conspiracy against us."

Mapa, like some other ministers we saw in 1983, including even the venerable Carlos P. Romulo—who to everyone's surprise had continued his tradition even during the martial law period of serving every Philippine President—was gentlemanly, urbane and highly intelligent on just about every subject that came up except anything that hinted there was something askew with the people in Malacañang. We found that every minister had a set piece to insert somewhere in any interview about how Marcos was cool and brilliant, and how the warm and intuitive Imelda provided a perfect balance.

The Mapa interview took place just after we had seen Imelda's royal Manila Bay edifices and such other of her constructions as the University of Life and the skyscraper that housed a discotheque. This was also the time, in 1983, when we had just had a close look at the fetid slums, the torn-up, garbage-strewn streets, and the new downtown hard-core sex scene in this once very different city of which Imelda was now governor. With a perfectly straight face Mapa was able to say he had just heard a piece of good news: "The First Lady has announced she's done enough for Manila and now she's going out to fix up the provinces."

One area where Imelda had already set foot in the provinces had been in the cities outside the Subic and Clark bases, where she had taken personal charge, as Minister of Human Settlements, of all development projects, which in most cases meant she was getting her hands on U.S. economic aid funds. These funds, being spent at the rate of about $100 million a year, were often earmarked for improving the areas used by

American airmen and sailors for fun. In virtually every country in the world where there are American bases, there is the usual array of brothels, girlie bars, massage parlors and roaming pimps offering their virgin sisters. The difference in the Philippines was the scale—and the age of the bodies being offered.

At Olongapo outside the Subic Bay base, where an average of 6000 American sailors headed into town looking for a good time each night, the number of licensed establishments selling sex, by official city count, was more than 350, and many more functioned without licenses. The city fathers' own figures had 8 percent of the 200,000 citizens of Olongapo as prostitutes. Inside Subic, U.S. Navy authorities told a reporter that the VD rate here was higher than at any American base in the world.

Recently a criminal case had been brought against an American petty officer, Daniel Dougherty, Jr., for running a child prostitution business in Olongapo. Although Marcos had said that under his regime Americans would always be tried in Philippine courts for crimes committed in the Philippines, Dougherty was hustled out of the country and tried by American court-martial in Guam. He was found guilty of thirteen counts of carnal abuse. The thirteen girls with whom he had had sex himself ranged in age from twelve to fifteen, and other members of their group were as young as nine.

These girls had come to the notice of Philippine authorities when two of them wandered into a health clinic and were found to have all the major veneral diseases at once—gonorrhea, syphilis and herpes. The authorities tried to keep the story quiet, but an Irish missionary, Father Shay Cullen, who ran a drug rehabilitation clinic, heard about it from some of the girls and went public. He began to receive death threats in the mail, which he showed us. At the same time foreign free-lance reporters who had lingered in Manila after writing about child prostitution there were slapped with criminal libel suits, sometimes by the military. As with the court actions concerning the political detainees, these cases dragged on. With hearings constantly postponed, the reporters did not get a chance to tell their stories in the Philippine courts.

The reporters periodically returned to Manila's Ermita sex scene. The most frequent line they heard from the children was how they preferred, in any of the sexual combinations being offered, an "all night" to a "short time," because it meant they would not have to sleep in the streets or in the slum homes many were supporting with their earnings.

The people who lived in those slums, where we saw the pictures of the Reagans and Marcoses together in formal attire, sometimes got to see Imelda herself, driving through in a stretch Cadillac limousine, wearing her jewels. "I am my little people's star and slave," she frequently told interviewers in statements so identical they must have been rehearsed and memorized. "When I go out in the barrios, I get dressed up because I know the little people want to see a star. Other Presidents' wives have gone to the barrios wearing house dresses and slippers." Impoverished people, she said, needed only to be embraced in "cradles of humanity, the generators and repositories of the human body, and the sanctuaries of the spirit of man."

When the government set out to address the problems of the urban poor more concretely, Imelda's Ministry of Human Settlements opted for treating slum dwellers not as people who needed food and medicine but as people who comprised an eyesore. Imelda's "slum clearance project," officially begun in 1982 but actually underway years earlier, remained linked to "beautification." Although precise figures were lacking, the human rights lawyers and nuns estimated some 100,000 Manilans had been evicted, their shacks demolished, during preparations for the 1974 Miss Universe Pageant. Another 60,000 were sent packing in 1976, the year the convention center and thirteen luxury hotels went up just in time for a World Bank–International Monetary Fund conference. In 1979, more slum people were moved out in advance of a United Nations Conference on Trade and Development for which the government imported more than 200 Mercedes-Benz sedans and limousines for the delegates' use.

In 1982, when demolition of slum shanties was officially announced, the poor began fighting back, building barricades to block the demolition crews and throwing rocks and bottles. The military appeared ready to fight if the people did not disperse. In the face of armed might the demonstrators stopped. With great fanfare Imelda ordered many four-story housing projects for, she said, resettling the dislocated people and "brightening their lives."

The rents were set, however, so that no slum dwellers could afford the projects. The main aim was still slum clearance for appearances. It was at this point that the shanty towns around the airport, which had been visible to all arriving foreigners, were demolished.

In 1983 in the Leveriza slum located south of Ermita, one of us learned at first hand the story of what had happened to a particular family uprooted the year before. Federico Adones and his wife, Gorgonia, had been ordered out of their shack and had been taken with their six children to Cavite, on Manila Bay south of the city, where thousands more had been resettled on Imelda's orders. The Adoneses quickly discovered what they had suspected: there was no means for making a living in Cavite. Soon they, like most of the others, had straggled back to another Manila slum quarter, where they built a cardboard and wooden hut against a stone wall located beside a still-water canal filled with human waste. The hut was too small to hold the Adones family all at once, so the six children slept by day, while the parents sold cigarettes, one "stick" at a time, to motorists stalled in traffic—their means of livelihood before they were banished from the city and still the only one they knew.

Federico, who had been coughing blood, died a few days after their return to Manila. As soon as Gorgonia had arranged for the disposal of the body, one of the children died. At a government clinic, which the Adoneses had avoided because the attendant demanded money for the supposedly free services, she was told the child had had meningitis. Nuns who worked among the poor of Leveriza told us the authorities always gave meningitis as the cause of infant deaths, even when it was clearly malnutrition. Gorgonia Adones stayed on, selling cigarettes in the streets, joined by the oldest child, and the family continued to live by the canal.

The way people were moved from the slums with no provision made for their livelihood exposed the regime as not being above trafficking in human flesh in order to pursue its ends, which ultimately amounted to nothing more than the enrichment and glorification of Manila's new superclass. Using child prostitution to attract any sort of foreigners in order for the rulers to make money on tourism was another example. Eventually prostitution became such an integral part of tourism— the only way to fill up the hotels the cronies owned—that the most typical form of organized travel to the Philippines became the literal sex tour.

There had been fads for such tours—German groups going to Bangkok, Japanese groups going to a health spa outside Taipei—in other countries of the region. But in other countries this was merely a sidelight to tourism's mainstream. Those countries built their hotels to keep up with increased tourism, whereas in the Philippines the rulers had to find ways to increase tourism after the hotels were built. Imelda established grandiose new consulates and embassies—such as the building in New York where Doris Baffrey had worked—in major cities all over the world to lure visitors to her islands. But because too many hotels had been built, and then urban terror had caused the cancellation of conventional tours to the Philippines, the sex tour became central to the country's whole tourism program.

The male tourists had at first come mostly from Japan, but the emphasis was switching to Australia and Western nations as even the Japanese sex tours slowed in the 1980s. In addition to the price for meals, food and transportation, the fee for the sex part of the sex tours, paid in advance, came to about $10 a day.

A new kind of establishment appeared that was neither bar, nightclub nor massage parlor, simply a vast room in which scores of girls, wearing numbers on their blouses, waited for the tour buses. The men from the buses would make their selections there, then return to their hotels, and the girls would be delivered later. Thousands of girls were taking part. Although prostitution was technically illegal—an absurd bit of hypocrisy in any time in this part of Southeast Asia—the sex tour girls were given health certificates by the city government.

The money was spread from the foreign tour operators to the Philippine tour operators to the girls and their pimps and madams. Sister Mary Soledad Perpinan, a Filipina nun, found that one Japanese tour operator used brothels in five different parts of Manila. At any one time there were 2000 to 3000 girls waiting with their numbers specifically for these Japanese. Because of publicity given to the Japanese trade, Japan Air Lines, which had increased its flights, decreased them for a time. The Ministry of Tourism began offering special deals to Japanese men who came to Manila with their wives and families. But soon the traffic was back to single men again. Regular groups began to arrive from Australia, the biggest operation being the one called the "Randy Rams." Even as far away as the Scandinavian countries and Germany, sex tours to the Philippines were being organized.

One Australian tour branched out and began busing its members to Olongapo next to Subic Bay and to Angeles City next to Clark Air Base. The men were taken to bars where they gathered around while a woman performed oral sex on one of the members as a free sample and advertisement of what was available. At other times, two women would appear and take turns performing their sample acts on the selected customer while the others watched.

Homosexual tour packages were also set up. These groups were usually taken to the resort of Pagsanjan, in a scenic tropical gorge with a white-water river and dramatic waterfalls, three hours' drive from Manila. In 1983, a church group estimated that some 5000 young Filipinos were at work as male prostitutes at the resort town.

But members of the government continued to discuss the new organized sex scene purely in terms of the bad publicity the country was receiving. Everything was image. A bad image meant press conspiracy. "Beautification" and grandeur meant a good image. Beyond railing against the prostitutes themselves, Imelda did not have time to give the matter her attention.

An example of the sort of thing that could hold Imelda's attention came to light in 1979 when people saw soldiers guarding a construction site that, strange though it seemed, was located on the leveled top of a mountain just east of Manila. No mention was made in the controlled media of what was going on, but this, it turned out, was the site of the basilica Imelda planned to build in honor of her twenty-fifth wedding anniversary. Foundation holes forty-six feet square were being dug on the leveled site in a circle more than a quarter of a mile around. The planned Basilica of the Holy Infant was to be topped by a dome 10 stories high and 450 feet in diameter, shaped like a Philippine peasant's straw hat. Imelda had said she expected Pope John Paul II to come here to preside as she and Ferdinand restated their wedding vows, an old Philippine custom. It all smacked of how a Pope had once gone to Napoleon for his coronation.

Cardinal Sin moved fast to bring her plans to a halt. "To put up a basilica while people are starving is not very Christian," he told the foreign press, and he sent angry letters to the contractors involved telling them the money should go to the poor. Imelda jetted to Rome to get Sin overruled, but she was turned down at the Vatican.

Yet, as we saw in 1983, with her cultural centers, elite clinics, antiacademic university, skyscrapers, hotels and convention center, Imelda did seem to have accomplished what she had said she would do: build a grandiose new "City of Man" that would last forever. At the same time, she had kept on adding from the public treasury to her personal possessions. After the basilica project fell through she was off to New York to start her annual Thanksgiving orgy of shopping. A *New York Post* columnist noted with fascination that year that she picked out a diamond necklace at Van Cleef & Arpels and paid for it with $1 million in cash. She used three floors at the Waldorf for ten days at $6000 a day, gave hundreds in tips to bellboys, sent $30,000 worth of flowers to UN delegates. Often the shopping became even more frivolous. In Honolulu, where she had had a department store closed to the public for use by herself and her entourage, she at one point paid tens of thousands of dollars for clothing she did not bother to try on. The dollars she used in payment were usually neatly bundled used bills, as in mob transactions.

Some of the shopping was for gifts to foreigners. "The chic thing to do just now," according to the *New York Daily News* "Suzy" column several years after the coup, "is to nip off to Manila to visit Madame Imelda Marcos who practically flings Philippine pearls to her friends." Palace guests "get to keep everything they find in their closet." *Cosmopolitan* included her among the ten richest women in the world, the only one from Asia, and said it was rumored she was at the top of the list. "Meldy is a charter member of the Jet Set, a long-time bosom buddy of Cristina Ford's, always favored couture by Dior and international shopping sprees at such outposts as Bergdorf's and I. Magnin's," *Cosmo* added. "[She] thinks nothing of flying her chums half way around the globe

when she's in a party mood. . . . And when Meldy travels—
to Washington, Osaka, Grosse Pointe, Persepolis—it's always
with [lots] of dear dear friends for diversion [and lots] of bodyguards to protect her from the enemy."

After she gave up trying to make a match of Imee and
Prince Charles—an undertaking begun when she and the
prince attended the same function in Nepal—she redecorated
a part of Malacañang to look like a throne room, where she
and her husband would appear sitting on the raised golden
chairs that had become familiar to the Philippines' television
viewers.

Back in 1965, on the night Marcos won the election that
made him President, Presy Lopez, later Psinakis, was present
at their home. She came upon Imelda in front of a mirror.
The new First Lady was watching herself make stiff motions
of greeting with her right arm. "How does she do it?" Imelda
wanted to know. "How does the Queen of England wave?"

From the start as First Lady, she kept around her many
of the wealthiest women in the country, whom she made wear
very plain blue dresses in contrast to her own costly gowns.
"Note the symbolism," said Ninoy Aquino. "Blue is for 'blue
blood.' "

Her jewel collection was legend. A former woman friend
of Imelda told us how back in 1967 she had visited Imelda's
palace dressing room and "there was an old Spanish-style
chest, and in the top were sectioned dividers." Although the
New People's Army later made much of an American magazine photograph that showed her with one particular diamond
rosary, the friend said that in each section of this chest "were
different rosaries, *all* made of precious gems. There was not
one but several diamond rosaries and others of emeralds, ru-
bies, sapphires. The larger 'Our Father' beads on the diamond
rosaries . . . were cut in several designs. Some of them were
heart-shaped."

Her jewels came from all over the world. The diamond

tiara she wore at state functions was, friends said, the biggest they had ever seen. Presy said that in 1966 Imelda boasted to the "Blue Ladies" that she was already rich, and marched them into a room in the Palace where they watched as she "pulled out from a metal filing cabinet one drawer after another" filled with gems. "She just wanted the Blue Ladies to know she had this from the beginning."

What she had before the coup was, of course, a fraction of what she got her hands on afterward. Inside the Philippines the Marcoses had many mansions, resorts, and private islands, but the biggest acquisitions were abroad. A close relative of Imelda's said he had, purely out of curiosity, with no criticism intended, counted up the houses, ranches, and apartment and commercial buildings bought by Imelda on four continents by the 1980s. The total of major pieces of property outside the Philippines came to forty-four.

In the New York area, according to *New York* magazine in 1983, the Marcoses had a Long Island mansion, an Upper East Side townhouse, an apartment building on Park Avenue, and an office building in the East Fifties. The magazine also noted a "huge farm" in Virginia, two more commercial buildings in London, more property outside London, office buildings in Hong Kong, and property in Australia.

It did not take a trained psychologist to deduce that—all her protestations to the contrary—Imelda did not come from wealth originally. In her own statements and in official biographical sketches about her, she was always "an aristocrat," even, in her own words, one who had come from the "oligarchy." Actually she was the offspring of an unsuccessful Manila lawyer, Vicente Orestes Romualdez.

By the time Imelda was born, on July 2, 1929, the servants had moved out because they had not been paid. The house was mortgaged. Then her mother, having quarreled with the children of her husband's first wife, moved with her own children to a converted garage, where Imelda spent her first years.

In 1938 Vicente Orestes Romualdez, widowed again and deeper in debt than ever, took all of his eleven children back to Leyte in the Visayas to the family's hometown of Tacloban, where they wound up living in a one-room country hut.

Imelda moved back to Manila in her early twenties, now a tall, striking young woman, arriving with about two dollars in her purse. She lived almost as a servant in the home of a wealthy uncle and worked as a salesgirl in a music store and later as a bank clerk.

In 1953 she got her first taste of celebrity as a disputed beauty queen. Judges of the Miss Manila contest gave the title to someone else. Imelda protested, claiming the judging was unfair, and was eventually awarded another title, "Muse of Manila."

This was as far as she had gone until she met Congressman Marcos, whom she married after an eleven-day courtship. Her life story became well known. It was recounted in detail in a largely sympathetic biography, *The Untold Story of Imelda Marcos,* published in Manila in 1969 by the journalist Carmen Navarro Pedrosa. Just after martial law was enacted the book was banned. Mrs. Pedrosa, then in London, was warned by friends not to return; there was an order out for her arrest. In 1983, still living in London, Mrs. Pedrosa described to us how after the coup, "Our house and that of our immediate relatives were raided and searched for alleged 'subversive manuscripts.' "

In her book Mrs. Pedrosa told in detail the same story we heard from Presy Lopez Psinakis, about how Imelda had said she could not adjust to the new world she had entered as a powerful congressman's wife. Early in the marriage she had a mental collapse. Marcos sent her to New York, where she underwent intensive analysis for three months. She came out of the treatment a changed woman, now starting to invent her story of an aristocratic upbringing and eventually moving with ease in circles of power. But Presy said she had never lost her inferiority complex. On a campaign swing through the Visayas when Imelda introduced Presy to a Romualdez cousin who was governor of Leyte, the future First Lady went away with "a smirk on her face." She told Presy how "members of my family have always looked down on me," and "those people are going to pay"—as the governor did, being replaced with Imelda's brother Kokoy after the coup.

Presy related how Imelda lorded it over the Blue Ladies, telling them, "See what I have done to all of you rich girls, all spoiled brats of Manila?" Presy said Imelda often told the Blue Ladies with glee about lowly tasks she was going to give them "and watch all your hands bleed."

But in 1983 Imelda told Ina Ginsburg, who was writing for Andy Warhol's *Interview* magazine, that the Blue Ladies were her "childhood friends," enlisted because she was comfortable with them, "especially since they came from prominent families."

She adopted the *terno,* the old butterfly-wing Spanish dress worn in colonial times, and had versions of it made for her by Paris designers, while still keeping her Blue Ladies in simple uniforms and placing lithe young girls selected purely for looks before them in the long train that followed her when she entered a room.

But there was more to her flamboyant style than a desire to humiliate others. Everyone with whom we talked who knew her, from her ghostwriters and privileged members of the Ministry of Human Settlements to bitter enemies of the regime, said she really believed what she said about her people wanting someone to look up to who was clearly their superior. When she, like others in Malacañang, got on the subject of what should be done about poverty, they sounded as if they had been guided by the same right-wing think tanks that had given the Reaganites their rationale for destroying, rather than promoting, antipoverty programs. It was not difficult to imagine Imelda saying that people who had food stamps used them to buy vodka, or that those who patronized soup kitchens were merely saving money by getting a free meal.

She touched on the poverty question in December 1980, during the six hours she spent with Steve Psinakis, warning him that the opposition leaders had better bow to Marcos because if they didn't Reagan would, as he had told her already, go after them. At one point she told a story, which Psinakis wrote from his notes, that went as follows:

Steve, I understand my people better than anyone. I study them all the time and even conduct experiments. I want to give my people not only everything they need but also everything they want to make them the happiest people in the world. But I know I should not give it to them all at once; it must be gradual. I have actually tested this by conducting an experiment. Let me explain. I found a small barrio of about fifty to sixty families where the people were very poor and just struggling to survive. I studied their lives and habits. They would work all day in the fields, from grandparents to grandchildren, trying to provide for their mere existence. But you will be surprised. They were not unhappy people. It was a happy little community. They all loved and helped each other like one big family. They were content being busy. They also managed to enjoy themselves. Every Saturday night they would have their barrio fiesta—roast their pig, sing, dance and so forth. The crime rate in that barrio—theft, rape, murder and so forth—was way below the national average; crime was practically nonexistent.

Well! I thought this barrio was ideal for my experiment. I gave these people everything you can imagine. I gave them electricity; I gave them a complete water system with tap water in every house; I started a small industrial project where everyone would be employed at high wages; I built a school and sent them a teacher—the children were now at school instead of in the fields; I gave them almost everything they could ever expect to acquire in their whole lives. What do you suppose happened? Do you think they were happier now? On the contrary, they now had all these things and didn't know what to do with themselves and their time. They were jealous of each other—of who had the better TV or the better house; they started to fight and steal, even to kill each other. In a short time, this community changed from a group of the most peaceful, contented, hardworking people to a barrio with the highest crime rate in our country. You see what happens when you give immature children too much too soon? That is why we want to give our people as much as possible, but *gradually*.

In the second year after the coup her husband had noted with pride at a Central Bank ceremony that "Our country now has one of the lowest average wage levels in this part of the world." U.S. Department of Commerce figures six years later listed 48 cents an hour as the claimed average wage for workers in the Philippines, which was lower than that claimed for any place outside Africa. Then Minister of Industry Roberto Ongpin made it a point in a report to the World Bank to mention that Philippine wages were lower by almost half than those in Singapore, where the stated average was 95 cents. In Taiwan, another authoritarian place where the government could set wages as it pleased, it was 85 cents, and in Hong Kong, the world sweatshop capital, the Americans put the average at $1.41 an hour.

A major reason for keeping wages down was that in the last two years of Marcos's legal presidency, with chaos all through the islands, there had actually been *dis*investment in the Philippines. Marcos was determined to bring foreign money back. His policy was best illustrated by his establishment of special duty-free export zones for labor-intensive manufacturing where foreign firms found they could operate cheaper than anywhere else in Asia, even places that had similar zones.

By the 1980s there were zones set up on Luzon's Bataan peninsula, in the resort hill town of Baguio north of Manila, and down in the Visayas near Cebu City, and another was planned for Cavite just south of the capital. Salaries had not come close to keeping up with drastic inflation—meaning they had dropped. Instead of the standard eight-hour shift, overtime was almost always required. In a peculiar twist, it was paid at a rate substantially lower than that for regular time. And in any case, few workers in the zones were covered by the minimum wage. By law, all were classified as probationary workers or trainees for the first six months, working regular shifts for about 22 cents an hour. At the end of the six-month period the workers would routinely be laid off, perhaps allowed to start again on a probationary basis sometime in the future.

These zone workers, mostly women from peasant families, typically lived six to a 6-by-6-foot room. When disease broke out, the women tried to hide it, since illness meant suspension without pay. In the towns surrounding the zones the infant mortality rate had doubled, church workers said. When strikes broke out, the armed forces were called in. Men from the banned unions who went to the towns near the zones to organize, according to the nuns of the Task Force [on] Detainees organization, frequently became victims of salvaging. Meanwhile, inside the zones the scene was often something out of Dickens. At several plants at the Bataan zone, an employee going to the toilet had to hang a ring with a large piece of cardboard around her neck so that trips to the toilet would be discouraged. At one foreign textile plant the normal work hours in peak months were from seven in the morning to ten at night; at another factory there were frequently twenty-four-hour shifts. At a Philippine-Chinese-British company, thirty-hour "stay-in" shifts were imposed, with doors and windows locked to keep the employees from leaving. At a German shoe factory, the German production manager always wore a .45 automatic pistol on his hip when he went out on the factory floor.

The trafficking in human flesh reached its most startling proportions in making use of overseas labor. By the 1980s more than 200,000 Filipino workers were to be found in the Middle Eastern oil countries, the terms of their contracts making them virtually indentured servants. According to the government's Ministry of Labor, 1.7 million Filipinos temporarily resided abroad, having left to find jobs in order to send money home. Many were college graduates working as menials. These Filipino workers abroad were, by presidential decree, required to remit home 50 to 70 percent of their earnings, depending on the job, via Philippine banks. The 1.7 million were abroad for set periods of time and planned to go home. No one knew how many had left the Philippines for good, including most in America's Philippine community of an estimated 1.5 million.

The authorities were speaking of Filipinos and Filipinas as if they were products. A Labor Ministry official, Jonathan de la Cruz, talking about overseas workers, said, "I would say it's about to become, if it hasn't already, our number one export earner, replacing coconut oil and sugar."

This blithe attitude toward human lives, so closely associated with Imelda and her theories, plans and gestures, went on even as the regime began to lose its grip. In the wake of the Aquino assassination, the people's lot was rapidly getting still worse. With capital fleeing the country, there were drastic further devaluations of the currency in 1983 and 1984, which meant yet another plunge in real wages. With a drastic decrease in imports, the factories had no materials to keep operating, and so more than ever before unemployment soared. Imelda, in canceling her 1984 film festival, was acting as if she were concerned. She even, after the assassination, went so far as to cancel her annual late autumn world shopping tour. But on closer inspection, the more things seemed to change at Malacañang, the less they did change.

In late November and early December 1983, Filipinos in San Francisco spotted some familiar faces. It turned out that Irene Marcos Araneta and her bridegroom, Greggy, were in town. Although they were staying with Greggy's father, Gregorio Araneta, at his large home in the Marina district, and although the father had made his personal position clear by erecting a large picture of Ninoy Aquino in front of the house, it appeared that Irene had been sent as Imelda's proxy for the shopping trip.

That the trip meant business as usual seemed clear to knowledgeable San Francisco Filipinos who spotted still another familiar face, that of the man serving as Irene's chief of security. Acting personally as her close-in bodyguard was the son of Gen. Fabian Ver, Rexan Ver, an officer in his father's Presidential Security Command.

Like mother, like daughter. Like father, like son. When the end seemed near, the New Republic, despite the scale of the extravagance and the scale of the terror, could still look like nothing more than a shoddy little family story.

15

RUNNING AMOK: THE WAR TO COME

Last Chance in the Philippines

AND yet the story of the Marcoses and their General Ver had been so much more than the sort of story usually associated with pretentious people who run entire countries as private preserves. It was a bigger story because of what had existed in the islands before them, and what was likely to come when they were gone. Before the 1972 coup the 1200-mile-long Philippine archipelago was so far from being a banana republic that Filipinos and Filipinas commonly complained when it was referred to as a Third World nation.

Leading its region in education, setting the standards and trends in everything from health to finance to entertainment, the old Republic of the Philippines had seemed proof that a democratic system could both endure and promote progress in a region where participatory government was rare. It could not be forgotten that here, for the first time in modern history, the people of a large Southeast Asian nation had taken control of their own destinies and proceeded to move into the future with confidence, zest, and even a sense of style.

The old Republic had had its faults. There had been oligarchs; there had been graft; there had been bands of body-guards that practically constituted small private armies. There had been remnants of flaws from the colonial and Common-wealth periods when, although America as a nation put far more into the Philippines materially than it took out, individu-als had been able to operate like robber barons and racism had been in the air. Yet before Marcos it was ballots, not guns, that ultimately decided the main, and potentially fratricidal, disputes. Before him there had been rights, and a rule of law.

In retrospect it now seemed clearer than ever that by the early 1970s, with a highly nationalistic Constitutional Conven-tion meeting to rid the islands of the last vestiges of colonial-ism, there had been a good chance that reform would carry the day again as it had back when the system was challenged by the Communist Huks in the 1950s. The spirit of reform had seemed to be everywhere—in the activities of the new farmer and worker associations and student groups, and in the actions of the more liberal traditional politicians. The out-look for the lame duck Marcoses and their crowd may have seemed bleak before the 1972 coup; quite the opposite had been the outlook for their people.

And so no matter how many books came out of Malacañang later talking about such concepts as "revolution from the cen-ter" and "martial law with a smile," the change that came when dictatorship replaced democracy fooled no one for long. The introduction of political detention, then torture, outright murder, massacres and salvaging had meant that sooner or later everyone except some *tutas*, the tamest government lap dogs, would be touched directly or through family by the new terror.

That the far left should emerge as the most potent opposi-tion force in the country, that the Philippines of the 1980s should be the only nation in Asia with a growing Communist guerrilla rebellion, were the direct results of the degradation brought about by the dictatorship. And aside from the terror, the fact that this dictatorship was the only strongman regime in all of Asia that was increasing poverty made the true nature of the New Society and the New Republic impossible to ignore.

The encouragement of foreign-owned Dickensian factories and a foreign-dominated plantation economy were but symbols of what was going on. With the destruction of all institutions except the military, and the elevation of a new class whose corruption was encouraged by the regime, the dictatorship was consciously moving the country backward in time. And then there was a new factor: after the inauguration of Ronald Reagan it became increasingly difficult even for Philippine conservatives not to see American collusion in the transformation of a numerous and once free people into a populace more akin to the lower orders in tiny Latin tyrannies.

With the now vastly enlarged military, which had been established in the first place under American direction and still received American training and arms, the wars of Marcos could easily be linked in people's minds to the bullying of a superpower. People were suffering. People were dying. Political detention, as introduced in 1972, remained a fact of Philippine life—as did the political killings that increased so sharply from 1981 onward.

The trafficking in human flesh continued. Tied to it were the massive forced dislocations, as in hamleting, and dislocations whose purpose could as often be frivolous, a matter of cosmetics or of making way for imperial structures in which the superclass could revel. Whatever the reason for treating people like objects, putting them out of sight, killing them when they stood in the way, encouraging them to prostitute themselves, looking upon them as an export commodity, it came to seem that forces bigger than any that had been developed inside the islands lurked in the background.

Then came the assassination of the country's only truly charismatic political figure, Ninoy Aquino, who because of his long years defying Marcos from a solitary cell in a military jail was a hero even to those in opposition who disagreed with his politics. Until that moment on the tarmac of Imelda's Manila International Airport on August 21, 1983, the perceived reality had seemed the only reality for most people in the Philippines. With displays of support from Washington, the calculating dictator, the showy First Lady, the cronies and the uniformed men around them had seemed invincible. But now that the people had seen how the dictatorship would stop at nothing, and now that the system seemed to be collapsing as they watched, suddenly individuals of all political persuasions were taking risks of the sort you take when you feel you have nothing more to lose.

Nobody believed the official story that a known criminal, Rolando Galman—who, it came to light, had recently been released from prison into the custody of Air Force Col. Arthur Custodio, an intelligence officer on Ver's staff—was the assassin. No one believed Malacañang's claims that Galman was a Communist agent. When Galman's body was released to his mother many weeks later, and then the mother was joined by Aquino's mother in the funeral procession, people turned out in the streets hailing even Galman now as a national hero.

High military officers were telling foreigners in secret that what the Japanese journalist Kiyoshi Wakamiya said he saw while looking between the legs of security guards was true. And by now, as ordinary Filipinos and Filipinas began speaking openly against the dictatorship for the first time, some of the Filipino airport witnesses, either coming forward at home or giving interviews while under protection abroad, were saying it was clearly a soldier, not Galman, who had fired the shot that killed Ninoy just before other soldiers shot at Galman. They had Galman being driven to the scene in the airport security van, and standing, or being held, in front of, not behind, Ninoy, making it impossible for him to have been the killer. And meanwhile careful analysis, with the aid of audio technicians and electronics engineers, of the tapes made by the Japanese and ABC television crews turned up the voices of soldiers speaking, just before the first shot, the Tagalog words, "I'll do it! I'll do it!" and "Shoot him! Shoot him!"

The regime kept changing its story. One official version, in 1983, had Galman as a Communist member of the New People's Army; another, in 1984, presented him as a professional assassin in the employ of the conservative former senator Doy Laurel. But it was hard to find anyone, whether a man on the street or a government figure speaking in confidence, who did not consider it unthinkable that the events at the heavily guarded airport could have taken place without the knowledge, and against the wishes, of Marcos, Imelda, Ver and many more Malacañang regulars.

With the government so thoroughly discredited in everyone's eyes, people began running for cover. The technocrats who ran many of the ministries were letting it be known that they had not for a moment believed the Marcos stories about a Communist or Laurel plot against Aquino. Low- and middle-echelon officials were making their peace with various parts of the opposition. Many high officials submitted their resignations. Some were talked into staying on. But by early 1984 some had quit anyway, including the Philippines' best-known elder statesman, Carlos P. Romulo, who had been saying for years he wanted to retire from his largely figurehead post as Marcos's foreign minister, and Minister of Education Onofre D. Corpuz, a scholar who by his presence had given the regime a measure of respectability and who had crafted statements used by Malacañang to justify authoritarianism.

Outside the ranks of the cronies, the Ilocano officers and some *tutas,* it was becoming as difficult to find a diehard supporter of the dictatorship in the Philippines as it had been to find a self-proclaimed Nazi in Germany after the surrender. Although there had been public exhortations to "Love your

New Society," "Honor the citizen-soldier," and follow the maxim "One nation, one thought," and although in 1984 Marcos was suddenly claiming that in addition to his armed forces he could call upon a reserve of 1.4 million, fascist ideology had never caught on. By now it was only naked power exercised by regular soldiers on behalf of the dictatorship, not persuasion through cajolery, that the regime was falling back on. Included in the new attempts at intimidation were Marcos's claims in 1984 that almost the entire mainstream clergy and almost the entire business community were now in league with the Communists. Each week, it seemed, more units were being withdrawn from the field to protect Manila.

The squalid side of Manila now, in early 1984, looked more than ever like something out of nineteenth-century travelers' tales. The crowds of the unemployed got larger. Some avenues that as recently as just before the Aquino assassination had still been kept clean and clear of beggars now looked like old-time bazaars, filled with mothers holding starving babies and people squatting on sidewalks and curbs trying to sell trinkets as others pawed through garbage.

When the government was found to be lying to its creditors about the size of its rapidly disappearing reserves of foreign currency, one of the most respected of the technocrats, Jaime Laya, was made the scapegoat and fired from his position as governor of the Central Bank. But the silliness that all along had characterized the regime almost as much as its brutality continued. Laya, it was announced at Malacañang Palace, was being promoted to a new catchall position as "Minister of Education, Culture, and Sports."

To help save the economy, Marcos announced, he was ordering postponement of completion of a recently begun Imelda-style project—the transformation of a mountain outside the resort town of Baguio into the Philippine equivalent of Mount Rushmore. The scaffolding was left standing on a 50-foot-high concrete bust of the dictator near the Marcos

Park Golf Course along the Marcos Highway—a bust meant to look more heroic than those of American presidents carved into Mount Rushmore since the concrete eyes of the dictator were actually above the peak looking down on the links.

But it was not silly ministries and silly Imelda projects that constituted the people's most immediate concerns. It was, rather, the increasing despair that sharply increasing poverty was bringing on in a country that military-backed dictatorship had already taken from the top to the bottom of the heap in Southeast Asia.

To many Filipinos looking to Washington it appeared many months after the Aquino assassination that the change in the Philippines had hardly been noticed on the highest levels. To Filipinos it must have seemed as if the men who controlled Washington were as inscrutable as Westerners supposedly found Orientals. The men who were in power there were, after all, the same men who had first openly blessed the dictatorship in the name of America and of democracy. More and more State Department officials were saying off the record that it seemed certain the Philippines would be the site of America's next foreign policy disaster, but the men at the top in Washington did not seem to be listening. And inside the Philippines yet more and more of the 53 million people were coming to look upon the Americans in the same way they looked upon the people in Malacañang.

And so, early in 1984, although Ambassador Armacost was making snide remarks about the Marcoses, although other Reagan emissaries were going through the motions of asking the regime to loosen up, although Reagan went to the Far East again and again by-passed Manila, the popular feeling against America grew more widespread. Those simultaneously real and symbolic pictures of the Reagans and the Marcoses smiling together could not be easily erased from the Filipino consciousness.

Before the killing the outlook for reconciliation rather than increased violence had not been bright. Now the last chances were fading away. Ninoy, although he had considered death at the airport unlikely, had thought his bid to talk Marcos into holding peaceful elections constituted "a long shot." He had seen as more likely other post-Marcos scenarios: a short-lived government of moderates, a seizure of power by some-one, probably Imelda, whom the military would eventually make a scapegoat, then an outright seizure of power by the generals and civil war, very likely resulting finally in the tri-umph of the far left.

There were still prominent and visible figures working hard for democracy. In San Francisco Steve and Presy Psi-nakis—like the publisher Alex Esclamado and his wife Lourdes—were blurry-eyed from their mammoth, largely suc-cessful effort to make certain the world held the people in Malacañang Palace directly accountable for Ninoy's death. And while Ninoy's widow, Corazon "Cory" Cojuangco Aquino, and his businessman brother, Agapito, known as "Butz," worked hard for the overthrow of the dictatorship from inside the Philippines, other members of his family worked equally hard from abroad.

Two of Ninoy's most trusted colleagues were younger sis-ters who had gone into exile. One of them, Tessie, the wife of a construction executive, Len Oreta, was nominally a house-wife, but she had served as confidant and go-between for Ni-noy for years, and her husband had been with her brother to handle security as he had darted about Asia, trying to keep ahead of possible government assassins, just before his return. The other sister, Lupita, now a TV producer in San Francisco, had been the Philippines' leading and best known television and movie director, as much a celebrity in the islands as her brother. During his years in jail, she had handled his relations with the foreign press in Manila, and represented him on the stump to try to get his message across in the course of Marcos's rigged elections. Her husband, Ken Kashiwahara, the American television correspondent, was the man who had

traveled with Ninoy in a private capacity as the family's representative on his last flight home. Lupita, noted for her energy
and endurance as well as her sparkling style, now redoubled
her efforts to try to see that the ideals Ninoy died for would
one day be put into practice through democratic politics in
the Philippines. Just as conservative and moderate opposition
figures in Manila, such as the former senators Salvador Laurel
and José Diokno, were stepping up their efforts, so too were
their counterparts who lived now in America—either increasing their activities in the United States or planning their own
return home to try to bring order out of the chaos into which
the country was falling. There were, naturally, fresh rumors
in Manila, such as that Defense Minister Enrile was to be
overthrown internally.

The exile representatives of the far left—communicating
with the Communist Party of the Philippines, the National
Democratic Front and the New People's Army—were also
working around the clock in America, as were their counterparts underground in the Philippines. Having striven for many
years to build what was now by far the most potent opposition
force in the islands—a fact still undetected by much of the
foreign press—they were being extremely careful, abroad as
at home, with their public statements. But they, like the moderates and conservatives, saw the collapse of the dictatorship;
they were not, if they could by any means avoid it, going to
let anyone seize control of what they knew in their hearts
was their own revolution.

Aquino himself had been conciliatory toward the militant
left, always staying in touch. Shortly before going back he
had said to Philippine leftist leaders in America that "the first
thing I will do if I ever become President is legitimize you
guys. You're going to be allowed your freedom. Amnesty for
all. Only one condition: don't pick up the gun. The moment
you pick up the gun I'm government, and I will hound you
worse than Marcos does."

But not long before, José Maria Sison, the jailed Communist

Party Chairman, had said at Fort Bonifacio that, although still willing to participate in a coalition, he was not willing to see the New People's Army disbanded. He had said that "without an army like the NPA the people have nothing. They have a few seats in a reactionary parliament. And to have no army in our country is to play a fool's game."

Who would win out in a government that included both moderates and Communists seemed to many to have become a question of purely academic interest with the killing of Aquino. His death, despite the forceful leadership provided by his previously retiring widow, Cory, and by his previously nonpolitical younger brother, Butz, and despite the new daring displayed by pre–martial law politicians, seemed likely to preclude a moderate solution on the old American model. It also seemed to preclude anything except a steady worsening of the old Philippine-American relationship.

Ninoy had spoken often of the leverage America could exert, since it had control of the money the Philippines needed to borrow to pay its mounting international debts and keep functioning. Even this issue became fuzzed after his killing, as foreign businessmen began to flee the islands, nearly all Filipinos with money worked out their escape routes, and most of the wealthiest immediately transferred their funds out of the country.

Just as few Filipinos believed there could have been martial law in the first place without some sort of consent from Washington, few believed Malacañang would have dared allow the Aquino assassination had any American in authority told Marcos to guarantee his rival's physical safety. Ninoy had described how in the Reagan years when he went to Washington, "I argue myself blue in the face. When you have a hard-nosed conservative who believes it's better to be dead than red, the only way to talk to a red is with guns, you're in bad shape." He spoke of how Marcos "had played this to the hilt. When he talks to Americans like Reagan, he tells them 'I'm the only one who can contain Communism in Asia. All these guys are fellow travelers. They're all pinkos. They're all liberals. I'm the only guy who can hold back the red tide and I did what I did precisely so I could check the red menace.' "

After Ninoy's death, Guy Pauker of the conservative Rand Corporation think tank, which had frequently done reports for the U.S. government warning of the dangers of embracing Marcos and keeping the bases in his country, said he had found that Reagan's State Department had not been taking Ninoy seriously. He said, "I think that if the United States government would treat opposition leaders in countries such as our old friend and former colony the Philippines the way we treat opposition leaders in Western countries . . . perhaps a leader like Aquino would not have felt that he had prematurely to rush back to his country to see what he can do. He would have been able to wait it out and let the political process take a normal course."

Former Senator Raul Manglapus, the anti-Communist middle-of-the-road reformer, put it much more strongly: "I point an accusing finger straight at the United States. Their support made repression and murder possible. Now they have to devise something very creative to withdraw the support."

There were no signs of such creativity, despite fresh information that was coming to America. An American group was sent to the Philippines to investigate the human rights situation on behalf of several scientific and medical organizations and reported that it was becoming worse as 1983 ended. So too did, among others, an investigatory delegation from the New York–based Lawyers Committee for International Human Rights, and the Geneva-based International Commission of Jurists. Malacañang denounced all such reports, issued statements saying Philippine human rights workers, from wealthy lawyer to brave nun, were all "in league with the Communists," and ordered military officers never to say a word to American investigators.

But it no longer mattered what the officials responsible for the terror and the degradation said, or whether they spoke at all. With the rulers staying out of public, with major commerce coming to a halt, with the people out in the streets again, what was most important was that a popular challenge had been made to Malacañang for the first time since the coup. It was something like a death watch as the people waited for the next response.

The old Malay phenomenon of running amok had not been limited in the past to individuals going into a frenzy. The other Malay countries had had major postcolonial bloodlettings that went well beyond the incidents of the turn-of-the-century Philippine-American War. The rivers had run red in Indonesia in its counterrevolution in 1965, and in Malaysia in that country's intercommunal riots of 1969. It had appeared that the Philippines had a system so strong that such carnage would be precluded, but that system had been overturned in 1972. Then in 1981 a new factor had been introduced as official America had come out openly in support of those most responsible for the Philippine people's plight.

Even the more conservative oppositionists were talking by 1984 of how no one could henceforth guarantee the safety of the estimated 80,000 American servicemen, businessmen and dependents who were in the islands. Yet in Washington there was not a hint of any change in a Philippine policy that came down to retaining Clark and Subic bases at any cost.

As members of the opposition bandied about post-Marcos scenarios, a new name was given to one that people had scarcely dared mention before. The label was "Operation Mad Dog." Filipinos love the neatly turned phrase, and suddenly the words "Operation Mad Dog" were being spoken all over.

It had to do with how the people expected their rulers to react when the crunch came. It had to do with something that would be like what had happened previously in the other Malay countries: General Ver and his men, the ones responsible for both the tactical and the random violence, going out and methodically killing off anyone they could find on any level who was leading opposition to the regime.

This was, after all, a land where national violence was vivid in memory. It was the land where General Aguinaldo—with other generals including Ninoy Aquino's grandfather, Servillano Aquino, and José Diokno's grandfather, Ananias Diokno—and their poorly equipped and trained bands had held off U.S. soldiers for three and a half years in America's first big overseas war. This was the only place in Southeast Asia where guerrillas from the mainstream population had consistently fought the Japanese throughout the World War II occupation. It was also a land where Communist guerrillas had nearly gained power just as the Cold War was beginning.

In the late nineteenth century it had been the first Asian country in the modern era to stage a national uprising for the sake of independence. Most recently, its right-wing regime had been the most visible oppressor in the region.

Now it was a place where a military coup, civil war and eventually a Communist takeover seemed inevitable to many who knew it best. Others saw a last chance in the possibility that there would be a change of administration in the old colonizer's far-off capital.

At the end most people believed the dictatorship had stayed in power only because it had American backing. Now to many the last hope was that a new American government would remove the U.S. bases and work with the last Filipinos who believed it was still possible to avoid a cataclysm in the islands. But Washington was doing nothing about moving its bases and its servicemen from this land again verging on revolution. The Philippines still remained a vital center for American military, intelligence and communications facilities meant to cover a large part of the globe.

It was not just Filipinos and Filipinas who could lose their lives if the wrong decisions were made now. It was not hard to visualize grieving families in America too.

INDEX

NISA (National Intelligence and Security Authority), 55–56, 92–93, 128–129, 220–221
  Presidential Security Command and, 221
Nixon, Richard M., 28–29
  Imelda Marcos and, 58–59
Nofziger, Lyn, 116
NPA (New People's Army), 52, 78, 96, 117, 133–149, 341
  arms for, 158–159, 230–231
  bases of, 134
  behavior code for, 163
  blood debts and, 141, 163, 228–229
  blood ties used by, 160–161
  Cellophil project and, 145–146
  CHDF and, 218
  Floirendo and, 260
  formation of, 154
  government services provided by, 142–143
  growth of, 135–138, 161
  hamleting and, 234
  hit-and-run attacks by, 137–141, 147–148, 163–164
  killings and, 100, 104–105
  Mindanao offensive against (1983), 136–139
  minor criminals and, 162–163
  Moros and, 206–207
  organization of, 137–138
  popularity of, 148, 161–162, 164
  Reagan and, 148
  social activities of, 161–163
  "sparrow" units of, 137, 163
  tactics of, 206–207
  teach-ins by, 138, 161–163

Octopus, the, 51–52, 246–268
  business opposition to, 246–247
  coconut market and, 248–252
  defined, 246–247
Olano, Alfredo S., 234, 242
Olongapo, 316
Ongpin, Roberto, 328
Operation Mad Dog, 343–344
Opposition, 29–30
  foreign press and, 109–111, 158

1981 election boycotted by, 60–61
  open, 111–120
  Reagan contacts with, 75–76
  silent, 115
  underground, 110–111, 118, 129–130
  U.S.-Marcos relations and, 76–82, 115–116
  (See also Exile opposition)
Oreta, Tessie, 339
Orsorio, Evilio and Margarito, 100–101
Ortigas, Fluellan, 94
Ortigas, Gaston, 198–200
Ortiz, Nida, 224
Osmeña, Sergio, III, 286, 292–293
Otis, Elwell S., 168–169, 172, 175

Paguio, Jemeliania, 102
Palma, Charlie, 91
Pan Pacific Commodities Corporation, 248–250
Pauker, Guy, 342
Paul VI, Pope, 311
Pedrosa, Carmen Navarro, 325–326
Peralta, Macario, 266
Peron, Eva, 307
Perpinan, Mary Soledad, 320
Pershing, John "Black Jack," 186
Philippine-American extradition treaty, 282–283, 305–306
Philippine-American War, 33–34, 132, 167–186
  atrocities in, 173–175, 182–185
  Batangas in, 180–182
  beginning of, 167–170
  casualties in, 178
  civilian reprisals in, 171–174, 180–182, 184–185
  end of, 185–186
  Filipinization of, 172–173
  guerrilla nature of, 172–175
  hamleting in, 180–182
  Moros in, 179–180, 185–187
  motive for, 168
  Philippine Scouts in, 172–173, 185–186
  prisoners executed in, 178, 180–181, 184–185
  racism and, 170–173
  Samar in, 182–185